Players in the Public Policy Process

Nonprofits as Social Capital and Agents

Herrington J. Bryce

Players in the Public Policy Process

First published 2005 by Palgrave Macmillan™
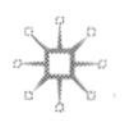
175 Fifth Avenue, New York, N.Y. 10010 and
Houndmills, Basingstoke, Hampshire, England RG21 6XS.
Companies and representatives throughout the world.

PALGRAVE MACMILLAN is the global academic imprint of the Palgrave Macmillan division of St. Martin's Press, LLC and of Palgrave Macmillan Ltd. Macmillan® is a registered trademark in the United States, United Kingdom and other countries. Palgrave is a registered trademark in the European Union and other countries.

ISBN 1–4039-6829–2 hardback

Library of Congress Cataloging-in-Publication Data

Bryce, Herrington J.
Players in the public policy process : nonprofits as social capital and agents / Herrington J. Bryce.
p. cm.
Includes bibliographical references and index.
ISBN 1–4039-6829–2
1. Nonprofit organizations. 2. Non-governmental organizations. 3. Political planning. I. Title.
HD2769.15.B79 2005
320.6—dc22
2004048838

A catalogue record for this book is available from the British Library.
Design by Autobookcomp.

First edition: April 2005

10 9 8 7 6 5 4 3 2 1

Printed in the United States of America.

To Simon J. Bryce and Myra Bryce-Laporte

and their children

and their children's children

and to those who in partnership gave them life and character

and to all the people of

LaBoca, Paraiso, and Gamboa

This book systematically develops the perspective of nonprofits or nongovernmental organizations (NGOs) as social capital assets and agents of public policy within the principal-agent paradigm and across public purposes—foreign or domestic, religious or sectarian, in developed or developing countries. The perspective has universal applicability and allows us to go beyond assumptions of market or government failure. Moreover, the perspective reflects the competitive situation in which nonprofits frequently find themselves when bidding against firms for government contracts. The analysis identifies five factors that could offer nonprofits a clear, competitive advantage over firms and governments in certain contract bidding. The perspective yields a set of implications for the strategic positioning of nonprofits in the public policy arena, and yields a new functional classification that includes nonprofits not merely as service providers but as managers of significant social risks, as market and transaction regulators, and as centers of collective action along the full spectrum of public policy issues.

Nonprofits influence our electoral choices of politicians (policymakers) and through the latter, nonprofits influence the appointments of those who design, plan, and administer policy within the public bureaucracy. Inside and outside the bureaucracy nonprofits influence policy choices, the protocols, the practices, and the success or failure of policy implementation. The central contribution of this book is the articulation of a perspective of how nonprofits play these varied roles as social capital assets and agents for the public's purposes and the subsequent theoretical, practical, and managerial implications of this functional view.

Insightful, innovative, and well-grounded; strongly recommended.

—*Julian Wolpert, Henry G. Bryant Professor of Geography, Public Affairs, and Urban Planning; Chair, Program in Urban and Regional Planning, Woodrow Wilson School, Princeton University*

The increasing role of nonprofits as agents of public purpose creates both opportunities and risks. This book helps us better to understand the sources of the opportunities and the nature of the risks.

—*Steven Kelman, Weatherhead Professor of Public Management, John F. Kennedy School of Government, Harvard University*

Timely, fresh, and innately significant.

—*Clarence Stone, author of* Regime Politics

This book raises all the important issues that the appraisal of nonprofits's role in governance should. Serious students of public policy ought not to ignore this theoretically sophisticated and empirically informed work.

—*Theodore R. Marmor, Professor of Public Policy and Management, Yale University School of Management*

Contents

Acknowledgments

A book like this does not come easily or quickly, and I acknowledge the experiences that shape it. I first met Emile Durkheim, Max Weber, Talcott Parsons, James Coleman, and Neil Smelser through their writings at the Maxwell School at Syracuse University through Professors S. M. Miller and Irwin Deutscher as I pursued a minor in sociology (theory) while getting a Ph.D. in economics (public finance). My interest in state and local governments came from professor C. Van Eaton at Minnesota State University. The blending of interest in these academic streams occurred over decades of both academic and public policy experiences on the local, state, and national levels.

In this book I draw from actual public policy experiences. I evaluated community development corporations for the Ford Foundation while a senior economist at the Urban Institute, and I paid particular attention to urban economics and local governance at the Joint Center for Political and Economic Studies. Through the auspices of the Joint Center and the Academy for State and Local Governments, I completed books on city planning, city revitalization, cities and firms, and the growth and decline of small cities, while simultaneously a fellow at the Institute of Politics at Harvard. And later I accepted faculty positions at the Massachusetts Institute of Technology and the University of Maryland in planning-related courses.

As vice president for research and operations at the Academy of State and Local Governments, I was confronted with policy from the purview of elected officials whose political careers depended on successful policy implementation while engulfed in strong, and competing interests. The Academy was operated on behalf of the National League of Cities, U.S. Conference of Mayors, the International City Management Association, Council of State Governments, the National Governors Association, the National Association of County Officials, and the National Conference of State Legislators. Part of my responsibilities was to coordinate their views with the views of private sector representatives such as the U.S. Chamber of Commerce in a forum, the National Urban Roundtable, which contributed to the annual report of the Secretary of the Department of Housing and Urban Development. Frontline exposure was also gained as a member of the board of directors at the National Council for Urban Economic Development—an organization of state and local economic development officials.

I am also grateful for the experience of being on a number of national, state, and local boards dealing with financing. These boards range from a budget committee in Montgomery County (Maryland) to the Treasury

Board of the Commonwealth of Virginia, which determines the terms of and issues all state-sponsored debt—exposing me to the financing side of policy and the responsibility of being a signatory trustee for such debt whether in the form of general obligation or revenue bonds. From the federal financing perspective, I was fortunate to be commissioned by the U.S. Bureau of Census (on whose advisory board I served) to analyze the impact of the decennial undercount on state and local government transfer payments and to have that exercise culminate in a manuscript introducing an alternative distribution method that published in the *Proceedings of the American Statistical Associations.*

Through Dr. Carole Neves (now Director, Office of Policy Analysis, Smithsonian Institution) and Scott Fosler of the National Academy of Public Administration I got to expand my appreciation of policy in the former communist countries by working with local officials in Russia, Estonia, and Georgia. It is in these countries that I became appreciative of how much the nonprofit sector contributes to the quality of life, lower budgetary burdens, decentralization, and greater local satisfaction in the United States, and that "the" market as we know it in the United States depends upon several nonprofit organizations for its efficiency and order, which are explored in this book.

This international experience was preceded by a project, financed by the Agency for International Development, to head a committee of educational officials in Panama to design a plan to implement a large-scale educational reform program and one in Berlin, financed by the German Marshall Fund, to design a study of cross-national urban development.

The nonprofit strain in this book comes from managerial, editorial, and advisor experiences, including the advisory boards of Guidestar and the National Council of Nonprofit Enterprise, being the special editor on nonprofits for the *American Management Association Handbook,* and as the editor and principal writer of *Not-for-Profit Financial Strategies,* a newsletter published by Harcourt Brace for CEOs, CPAs, and CFOs of nonprofit organizations. With respect to specific classes or organization, I am grateful to Frances Kuecker and the editors of *Health Care Management Review,* and Russell Taylor of National Arts Strategies

My interest in the law and contracts and in nonprofits as market regulators arose in my CLU and ChFC studies through the American College. But it also comes from having so many lawyers in the immediate family—Beverly, Marisa, Herrington Simón, and Shauna Bryce and then Matthew Queler, Henry Morris and Rene Bryce-Laporte—and so many law books and journals around. I am pleased that the most recent edition of my book *Financial and Strategic Management for Nonprofit Organizations* is listed among the suggested references by the American Bar Association (Business Law Section) and the American Society of Corporate Secretaries—the second edition having been recommended by the *Journal of Law and Arts Management.* This type of acceptance emboldens and encourages investigations such as those represented in this book.

Having struggled with this manuscript for several years, I was presenting a paper at the Network of Institutes and Schools of Public Administration for Central and Eastern Europe in Bucharest, Romania. Jane Finlay of ELS/LEED of the Organization for Economic Cooperation and Development (OECD) asked me what I knew about social capital. That generated a deeper interest in that subject, which is reflected herein. Sometimes a rare challenge helps, such as when Stefan Gougherty, a freshman design student, asked me to explain what my book was about so that he, under the tutelage of his mother Edeltraud, a designer, could try replicating its concepts in a design—the challenge of representing theory in art. I am grateful to Allan Rosenbaum for his comments on this book from the perspective of his extensive experience across the globe, and to Magnus Lofstrom and Clarence Stone for their views as to how this book may apply to a public policy course such as the ones they teach. A parking lot conversation with my colleague, John Strong, helped me to sharpen one theme of my thinking. I thank Michelle Semones for being sure that I did not misrepresent his organization, the National Beer Wholesalers Association in Chapter 10.

I am grateful for the facilities at the College of William and Mary, where I teach both corporate finance and nonprofit finance to a combination of questioning graduate business, law, education and public policy students, and to my colleagues such as Charlotte Brown, Ronald Sims, and Dean Larry Pulley and to Dean John Boschen, Tricia Whisnant, and Tammy Gainer for scheduling my courses so that this work was possible even while carrying a regular load. I am grateful for University College (University of Maryland), Dean Milton Grodsky and Dean John Jamison, who provided working environments for the cultivation of this interest.

Finally, I am grateful to the people at Palgrave Macmillan, particularly Anthony Wahl and Heather Van Dusen, for their responsiveness, and to their reviewers; to Autobookcomp (design and composition); to Rick Delaney (copyeditor); to Jen Simington of CopyRight Packaging and Editorial; to Jana Rhone and Sharon Valentine of the School of Business at the College of William and Mary for assistance in the final preparation of the manuscript; and to Joe Gilley, also from William and Mary, for his graphics and tables.

Herrington J. Bryce
August 30, 2004
College of William and Mary
Williamsburg, VA

Preface

This book is about the nonprofit or nongovernmental organization (NGO) as a social capital asset and player in the public policy process. It covers (a) policy conceptualization through research; (b) policy formulation through advocacy, lobbying, and other collective actions; and (c) policy implementation through performances in the arts, sciences, capital and consumer markets, social services, and foreign policy, and other activities that shape the welfare of entire communities and countries.

The book views these public policy purposes through the principal-agent paradigm, the contractual relationship between the nonprofit and the public, and the risks and rewards associated with this connection. It also addresses the following: Since federal and state contracting laws (as cited), require competitive bidding between nonprofits and firms, why would the government choose a nonprofit over an equally competent and competing firm? What are the five factors with which nonprofits are endowed that are within the capacities of their management to further cultivate, that could improve their competitive and market positions for government contracts? From this perspective, the book speaks to the future of contracting opportunities for nonprofits as firms further compete for contracts, including those in the social services, and as the fiscal capacity and willingness of governments to fund these programs shrink.

While recognizing the continuing importance of market and government failure theories of the rise of nonprofits, this book demonstrates the operational, theoretical, and managerial utility of using the principal-agent framework for viewing nonprofits as agents of the public's policies as articulated by representative governments. This book provides and captures an interdisciplinary but systematic approach to the role of nonprofits in all modern societies, even those that are struggling with poverty, and those that are not fully market driven, as in the current social capital initiatives of the World Bank. The book is accessible to the undergraduate, graduate, and professional reader in public policy, public administration, economics, sociology, social welfare policies, and planning, and it draws on these fields both in its narrative and in its illustrations. It is also directed to the practitioner community. To that community, it speaks of public purpose, the systematic risks associated with that purpose, and a new five-factor perspective of the competitive advantage of nonprofits in contract bidding and performance.

The book's key concepts are: social capital assets, nonprofits, public policy process, and the principal-agent paradigm. These key concepts, being temporally and culturally neutral, are applicable to describing the role of nonprofits in the public policy process universally. Moreover, they are applicable to any public policy—foreign or domestic, scientific or nonscientific, sectarian or religious, artistic or educational, developed or developing societies.

Accordingly, among the key questions of this book are the following: Why should the nonprofit be considered a social capital asset? Why should the nonprofit be considered a public policy agent? How can the agency relationship between the nonprofit and the society it serves be represented in a way that is not culture- or mission-bound? What are the advantages of this formulation to the nonprofit sector, its management, and to those interested in increasing the effectiveness of nonprofits in every phase of the policy process? What are the risks and advantages to both the nonprofit and the public that this paradigm exposes? How can they be treated? How does society keep its agent, the nonprofit, in check? Can any of this be illustrated by real-world experiences—what is the evidence? How does this perspective fit within current empirical and theoretical knowledge across the social sciences? What are the key insights for managers of nonprofits in terms of positioning their organizations in a competitive environment?

This book is born at a time when three long-term core issues confront the nonprofit sector in the United States:

1. The performance of faith-based organizations, and the extent to which they should receive government funding;

2. The Congressional outcry, hearings, and drafting of bills to regulate nonprofit organizations, and the need for greater self-regulation;

3. The increase in successful bidding by corporations on social services, job-training, and other contracts traditionally thought to be inherently nonprofit and the competition that this implies.

Addressing these three core issues is an inescapable responsibility of a book such as this, though its theme is larger. Therefore, these three issues are clearly addressed within the principal-agent framework. What insights does this yield?

Given the competitive realities of contracting generated partly by specific government regulations that promote contracting competition between firms and nonprofits, a key question in this book is why would the government choose a nonprofit over an equally qualified firm? In this context, some of the common answers, such as politics, transaction costs, unspecified contracts, charity, and trust, all beg the question: Why should these be more advantageous for nonprofits than for firms? And if trust is so central, shouldn't this be a "slam dunk" decision for faith-based organizations to which faith and trust are almost always automatically ascribed?

To answer these questions, the book systematically goes through federal and state regulations and contracting practices and emerges with a five-factor description of the competitive advantages of nonprofits based on their special endowments. The result is analogous to a theory of comparative advantage of nonprofits over firms and governments in parts of the public policy process. The foundation of this approach is in law, public choice theory, classical economics, the role of economic sociology (particularly as it relates to social capital), and in the contracting rules of state, federal, and local governments. The application of the approach is demonstrated in the social services, science, business association, community development and housing, and the management of acute care hospitals. The utility of any theoretical approach is based, in part, on its applicability across situations—including, in this case, its application to comparing secular and faith-based organizations.

The book initiates its mission by explaining why a broader perspective (beyond market, contract, or government failure) is needed in today's world, where the nonprofit plays so many key roles in public policy and in politics that cannot be adequately captured in the "failure" theories. It then recognizes the discomfort that the concept of social capital leaves with many scholars, and addresses this by setting criteria that a nonprofit must meet to be considered a social capital asset with the capacity to contract as an agent to the public.

These criteria do not admit to certain types of common uses of social capital, such as norms and networks, for while they may be social capital, they cannot fulfill the role of an agent within the principal-agent paradigm. Yet, these concepts play determinative roles within the paradigm and throughout this book.

The book proceeds to lay out and to develop the principal-agent paradigm and to isolate concepts, such as the mission as a contractual promise and what that implies, the roles and expectations of different parties to the contract between the nonprofit and the public, and other concepts drawn from contract law.

What is the competitive advantage of the nonprofit as an agent of public policy over a firm within this paradigm? By going through the major steps in government contracting processes, does it make sense, as we often state, that the government has greater trust in nonprofits than in firms? What is the basis of that trust when the government is seeking specific performance and it has no more intimate knowledge of a nonprofit than it does of an equally qualified firm and when, as it does, it pays both a fee above the contract cost?

The book then turns to the application of the principal-agent paradigm, the five-factors that are distilled as giving the nonprofit an inherent competitive advantage, and the concept of social capital to demonstrate them in housing and community development and in hospital administration. By doing this, additional concepts, such as (a) the conflict between public expectations and organizational survival and managerial self-interest, (b) organizational capacity and actual performance, and (c) the incentives to perform, such as penalties, risks, and associated moral hazards, are explored.

The book then turns to the argument that, as agents of public policy, nonprofits are not passive purveyors or implementers of policy, but they are also instrumental in shaping public policy. In this role, they are often double agents—for the public at large and for specific interests, including business interests. This book focuses on business associations. What is their nonmonetary source of power? Is lobbying, a common tool of these associations, a net good or bad to society? What do extant theory and research imply?

The concept of control is part of any principal-agent paradigm. The book reminds us that the public seeks to apply some controls over its agents through controlling their finances. What is the hazard of doing this? What is the incentive of nonprofits, what type of nonprofits are prone to noncompliance when these rules are voluntary, and why? Lastly, the book looks at some nonprofits as regulators—the nonprofit as a legislative body (writing rules), a judiciary body (assessing public penalties and disbarment), and an executive body (implementing and enforcing policy)—and it illustrates this with examples from the capital market where stocks and bonds are issued and traded.

The final chapter of the book gives a general summary of its findings, itemizes its 20 major perspectives, and addresses the following questions: What are the implications of viewing the nonprofit as a social capital asset and agent within a principal-agent paradigm? How does this help the nonprofit manager's perspective in a competitive environment in which nonprofits must compete with better-situated firms, other nonprofits, and government agencies by virtue of pubic policy as described in this book?

This book is intended to be useful and accessible to the advanced reader inclined to the exploration of thought and perspective. It might provide those interested in the theory of nonprofits, social services, and public policy with a framework or paradigm that views the nonprofit as a policy agent across the full spectrum of policy involvement. Chapters 1 and 2 explain why the perspective of this book is needed. Chapters 3, 4, 5, and 11 contain the core arguments. Chapters 6–10 give specific types of applications and the attendant policy-related problems across a spectrum from housing to hospitals, from business associations and other nonprofit lobbying agents to public regulation of nonprofits, and discuss the foundation needed for the nonprofit as a regulatory agent in asymmetric markets.

Those interested in contracting only will find chapters 4 and 5 and parts of chapter 2, especially under "Government Contracting of Nonprofits as Agents of Public Policy: Protecting the Public Interest,"of special interest because they explore in some detail the contracting procedures of governments and how selections are made. Those interested in economic sociology, social capital, or the sociology of institutions will be interested in chapters 3–5, and in the concrete illustrations in chapters 6, 7, and 8. Readers interested in policy formulation only will find that addressed in chapter 8 with respect to business associations and their lobbying purpose and structure. Readers interested in fundraising and its regulation will find that chapters 9 and 10 relate to those issues. Chapter 10, however, deals with the creation of a broader watchdog or self-regulatory function—not unlike those in the fundraising world, although the question is a broader one dealing with what it takes to be successful. Chapter 11 is especially for the reader interested in management and the perspective that this approach gives for better positioning the organization in a competitive environment. Readers interested in markets will find that chapter 2 is about the regulatory and facilitating roles that nonprofits play in large, consequential markets as a matter of public policy, with illustrations to make the singular point: Markets as we know them today are shaped partly by nonprofits carrying out assigned or acquired public policy functions. The remedial approach to nonprofits, even when demonstrably applicable, is insufficient in capturing the public policy functions and performances of these market-modifying nonprofit organizations.

Except for chapter 11, this book is more about a perspective or vision than about achieving excellence in operating a nonprofit—the objective of my *Financial and Strategic Management for Nonprofit Organizations: A Comprehensive Reference to Legal, Financial, Management, and Operations Rules and Guidelines for Nonprofits* (Jossey Bass 2000). I hope it serves its intent.

Herrington J. Bryce
Life of Virginia Professor of Business Administration
College of William and Mary
Williamsburg, VA
herrington.bryce@business.wm.edu

Part I

The Need for a Policy Perspective of Nonprofits

Markets, as we know them, are influenced by nonprofit organizations discharging a public purpose. This is evident even in capital markets. The New York Stock Exchange and the Chicago Board of Trades are nonprofit organizations. In product and service markets, nonprofits are more than consumers or employers. They address issues of asymmetric (one-sided and often unfair) information, and they are facilitators of transactions. They enable markets to operate more efficiently on both sides of a transaction. In noneconomic markets, nonprofits are kernels of collective action and agents of public policy, be those sociological, political, religious, educational, scientific, domestic, or foreign. Nonprofits not only discharge humanitarian action on behalf of the American public, but they generate public concern, shape the debate, shape the formulation of policies, and often influence who (the selection of agency), by whom (the selection of officials such as judges, ambassadors, and other political appointees), and how they will be discharged. We need a paradigm that incorporates playing in this extensive field of public policy.

Chapter 1

The Significance of the Principal-Agent Paradigm

Citizens voluntarily form nonprofit or nongovernmental organizations (NGOs) for the expressed purposes of advancing public and community welfare. These organizations are rapidly growing and becoming a significant part of modern societies everywhere. They are blossoming throughout the world and dependence on them is increasing by citizens, governments, and by international organizations such as the World Bank and the Organization for Economic Co-operation and Development (OECD)—both of which have commissioned expert manuscripts on the roles that NGOs as well as social capital may play in increasing the effectiveness of their programs.

The concept of social capital has become so important to policy and planning that the American Planning Association convened a group of experts to consider "social capital" as an integrating concept in planning theory, research, and practice. The concept also appears in other professions, as well as in leading economic journals, as will be cited in this book.

In the United States alone, nonprofits known as 501 (c) (3)s grow at an average decennial rate of 50 percent.[1] The 501 (c) (3)s are the educational, health, scientific, arts and cultural, religious, civic, charitable, and sports organizations and account for well over 60 percent of all nonprofits in the United States, where they are both the largest and fastest-growing group of nonprofits. They, along with civic, labor, business, and professional organizations, are the organizational foci of this book. The first group works directly to advance public welfare and may or may not have individuals or entities as members. The second group always has members and works on behalf of the public's welfare or interests primarily through service to the association's members—improving their performance in service of the public.

Both types of nonprofit organizations are playing an ever-increasing role in societies across the world—even though at a snail's pace in some countries. An irresistible challenge is to characterize this role in a meaningful way that is applicable across countries, cultures, and parochial purposes. It is not enough to assert that these organizations are social capital assets. It is necessary to develop an argument why such a controversial[2] sociological concept may well apply. This argument, as chapter 2 will show, is best made in the logic of economics or business rather than in sociology; but the sociological implications are strongest in supporting the economic as well as the sociological advantages of these organizations, as chapters 5–8 will show.

From the perspective of public policy it is insufficient to conclude that these organizations that are blossoming everywhere owe their existence simply to market or government failure. Public policy is concerned with what the organization does, how it does it, when it does it, and for whom. These are core policy questions whether in the idiom of Lindblom,[3] Dahl and Lindblom,[4] Etizioni,[5] Wilson,[6] or Forester.[7] Therefore, from a public policy perspective, the paradigm that is used to generalize the role of these organizations should be one that allows us to respond meaningfully and systematically to those questions.

In this vein, this book carefully develops the perspective of nonprofit organizations (NGOs) as social capital assets and agents of public policy within a principal-agent framework. It takes an interdisciplinary approach, drawing on economics, sociology, political science, and public choice theories to systematically develop its perspective. The book shows the practical as well as the managerial and marketing advantages of such an approach, drawing heavily from the legal theory of contracts. This approach also enables us to assess the role of faith-based organizations from a fiscal and sociological—and not faith-based—perspective. Enforceable contracts are not based on "faith" but on the promise of performance. The principal-agent framework provides a positive (if not aggressive), cross-national, and inclusive perspective that can be substantiated in a developed or developing country and across public policy purposes.

What Does the Paradigm Contribute That Will Be Reflected in This Book?

The paradigm puts the relationship—the nonprofit in service of the public—into a particular framework or structure applicable to all nonprofits, secular or religious, foreign or domestic, in developing countries or advanced countries, in scientific or nonscientific enterprises. Structure is important not only in giving perspective, but also in developing theories, testing hypotheses, and in assessing the operating ties between the nonprofit and its public.

These connecting ties deal with channels of communication, responsibilities, dependence, expectations, the exercise of discretion, trust, compensation, choice and the specificity of contract terms, penalties for violation of trust and contracts, and much more. Thus, the relationship between the nonprofit and public is a structured one in the same way that the relationship between an employer and an employee, or any two parties subject to a contract or a promise that one would work on the behalf of the other, is a structured relationship. As a consequence, by placing the relationship between the nonprofit and the public in a principal-agent paradigm, we can focus on a common structure (one in service of another) and those things that may be attendant to such a structure regardless of the nonprofit, its purpose, or its location.

I have listed the basic building blocks of the principal-agent paradigm that will be used to explore the nonprofit as an agent of public policy. Key terms are in italics:

1. There is a *relationship* between the society and nonprofits in service of the society.
2. This relationship is based on mutual *expectations*.
3. Expectations are based on specific *performance*, upon which both parties agree.
4. Being connected, both parties assume certain *risks* caused by the *discretion* and actions of the other.
5. At some pre-agreed time and manner an *evaluation* or *determination* is made of the performance.
6. A determination can be made to *keep*, *modify*, or *terminate* the relationship.
7. The parties can *agree* to all of the above.
8. The parties can *communicate* a *common* understanding of the agreement among themselves.
9. All of the above actions are *voluntary*.
10. The parties have a *free* choice and *alternatives* to entering into this *contract*.

Placing the relationship between the nonprofit and the society into this common but inherent structure gives a universal framework for analyzing how, how well, and why the relationship works; and, consequently, how its details can be modified to meet particular circumstances while keeping the structure intact. Thus, the relationship between a school and the public it serves has a basic expectation (the school educates the children for the betterment of society), whether in Uganda or the United States, although the capacities of the two are clearly different. The principal agent paradigm focuses not on the capacity, but on a structure (the relationship between the school and community) and those things attendant to the structure—given, but not ignoring, the realities of differences.

To illustrate, financial and technical capacities or administrative or pedagogical strategies or content do vary from place to place (e.g., Uganda and the United States) and between nonprofits (e.g., a school in Uganda and a school in the United States), but the core responsibility to educate the children, and therefore the role of the school to serve the public, is no different. The principal-agent paradigm focuses on this responsibility or promise; and, specifically, the way the relationship between the school and the public is structured to meet that promise.

The paradigm not only gives a structure to relationships between an agent and its principal and the problems or improvements attendant to that structure; it also focuses on the transactions (what transpires) between them regardless of the content of that transaction. Thus, the paradigm may apply to all public policies regardless of content, place, or purpose.

Why is the concept of transaction important and deserving of attention regardless of content? It is important because the relationship between a nonprofit and the public is no different (in some respects) from the relationship between two people or two entities. The parties incur and impose costs on each other to establish the relationship and to make it work to their expectations. The consideration of these transaction costs influences whether and how the relationship is established, kept, and operated. Thus, the nature of the relationship and its attendant costs are a focus of the principal-agent paradigm—no matter what the content or mission being served.

Of course, the content cannot be ignored because it determines how the transaction is performed. A housing and community development agency is not different from a hospital in the sense that both serve the public. In both cases, the public and the nonprofit incur costs to establish and to maintain a relationship. But the content of the mission and, therefore, what each promises the public, is different. And because each promise is different, each causes the public and the nonprofit a different set of problems and creates a different set of expectations.

The cost of ensuring that the apartments meet code and are occupied by targeted residents is less than the cost of ensuring that the beds are filled only with patients who ought to be there for the length of time each patient should, given the peculiarities of that patient's physical and financial situation and the assurance that care and the hospital environment rise to the level of best available practice. Thus, the content of the mission affects the cost of the relationship (in this example, monitoring and ensuring the results); but the basic relationship (one in service of the other) does not change. The principal-agent paradigm allows us to distinguish between the cost of the relationship and the cost of the content of the relationship and to focus on the latter across and within mission contents.

Another contribution of working within the paradigm is that it forces confrontation with the infinite possibilities for conflict between the interests of the nonprofit and the public it serves. Getting behind concepts such as moral hazard and going into the daily operating realities of management places a more objective light on the sources of this conflict. Accordingly, self-interest becomes an issue of managerial incentive and method of operation, not merely of morality and ethics.

One of the contributions of public choice theory to this discussion is its recognition of how ubiquitous self-interest is in motivating management. The principal-agent paradigm alerts us to the fact that any service relationship is vulnerable to the omnipresent and ingrained selfishness of the agent, especially when the principal lacks relevant information and is ignorant. But this begs the question constantly raised in this book: Is this always bad?

And How Does the Paradigm Differ from Extant Theory and Operational Emphases?

The paradigm is inclusive. Some of its key concepts are shared by all social science disciplines. Understanding the paradigm from the perspective of law, particularly contract law and employment law (the principal employs the agent), expands the usefulness of the paradigm. But borrowing from economic and other social sciences also expands its usefulness because the paradigm is ultimately about human interaction or the interaction of human organizations. The challenge, particularly of this book, is to demonstrate how these cross-disciplinary concepts can be integrated into a credible and compatible characterization of how the nonprofit serves the public as an agent of the public's policies.

The paradigm is neutral without the need for interdisciplinary warfare. The literature on social capital makes note of the criticism by economists of the concept. As Arrow[8] asked, how can a norm or an interaction be capital? On the other hand, other social scientists would ask of nonprofit economists: How can everything that exists be the result of market failure even though they may well have predated the concept of "market" as we know it in economic theory?

The plain truth to this author is that the use of "social capital" can at times be so all-inclusive that virtually everything falls into it and there is no need to prove that anything should be included or excluded. This is what is at risk (see the essays in Dasgupta and Serageldin cited at the end of this chapter) when social capital is defined as norms and institutions, formal or informal, weak or strong, good or bad, cognitive and noncognitive, associative or nonassociative—all at the same time.

The only things excluded from this definition of social capital are animals and inanimate things, such as buildings. Yet, isn't a zoo of rare animals, financed by the public with the expectation of attracting congregations of people and a stream of revenues, social capital? Is it not an investment to advance public welfare? Is it not an economic institution having costs and revenues? Does it not have a measurable rate of return, even if only in the monetary measurement of a stream of income and a stream of expenditures over time? If it didn't, how come structures of zoos, like universities and hospitals, can be financed by borrowing—specifically by the issuing of bonds? To whom does the zoo, excepting private zoos like Neverland, belong? Is it not the public?

Yet, this author believes that when "social capital" meets the challenges of Arrow [9]or Solow,[10] it can be powerful in depicting the role of nonprofits as agents of policy and in explaining their inherent power based not purely on economics but on sociology as well. This book, therefore, argues early in chapter 3 that nonprofit organizations should be considered social capital—beyond the notion that they are institutions and/or associations. Later in the book the cognitive definition is also used. In each case, care is taken to avoid these all-inclusive traps and to answer the question: What makes this argument hold?

The paradigm places an emphasis on the organization's performance. Within the context of a principal-agent paradigm, the manager of the nonprofit and the manager of a firm have a strikingly similar challenge. The manager of a firm is judged partly by his or her producing a good or service that satisfies the consumer and is evidenced by consumers paying for it. This is the revenue side of profits. If the nonprofit is an agent of the public, then its value depends upon public acceptance of what it produces. Therefore, public expectations and acceptance are important. As a result it is not just "producing" or "marketing" that matters. It is also the discovery of what the public expects or wants, the ability to produce it, and the ability to make it available; also important is the repetition of these actions over and over again since public expectations and requirements change. The principal-agent paradigm provides for the dynamics of change.

In this vein, an emphasis on how well management (including the trustees) performs—not merely in how well it collects—is important. Every additional dollar collected is a dollar's worth of expectations added. Fundraising is connected to future and foreseeable objectives. The fundraising strategy may well be doing more of the same or better in wider markets—as long as it meets a public need.

Every dollar collected increases the claim of the public against the future performance of the organization. Therefore, the paradigm encourages those responsible for the governance of the organization to be particularly concerned with questions such as: Are we keeping our promise to the public and, specifically, are we meeting their expectations—are we relevant to public need? This question may require the management to be proactive—anticipating and shaping public opinion through the marshalling and dissemination of information.

The question of "in service of whom" is front and center to the purpose and mission of associations, because their members and members' interests are the reasons for the creation of associations. Business associations, chapter 8, exist and are financed by members (not the public at large). Membership is taken because of a deeply held self-interest—the business. Members have strong views about what they expect to get from these associations: Through collective action, such as lobbying for or in opposition to a proposed policy or regulation, members are able to achieve what they cannot effectively do on their own but is necessary for the success of the business.

Thus, the contract content, the transactions, the structure of the relationship, and strong accountability to members—all of whom are at risk and have a direct stake in the association—are more individually and critically monitored in associations than in non-membership forms of nonprofits. All the stakeholders in a business association are at risk with what counts most for each—the success of their businesses and their personal, professional, and financial success as individuals. The continuous failure of management to meet expectations is not without consequence for management, members, and the organization.

The principal-agent paradigm places the organization in a competitive environment. Why? Nonprofits (probably with the exception of authorities discussed in chapter 6 and some self-regulatory bodies discussed in chapter 9) do not have monopoly control over markets. Nonprofits and for-profit competitors exist in or can easily enter the market. The American Red Cross does not have a monopoly in supplying blood or blood products. Therefore, the question for the management should always be: How can we be the most favored or, at least, one of the favored agents?

Accordingly, one of the tasks of this book is to identify what it refers to as the five factors of confidence in contracting with a nonprofit. Why would the government choose to contract with a nonprofit rather than with an equally qualified and situated firm? Is greater trust a reasonable explanation? Or the lower transactions cost? Or the unspecified nature of contracts? Standard answers to these questions are laid to scrutiny. Can one really believe that the government trusts a nonprofit more than an equivalent firm? If trust were so central, why is it that most government contracts in dollars and in numerical terms go to firms? Why wouldn't more firms change their corporate status and become nonprofits—rather than the reverse? Why wouldn't competent faith-based organizations not have an advantage over other bidders, since trust is almost always automatically ascribed to them? What is the competitive advantage of a nonprofit? The principal-agent paradigm forces similar questions since the principal is free to choose agents.

And How Does the Paradigm Deal with Accountability and Control Once Entrusted with the Public Good and Its Assets?

Unlike a firm, the nonprofit is a public or social asset. It does not belong to a group of investors. Therefore, the issues of social accountability, responsibility, and control are inherent in the principal-agent paradigm as applied to the nonprofit as an agent of public policy.

When a professional athlete signs with a team, the team exercises some control over that person. But the team does not own the person. The same thing is true of an employee in any other sphere. Yet, the employer or team owner pays that person (often times handsomely) to do something that person may have done anyway—the principle of economic rent. Hence, one of the elements of the principal-agent paradigm is that it places an emphasis on control of the former over the latter and the limitations imposed by the latter on how that control may be exercised. Moreover, both parties are subject to some sanction if these agreements are violated. How does this work when the nonprofit is in service to the public and entrusted with the public's assets?

Summary and Preview

The basic theme of this book is that nonprofits or nongovernmental organizations (NGOs) are institutional forms of social capital. They foster, formulate, perform, and evaluate society's policies that are in the furtherance of the public good. Inherent in this relationship is the concept of the nonprofit acting as an agent of public policy. This is the concept explored in this book and is applicable whether the public policy is economic or social, religious or secular, scientific or nonscientific, peaceful or militaristic. To do this, a principal-agent paradigm is proposed as a framework and explored in this book. This chapter discusses the key questions the principal-agent approach will answer.

The principal-agent paradigm articulates structures, connections, transactions, problems, and advantages common to all nonprofits in relation to the public and the public's policies. The use of the paradigm is natural and inherent to the purpose of every nonprofit based on the promise required in its mission statement that is used to obtain an operating charter and to obtain tax exemption. The paradigm is inclusive of contributions from various disciplines. To develop this theme is the principal charge of this book.

The reality is, however, that the most common and articulated explanation for nonprofits is in economics. Therefore, chapter 2 begins with a discussion of the economic theories of nonprofits, and why such theories are insufficient. The remainder of the book builds on the book's theme: nonprofits as social capital assets and agents of public policy.

Chapter 2

The Policy Significance of Nonprofit Organizations

Beyond the Limits of Failure

It is remarkable that while a substantial part of the burden of dealing with social maladies, social advancement, social planning, social arbitration, political and social advocacy, and the enforcement of social laws falls on nonprofit organizations, and that many who practice in the resolution of these social problems are not economists, the principal explanations for the existence of nonprofit organizations are in economics.

Yet, sociological theories of social capital and embeddedness, organizational theories such as resource dependency, political theories of advocacy, public choice theories of collective action, the legal theories of contracts and principal-agent relationship have much to offer in explaining the roles of nonprofits as public policy agents. But these theories are less than fully applied in the current nonprofit literature. A survey of the nonprofit literature reveals that the emphasis is on a few concepts: asymmetric information, adverse selection, transaction costs, and moral hazard drawn from principal-agent theory. Even in these concepts, we could advance our appreciation and knowledge of nonprofits by thinking outside of the economic box—while admitting to its continued furtherance of our understanding of the nonprofit sector. That is the mission of this book.

There are both benefits and shortcomings in relying on economic theory to describe the nonprofit as an agent of public policy. The principal contribution of these theories is that they identify the types of products and services, contracts, and transactions, that make the nonprofit better than the firm as an agent of public policy. Their major shortcoming from this book's perspective is that a number of significant and powerful nonprofits are probably best described otherwise: as prominent players in the public policy process.

As we proceed in this chapter, bear in mind that the issue is not which theory is right and which wrong, which is superior and which is inferior. The simple issue is this: To describe the nonprofit as an asset or as an agent or both, we need to describe its purpose in more specific terms than to say it exists because of the failure of the government or the market. What does it exist to do? It is an agent, and for whom and to do what?

C-SPAN, PBS, and NPR: Significance of Perspective

This book is about a single perspective: The nonprofit as a social capital asset and agent of public policy. The mission of the C-SPAN network of radio and television channels (www.c-span.org) is "to air unedited, balanced views of government and public policy forums, and to provide viewers with direct access to elected officials, decision-makers and journalists." To maintain its independence C-SPAN (Cable, Satellite, Public Affairs System) is funded from fees paid by the outlets that carry its programs. While created by the cable television, with a board of directors made up of members of that industry, this board does not influence the programming or programming content of C-SPAN. The industry's voice is its association, the National Cable and Telecommunications Association. The NCTA (www.NCTA.com) claims that its "primary mission is to provide its members with a strong national presence by providing a single, unified voice on issues affecting the cable and telecommunications industry."

National Public Radio and public television describe themselves as offering programming that is noncommercial—programming that has the length and depth that one could not get on commercial radio or television. This includes not only news and analysis, but quality music, drama, and documentaries. C-SPAN describes itself as a window to public policy throughout the world—as a forum through which public policy is discussed at length and in depth through various forms ranging from halls of governments to books and lectures and interviews. Both are nonprofits 501 (c) (3)s providing excellent service.

One organization, NPR, implies an existence due to market failure—the failure of the commercial media. Hence, public radio and television are always on the defense to the U.S. Congress, from which they receive funds, and to their audiences during fundraising to demonstrate how they differ from the commercial media. The second, C-SPAN, implies an existence to fulfill a public policy purpose—the involvement of an audience in the formulation, explication, and evaluation of public policy and in taking the pulse of the audience on such policies. Its defense is in the continuity of its public policy–related programming. Yet, the former is more public than the latter since the former relies on public funding whereas the latter is paid for, almost completely, by the cable industry. Yet, one is more likely to see a cable industry–related sponsorship announcement on public television than on C-SPAN. Perspectives matter.

Similarly, any focus on nonprofits as consequences of market failure risks understating the reliance of major markets on nonprofits as a matter of public policy. On a macro level, nonprofits affect the performance of the economy as well as markets and may do so through the operation of social capital. In the *American Economic Review,* Goldstein and Justman[1] suggest that a public education system is more likely than a private system to make a greater contribution to economic growth and to building social capital that instills common values, lowers economic transaction cost, and reduces social tensions. Thus, they imply, a shared public education system is likely to make a greater contribution to economic growth than a fractured, polarized private system reflecting different group beliefs and orientations. As this and the following chapter will illustrate, on a micro level social capital and nonprofits affect the performance of entities involved in a myriad of major market transactions as a matter of public policy. But first, we need to fully appreciate the contribution of the concept of market failure as it relates to nonprofits advancing public welfare.

The Contribution of Market Failure Theories

To say that the market fails means that the motives and the terms under which consumers and firms make decisions and carry them out may not lead to the best results for the community or the society—even though it may well satisfy the objectives of individual firms or consumers. The individual may be better off but society or a specific collectivity such as the local community is not.

The two leading theories of the rise of nonprofits relate to market failure—the incentive for firms and for individuals under certain circumstances to do what is best for themselves even though it may not be best for society. This leads to the need to create an organizational alternative to satisfy society's requirements. Because these two dominant theories see the nonprofit organization as an alternative form when the market fails, they are referred to in this book as market centric. Their principal utility for this book is that they describe the types of goods or services, contracts and transactions that are in society's interest and may be better served by nonprofits as agents of public policy rather than by market forces.

About market-centric theories, Ben-Ner and Gui write[2]: "These theories therefore predict that nonprofit organizations will not arise in perfectly competitive markets." One market-centric theory is based on the concept of market failure and the other on the concept of contract failure. When does market failure lead to the formation of nonprofits and in what respects are these nonprofits agents of public policy?

Public and Collective Goods and the Formation of Nonprofit Agents

One version of the market failure theory says that because the principal motive of firms is to make a profit, there are some goods or services firms (the market) will not provide. There are others that they will provide but in smaller quantities than the society needs. The first of these goods are public goods. These are goods that all persons in the community can enjoy without paying; and, therefore, many will not pay (except through compulsory taxation). Rather, they will choose to go along on a free ride—enjoying the good without paying for it. Since the firm cannot collect, it cannot make a profit and has no interest in providing these goods.

Public goods have two properties: (a) the amount consumed by any one person does not diminish the amount available to others; and (b) there is no way to deprive or deny anyone the right to consume that good. The first is known as the principle of nonrivalry or nonsubtactibility and the second as the principle of nonexclusion.

Two public policy implications follow: (a) the good, even though necessary, will not be produced by the market; and (b) some way has to be found to produce and pay for it since, in the extreme, if everyone free rides there are no revenues from the sale of the good to finance its production even though it is socially necessary.

One version of the market-centric approach argues that nonprofit collectivities may organize to provide these public goods. Thus the good or service may maintain its characteristics of nonexclusivity and nonrivalry but within a defined boundary or space and with respect to a defined collectivity or community. For them, it is a collective or community good. Neighborhood watch, neighborhood preservation and restoration, neighborhood cleanup, and infrastructure improvements are some examples. They are all goods that any member of the community can enjoy without diminishing the amount available to others and from which no member of the community can be excluded from enjoying even if such a person does not pay.

Olson[3] argues that firms will have no interest to provide goods or services where a price cannot be charged because no one would have an incentive to pay and therefore the firms will not be able to have revenues or profits, which is their principal motive. Therefore a market solution relying upon firms will not work.

An alternative form of organizing the production and financing of these activities is the collective or nonprofit mode where profit-making is not the objective—community or collective satisfaction is—and charging individuals is not necessary since the good can be financed through donations or taxation or a combination of the two. Accordingly, one form in which a nonprofit can be viewed as an agent of public policy is as an alternative to or an ancillary to government in the provision of collective or public goods. Thus, a nonprofit, the Chesapeake Bay Foundation, protects the environment of the Chesapeake Bay. The bay's benefits are available to all (even those who do not pay) because the foundation is financed by gifts and donations, a tax-exempt subsidy, and fees that may exclude some persons are charged for only a small portion of the offerings of the bay.

Goods with Substantial Positive Externalities and the Formation of Nonprofit Agents

Public policy is also concerned with goods or services with significant positive externalities. These are goods where the society as a whole would benefit if larger amounts were consumed by persons who cannot pay. This is so because the consumption by each person has a positive effect on the society as a whole. The benefits to the society exceed the benefits to the individual consumer. But the firm, being profit-making would only produce for those who will pay the market price. Those who can pay will consume only as much as they can justify given the price and they would be unconcerned that greater production and consumption would benefit the society. Thus, the society is better off if every child is properly inoculated and examined before starting school whether or not the family can pay.

The public policy issue connected to public or collective goods has to do with whether or not the good will be provided, but the externalities question has to do with whether it will be provided or consumed in sufficient quantity. Given the profit motive, firms will only produce the quantity of each good that they can sell at a price that assures them a profit even though at a substantially lower price (one that could lead to a loss); more people would buy and therefore the community would be better off. More people may need inoculation to reduce the risk of spreading a disease but only a few can afford it. The market will supply the portion of the need that people will pay for and only to the extent that they will pay even if more people taking more shots each will help. Thus, the market fails to fully meet society's needs. The nonprofit organization not motivated by or dependent upon profits can meet society's needs and finance it through donations and a subsidy such as tax exemption.

Trust and Club Goods and the Formation of Nonprofit Agents

The common nature of trust and club goods is that the market fails because the purchase of some goods is heavily dependent upon the consumer having trust in the producer. This trust may be absent because of asymmetric information, meaning that one side of a transaction has less information and a different motivation than the other and therefore the former may be subject to abuse by the other or may simply be insufficiently informed to have confidence in the transaction and make it work. One will not buy kosher food from a market where one is not certain that the food is kosher.

Trust may also be lacking because the consumer may not be confident that the producer, whose principal motivation is profits, has the best interest of the consumer at heart. If a religious educational environment is important to a family, it will seek a religious school—not a public school or a secular private school. It will join with other members of its community with similar orientation to form a religious school that is set in the religious doctrine it prefers and where it can trust that its religious beliefs will prevail. Clubs are formed with the same particularistic motivations. In these instances, the nonprofit is an agent to satisfy particularistic needs.

Multiple Market Failures and the Formation of Nonprofit Agents

Weisbrod[4] enumerates four conditions when the market or government fails and nonprofits offer a better way:

1. When there is informational inequality: Where consumers are poorly informed they "may be ill served by opportunistic sellers."
2. Even when consumers are informed about their needs for a particular product or service they may not reveal their preferences if they receive the benefits whether or not they pay. Even if they don't pay, they cannot be excluded.
3. When there is a diversity of consumer demands and government is responsive to the majority, various nonprofits may arise to respond to the specific and peculiar needs of the minorities.
4. Because firms rely on profits, they cannot provide goods and services that are valuable to society but provide no profit. But nonprofit organizations can because they rely on and are responsive to donors and neither they nor the donors rely on the organization's profits.

Weisbrod[5] argues that government generally supplies goods that are large and must be available to all. As a result, attempts by government to broaden the availability of its services to all those who need it means that in so doing, many not in need are included when the net is so wide. Alternatively, to reduce this inefficiency by restricting the range of inclusion means that some that are in need could be bypassed. Accordingly, the nonprofit is, to him, a form of decentralizing, focusing, and tailoring these offerings to meet diverse needs. From this perspective, the nonprofit may be viewed as an agent of public policy not only because of market but because of government failures as well. This and other of his theoretical approaches have empirical support and have been used to explain among other things managerial compensation,[6] charitable donations,[7] and volunteerism.[8]

Market Failure and Individual Initiative to Form Nonprofit Organizations

Ben Ner and Gui[9] argue that it is not enough to explain why market failures create a demand for nonprofits; one must also identify what motivates individuals to create the nonprofits. They summarize Young's[10] argument that certain entrepreneurial types are drawn to the nonprofit sector and James's[11] argument that some individuals are drawn to the nonprofit sector to develop the prestige they can later use especially in a political career. Both types of individuals tend to create nonprofit organizations to respond to the failure of markets to attend adequately to society's needs.

Ben-Ner and Van Hoomissen[12] argue that the operation of nonprofit organizations sometimes boils down to the ability of their consumers or stakeholders to control their organizations and therefore be assured that they operate for the purposes for which they were intended. Entrepreneurial types may start or manage organizations, but the control of the organizations is by those for whom they are intended—the consumer or beneficiaries. This control may be direct or indirect. Thus, Ben-Ner and Gui[13] conclude that those who start organizations do so fully recognizing the need to "cooperate with key high-demand stakeholders and de facto make them controlling stakeholders." From this perspective, the nonprofit as an agent of public policy represents a mechanism over which the stakeholders have more direct control.

Contract Failure Theories

The second major market-centric approach to nonprofits is called contract failure theory. It addresses questions such as: Why would the profit motive be a detriment and cause the market to fail, even when goods can be priced, consumers who don't pay can be denied, and consumers are willing to bid? Why, in these instances, may the market not lead to transactions at the end of which both consumers and producers are satisfied? Why may the consumer resist purchasing the product at the price offered by the producer? The market may fail in these situations because the nature of the contract or the character of the transactions that it takes to transfer those goods from the seller to the buyer fails. Contract failure theory focuses on the nature of the contract or transactions that makes nonprofits more suited than firms to be agents of the public's policies.

Hansmann[14] developed the contract failure theory. He writes, "I am suggesting that nonprofit enterprise is a reasonable response to a particular kind of 'market failure,' specifically the inability to police producers by ordinary contractual devices, which I shall call 'contract failure.'" Unlike market failure theorists, Hansmann's focus is not on the type of good or consumer, but on the type of contractual understanding or arrangement that makes the market work. The norms by which market contracts are understood, arranged, and implemented do not work under certain circumstances.

Where would market contractual arrangements fail? Here are three of Hansmann's situations.

1. Where there is a separation between the purchaser and the recipient of the service and the purchaser wishes to control his or her contribution and maximize its use on behalf of the recipient.

2. Where there is voluntary price discrimination, such as at a museum, where some people would gladly pay more than others for the same exhibit.
3. When consumers have choices to be made but cannot exercise discretion, perhaps for lack of information or asymmetric information, which places them at the mercy of the supplier.

Illustrations of Contract Failure Due to Asymmetric Information and Other Factors

But why wouldn't the market contract work? In item number 1 it would not work because the profit motive provides for investors to be paid dividends. A payment of a dividend means that money leaves the purpose for which the donor gave it and enters the pockets of the dividend receivers, who in the market contract are the owners who have rights or claims over the net assets of the business. In addition, the donor does not make this decision—the managers do. In a nonprofit no dividends can be paid and all earnings must be used for the purpose intended. Moreover, the organization must honor the wish of the donor when it accepts the donation. Under these circumstances, the market contract fails and a nonprofit is indicated as a superior organizational form to meet objective number 1.

Objective number 2 may be explained this way: All consumers are price takers in a market contract. They face a common price and they all pay it. The store sells its bread for so much to everyone who purchases it. In some cases, however, consumers may gladly pay more for the same good; and some may wish to pay less. It is not atypical for a museum to "suggest" a range of prices and for people to voluntarily elect which they wish to pay—voluntary price discrimination. Those who pay more than others may see themselves as making a gift to the organization or as subsidizing poorer persons who pay less. Because the market charges all the same price, the market contract fails when voluntarily differential pricing may be advantageous.

Objective number 3 is essentially described earlier. The market contract presumes that both the seller and the buyer have similar information about the product and the transaction. If they don't, the transaction is likely to be less than satisfactory if it occurs at all. Indeed, the consumer may be so distrustful knowing that what motivates the seller is making a profit that the consumer may simply walk away. Joining like-thinking consumers, they may produce their own product for their own satisfaction and jointly control the operation through a nonprofit organization where the profit motive does not exist.

Easley and O'Hara[15]add to the contract failure theory by arguing that when outcomes are hard to observe or can be observed only at great cost, a nonprofit organization that pays management on the basis of a fixed-fee contract is better than a firm using a "typical" incentive market contract. Under a "typical" market contract, the compensation of managers varies by performance and therefore they would have an incentive to "lie." In this instance, the market contract fails.

Merging Contract and Market Failure Theories

In a sense, market failure theories focus on the types of goods and services while contract failure theories focus on why the standard way of doing business in a for-profit market fails. They both recognize the importance of asymmetric information and they both recognize that the for-profit motive can cause consumers to be distrustful of sellers.

Market failure theory focuses on donations as a means of paying for nonprofit services. Contract failure theory sees donations also from the perspective of who controls it. To illustrate, without attempting to place them in one category or the other, we quote Fama and Jansen[16]: "the absence of a residual claimant avoids the donor-residual claimant agency problem and explains the dominance of nonprofits in donor-financed activities." In short, nonprofits thrive in sectors where donations cannot be claimed or diverted to stockholders or partners (residual claimants, in Williamson's terminology)[17] but must be retained for the purposes for which they were given.

Ben-Ner[18] has tried to merge both market and contract failure theories to distinguish a nonprofit organization from a for-profit firm. He notes that the characteristics of a nonprofit are:

1. Control by the stakeholders for whose benefit the organization was formed.
2. Specialization in goods where asymmetric information works against stakeholders (trust goods) and collective goods where people cannot be excluded and consumption is possible by all.
3. The lack of ownership shares.
4. Profits may not be distributed.
5. The open-books policy gives access to information leading to trust in the organization.

Why is the distinction between the firm and the nonprofit important to this book? Because a principal question in looking at nonprofits as agents of public policy is to ask: Why does the government choose to contract with a nonprofit to implement a public policy when it could contract with an equally qualified firm? This question will be addressed in chapter 5.

The Public Policy Impact of Nonprofits on Markets

The market-centric approaches described in the previous two sections emphasize the forming of nonprofits or collectivities to meet needs insufficiently or inadequately met by the market either because of the nature of the good, service, contract, or transaction. Because this book is about the nonprofit as an agent of public policy, we must go beyond that. Public policy is far more than an alternative to the market. In this opening section we shall discuss (a) how nonprofits impact an imperfect market and move it toward greater efficiency; (b) how nonprofits make large-volume markets and regulate them; and (c) how nonprofits treat the negative social and economic consequences of the market—all for a greater public policy purpose. The point here is that even in markets, the nonprofit is not a passive consequence. It helps shape the market; and is no more a product of the market than the market is of it to the extent that public policy determines the behavior of market forces.

Nonprofits that Assist Markets toward Perfection as a Matter of Public Policy

Several nonprofits serve as the public's agent to improve market performance. The following typology is created by going through all of the public policy functions that qualify for tax-exemption under the Internal Revenue Code and categorizing them.[19]

1. Assisting Consumers: Nonprofits that test for product safety, provide information on product prices and product quality, and advocate on behalf of consumers.
2. Assisting Workers: Nonprofits that provide job training, counseling and placement assistance, and day care centers, and advocate on behalf of workers and other employee associations.
3. Assisting Producers: Nonprofits that do scientific research and advocacy on behalf of firms and assist in the development of firms through incubators and nonbankable loans and lease technology to firms.
4. Assisting Savers: Nonprofits that provide credit counseling and assistance; credit unions, pension, and retirement benefits associations.
5. Assisting Investors: Nonprofits that provide information and advocacy for investors and that encourage area development and renewal and attract and retain new investments in local areas.
6. Assisting in Improving Industry and Economic Environment: Nonprofits that promote fair business practices, trade shows, business leagues, chambers, and associations, tourist bureaus, farm bureaus, community development and crime prevention, and provide industry-wide information such as real estate prices.
7. Assisting Employers: Nonprofits that provide training and counseling, certification and screening, and employee benefits.

Nonprofits that Assist Markets in the Problem of Asymmetric Information as a Matter of Public Policy

Arrow[20] explains the formation and continuation of nonprofit hospitals on the basis of asymmetric information. The patient knows less about medical care than the hospital provider. The patient also knows that a for-profit hospital is interested in profits and the patient may accurately or not link the method of treatment with the making of profits. Alternatively, the patient may go to a nonprofit hospital where there is a convergence of interest between the patient and the hospital (a religious or fraternal hospital of like thinking with the patient) and where there is no profit motive to cause a perception of conflict of interest. The patient may not solve the asymmetric information, but its existence is more tolerable because of the greater trust.

Some nonprofits exist to reduce the asymmetry of information and to make consumers more aware as a matter of public policy. *The Consumer Reports* is owned and operated by the Consumer Union—a nonprofit organization founded in 1936. It is an example of providing information to consumers—information they would not otherwise have. Highly reputable and consulted, it provides comparative information to the consumer about the performance of a wide range of products. It increases the trustworthiness of its report by never taking corporate contributions as a matter of policy and by creating an endowment that it uses to help finance its work. Another nonprofit, The Center for Science in the Public Interest, has been instrumental in getting proper food labeling and more accurate advertising of food and the nutritional content.

Before the Fair Packaging and Labeling Act of 1966, most consumers had not the foggiest idea what the nutritional content was of the food they were consuming. National Consumer League, started in 1899, still provides consumers with information on a wide range of products. The Center for Auto Safety provides information on new and used cars, has a mechanism for consumers to share complaints about cars, and maintains a library on cars. These are examples of nonprofits that try to reduce the scope of asymmetric information rather than produce an alternative supplier of goods and services.

Spence[21] and Akerlof[22] argued that there are times in which potential buyers consider a product to be of lower quality than the seller knows. The buyer, not having this information, is only willing to pay a lower price than the seller wants. The price of the product will be driven down and the sellers would no longer offer it. Spence noted that a screening strategy maybe used by the seller to inform the buyer of the quality of the product. This strategy may be so expensive that the low-quality provider cannot compete in disseminating information about their product. One of the functions of professional and business associations (nonprofits discussed in chapter 8) is screening. By certifying and licensing members, they signal to the public that those who bear these "approvals" are of higher quality, justifying, perhaps, a high price and confidence. The certificate, not the advertising, justifies the price.

Stiglitz[23] and his associates studied various types of situations involving asymmetric information, including universities operating as a screening mechanism for markets, and the effects on credit, including the possibilities that the risks associated with asymmetrical information can be dealt with through the formation of nonprofit risk pools in which members induce each other to pay and to protect the lender as a group. Nonprofit organizations involved in micro lending are examples and form a basis of development policy in many countries.

Nonprofits that Assist Markets as Market Regulators as a Matter of Public Policy

The Financial Accounting Foundation is a 501 (c) (3). It selects the members of the Financial Accounting Standard Board (FASB). It oversees the board (except its technical decisions) and provides its managerial and financial support as an independent arm. Since 1973, the Securities and Exchange Commission has accepted the rulings of the FASB and has yielded its statutory function of setting accounting rules to FASB.

The rulings of FASB cover every aspect of accounting and financial reporting done by public firms. These include accounting for mergers and acquisition, for inventory, for profits, for revenues, and all manner of expenses and compensation. According to the board's brochures, "Such standards are essential to the efficient functioning of the economy because investors, creditors, auditors and others rely on credible, transparent, and comparable financial information."

The National Association of Securities Dealers (NASD) controls the education, certification, and registration of all individuals and brokerages dealing publicly with securities in the United States, whether as issuers or sellers. It also controls the relationship between these people (known as agents) and their principals (firms). It controls the behavior between these agents and customers. It controls advertising by firms and sales practices. It disciplines by fining, suspending, and barring agents and firms from further practice. It owns (or owned, if the proposed sale proceeds) the Nasdaq that gives daily price, volume, dividend-payout, and provides information for clearing securities markets. It is a nonprofit and is tax exempt.

The historical fact is that NASD grew out of what may be a combination of market failure (the existence of externalities), contract failure (the certainty that individuals and firms could not trust each other on economic transactions), and government failure (the inability of the government to form a regulatory organization to the likings of the brokerage firms and the Supreme Court in 1933). It operates as a substitute for government with formal contractual terms with the SEC and the U.S. Congress. What is important about the NASD and other similar organizations is the power they exercise over financial markets as a matter of public policy for the smooth functioning of financial transactions and for public protection.

A final example is taken from the insurance industry. Each and every type of insurance product offered by any insurance company has to be approved in each and every state in which that individual product is offered. Each insurance company has to file extensive and detailed accounting information in each state in which it wants to sell its products. Sales agents have to be examined and authorized to sell various lines of insurance products. State commissioners of insurance bear this responsibility. They license companies, products, and agents.

In 1871, the commissioners formed the National Association of Insurance Commissioners (NAIC) to which the insurance commissioners of 50 states, the District of Columbia, and 4 territories are currently members. According to its brochure, the mission of the NAIC is to assist state insurance regulators, individually and collectively, in serving the public interest. Accordingly, the NAIC undertakes these regulatory actions described on its website:

> Protect the public interest
> Promote competitive markets
> Facilitate the fair and equitable treatment of insurance consumers
> Promote the reliability, solvency, and financial solidity of insurance institutions; and
> Support and improve state regulation of insurance

All three organizations cited above play a key regulatory function in the interest of public policy, improving market performance and protecting the public interest.

Nonprofits That Facilitate Corporate Liquidity as a Matter of Public Policy

Companies throughout the world need liquidity, and investors throughout the world need a market place to buy and sell the financial instruments that provide such liquidity. Some of the principal exchanges where financial securities (stocks, bonds, options, futures contracts, and futures options) are bought and sold, such as the New York Stock Exchange and the Chicago Board of Trade, are nonprofit organizations. They provide the facilities, the place, the electronic communications, and the rules of conduct and reciprocity that enable such transactions to move fairly smoothly. They may also operate, own, or coordinate the activities of the corporation (called a clearinghouse) that actually clears the market, that is, that does the actual transfers according to the orders obtained on the floor of the exchanges or holds the securities (called depositories).

The New York Stock Exchange, for example, is incorporated under Section 102 of the New State Not-for-Profit law with a mission to provide rooms, rules, and facilities that enable its members to receive and make orders (market making) in various financial securities and to provide a forum for the discussion of public policy. The Chicago Board of Trade is also a nonprofit organization and clears its trades in options, futures, and option futures through an independent clearinghouse once its subsidiary. Exchanges are variously linked electronically so that orders may move from one to the other and across the globe.

Nonprofits that Reduce Negative Externalities and Social Consequences of Markets as Public Policy

Coase[24] explains that when transaction costs are low, there is no need for taxation, fines, penalties, and other social or governmental actions when the negative consequences of one party's behavior affect another. The parties are capable of working it out efficiently and satisfactorily without government intervention. An implication of this is that nonprofit organizations, as substitutes for government to adjudicate in these situations, may also not be needed in these circumstances where individuals can resolve their differences.

The need for organized intervention exists when transaction costs are high and the stakes are big. For example, it is literally impossible for each person to work out an agreement with all potential smokers he or she may encounter, to monitor that agreement, and to enforce sanctions against those whose smoking may have a negative effect. When many people in a community are faced with the same problem, then, organized community action may be needed.

In this vein, a number of nonprofits are created to deal with the negative impacts on individuals and society because consumers as well as producers are motivated by their own private benefits and ignore the costs they impose on others. These nonprofits include those dealing with substance abuse, driving while drunk, threats to wildlife and the wilderness, pollution, conservation, and nitrogen and pesticide runoffs. Thus, the environmental-conscious design of cars is not the product of consumers creating their own suppliers, but of nonprofits impacting manufacturers not withstanding prior claims of asymmetric information about what was technically cost-effective to do.

Government Failure and the Failure of Trust

Another theoretical approach for explaining the role of nonprofits in society is government failure. Some outside the economic profession argue that nonprofits owe their existence not to market but to government failure. Lohmann[25] has noted that, either way, both approaches are based on failure. Salamon[26] has noted that the emphasis on market-oriented explanations of nonprofits seriously limits the debate. His theory is that government and firms are the results of the failure of the nonprofit sector due to the amateurism, the dominance of founders, insufficient funding, and the tendency of nonprofits to focus on special groups. These "failures" create the need for government and sometimes firms.

How does government failure lead to the formation of a growing nonprofit sector? Weisbrod[27] argues that by its nature, government tends to provide large goods for which the public as a whole pays. Therefore, in a country where groups have different preferences, many nonprofits would be formed to offer these smaller, more diversified goods. In short, the number, growth, and diversity of nonprofits increase as population diversity increases.

Douglas[28] argues that there are five reasons for government failure:

1. Government provides goods on a universal basis and therefore persons with particular needs are not likely to be satisfied.
2. Government responds to the majority rule in satisfying needs but leaves the particular needs of minority groups unsatisfied.
3. Government officials are elected for short terms, hence they tend to focus on short-term needs, leaving some long-term needs unattended.
4. Government bureaucrats do not have all of the relevant information.
5. Government is too large and impersonal, and therefore there is a need for mediating (nonprofit) organizations.

In Douglas's view, any of these conditions represents a failure of government and creates a role for nonprofit organizations.

The Failure of Trust in Government as a Probable Cause for the Rise in Nonprofits to Deal with Public Policy

All of the above government-oriented failures refer to failures in operation. There may also be a failure of trust. Nye, Behn, Ostrom[29] and others itemize why people distrust governments. These reasons range from corruption to issues of efficiencies, to lack of responsiveness, to lack of accountability and commitment. Hardin[30] reviews the use of the concept of trust and arrives at the following: A person places trust in others who that person believes will act in that person's best interest, and the main incentive of one to act on behalf of the other is the expectation of some benefits in return. At least from this individual-to-individual perspective, Hardin argues, what is significant is not how much people trust government, but how much they distrust government—whether the majority feel that government will not act on their behalf. This argument seems to say that people may trust government without taking action, but that distrust stimulates action. Could it be that a lack of confidence in government leads to the formation of nonprofits in the same way that distrust of firms leads to the formation of nonprofits?

The Rise of Nonprofits to Deal with Public Policy Issues of Stability and Tranquility

A primary role of government is the security of its citizens. Boli and Thomas[31] have shown that the growth in international nongovernmental (nonprofit) organizations (NGOs) correlates with world economic and educational development, globalization, and the development of interstate systems. It declines during world wars and rises vigorously after. They conclude on page ten of their article that international nongovernmental organizations "have expanded in the interstices of power networks." These include international organizations in science that provide for international cooperation and sharing of information and organizations in human rights that, among other things, influence the agendas of international organizations.

Some political scientists have noted the rise in the number of international protest groups dealing with economic and political matters.[32] One political scientist suggests that the rise of some protest groups in some countries is in part related to a moral hazard—the greater the probability that outside forces would intervene to protect the protestors, the greater the willingness to risk the penalty of protest.[33] The fundamental question here is the extent to which nonprofits rise or fall in environments of instability and their contribution to the establishment and permanence of stability, even in former communist[34] and in developing countries,[35] and to civic discourse.

Local, not just international, nonprofits may be agents of peace and tranquility even when their missions are not. The island of Cyprus is divided between people of Turkish and of Greek origins, with only the latter portion having international status as a nation. The United Nations has tried to bring about unification between these two peoples, who are separate in language, culture, religion, and wealth, in addition to being physically separated. Through the assistance of the U.S. Agency for International Development a set of nonprofits has been financed and much effort has been made to increase their operating capacities.[36]

These nonprofits are the typical economic development, artistic, cultural, and family mediation organizations. However, no project is funded in this program unless it involves peoples across both borders. There is a historic wall that separates both sectors; hence, one project involves the restoration of that wall. Each community works on its side of the wall. The principal public policy that is being promoted is not economic development, but peace and civility—conditions for orderly governance and intercommunity discourse.

The Nonprofit as a Mediating Structure in Public Policy

Berger and Neuhaus[37] define mediating structures as those entities that interface between the private lives of individuals and the remainder of the world. Thus, all forms of nonprofit organizations including the church may be considered mediating agencies. They enable the individual to cope with other entities including the government. A natural but unmentioned extension of this notion is that nonprofit organizations originate and are created by the individuals to allow them to cope with aspects of their environments in a more efficient manner than the individual can by him- or herself.

The Nonprofit Agent as a Regulator: Rules, Public Policy Regulations, and Asymmetric Information

Earlier in this chapter, we visited nonprofits as regulators of markets. Some of these facts lead to another perspective—the nonprofit as a self-regulator. In this sense, nonprofits also play a role in governance. In this role, they are not attempting to regulate a market (i.e., to establish a predictable order in which transactions occur freely) but to enforce public laws and to protect the public interest by regulating the behavior of their members. This includes determining whether they are suited to or do perform competently and ethically in the public's interest. These organizations are involved in governance; they substitute for government in regulating their members. This regulation can be subtle or very direct.

The first example is the College Board. Formed in 1900, the College Board is an association of over 4,500 colleges, universities, and other educational institutions that is best known for administering the SAT and PSAT exams, which significantly influence colleges' selections of their future students. The College Board works as a powerful "invisible hand" in influencing the allocation of students and student-opportunities among its member schools. It influences rather than regulates its members' behavior. It influences their choices, and the results of these choices influence their reputation; that is, "good" schools enroll students with top SAT scores.

The American Board of Anesthesiologists—and ultimately the Accreditation Council for Graduate Medical Education (another nonprofit)—sets standards for the training of anesthesiologists. Schools of medicine follow these standards in order to acquire and maintain their accreditation in the training of anesthesiologists. A principal purpose of certification in this and all other cases, including 24 medical specialties, is to provide signaling information to the public that certain standards have been met by the certified so that a professionally acceptable outcome may be expected from them.

The Federation of State Medical Boards of the United States, Inc., describes itself as a nonprofit organization made up of the 70 medical boards of the United States, the District of Columbia, Puerto Rico, Guam, and the U.S. Virgin Islands. Its members are government agencies or commissions comprised of boards appointed by the governor to protect the health of the consumer public through the proper licensing and behavior of physicians and some related medical personnel. The boards judge physicians based upon state laws falling under the general title of the Medical Practice Act. The act is concerned with finding evidence that a physician's performance was impaired, including by the commitment of a felony.

The mission of the federation is to improve the quality, safety, and integrity of health care through the development and promotion of high standards for physician licensure and practice. In its April 6, 2004, news release, the federation reported that its members had taken over 5,230 disciplinary actions against physicians in 2003 and some 4,590 were of the type that jeopardized, suspended, or revoked a physician's license.

These are various models of nonprofits operating in a regulatory manner. The most complete power to so act that this author knows of is in the securities business, where the nonprofit as a self-regulator controls the registration, advertising, transfer through sales, hiring, supervising, educating, arbitrating, assigning of penalties and expulsions, recordkeeping, and virtually every significant aspect of the securities market. There is at least one in every country, large or small, in which there is a capital market. This topic is left to chapter 10.

Self-regulation, to the extent that it works, reduces the burden of government. It reduces the need for an additional government bureaucracy and government financing since these groups do not depend on government subsidy but are self-financing mostly through dues and fees charged to their members or clients. Self-regulation also addresses the problem of asymmetric information; for example, the College Board serves as a screening device to sort of even out the risk that a college would take because it would otherwise know less about the student than the student would about the college. The credentialing nonprofits, such as those in medical specialties, give certificates that "signal" to consumers that the physician has qualified and demonstrated a level of competence acceptable to his or her peers. Absent this, the patient would know less about the qualification of his or her physician.

The Risk of Overstating or Overreliance on Market and Government Failure

Finally, one of the problems of relying on failure theories is that failure is neither a permanent nor an exclusive state. In a dynamic world, failure is an unstable platform upon which to justify an organization's existence—particularly within the public policy process. First, in virtually every sphere in which nonprofits work, there are successful for-profit competitors—in some spheres such as higher education, hospital care, job-training, and social services, the inroads being made by firms are not trivial and the products and processes not necessarily fundamentally different. A distinction, as we shall see throughout this book, is the risk exposure to which the nonprofit is subjected and what this book develops as the five levels of contracting confidence that are intrinsic to nonprofits but not to firms.

Second, a number of nonprofits have converted to for-profit status—undoubtedly concluding that the former status is no longer an advantage and operating under the latter is not only possible but profitable. The reverse conversion is rare. Under these conditions, one cannot rely on (at least forever), or gain sufficient competitive advantage by, resting one's claim for being on the failure of others. There must be a more intrinsic value for the nonprofit—a purpose of their being regardless (not just because) of the failure of others.

In closing this chapter, two essays are worth keeping in mind because they remind us of the risk of overstating market and government failures and, by implication, the rise of alternative organizational forms to substitute either for governments or markets. Kelman[38] writes: (a) that there is nothing unique about government failures—firms also fail; (b) that much of government failure can be attributed to the politics of policy that impede policy implementation; (c) that some government failure is an over generalization of one or a particular failure to a characterization of how government operates; (d) that some government failure is attributed to the inherent conflict between liberty and efficiency in governmental management; and (e) some of government failure is due to the difference between citizen expectations and government performance and to the intellectual tools by which we judge governments. Particularly through chapters 5 to 8 of this book we shall see that some of these issues also apply to nonprofits and that through organizational learning, even governments can learn and become formidable, efficient competitors.

With respect to market failure, Zerbe and McCurdy[39] write that market failure theory fails in part because it is "ubiquitous" and, in part, because it may only be explaining the transaction costs to enforce and exercise property rights. By extension, to the extent that these property rights problems can be solved, market failure disappears as a justification for nonprofits or government intervention. They argue that some prominent economists have long recognized the limitation of market failure theories.

Together, these two essays are interpreted in this book to imply that the exclusive reliance on failure theories is intellectually risky and may obscure appreciation of the role of nonprofits in the public policy process. If failure is significant, but not sufficient, what other paradigms work to portray the social function of nonprofits?

Summary and Preview

The principal purpose of this chapter is to lay the foundation for the remainder of this book. It does so by reviewing extant theories about the role and proper purpose of nonprofit organizations primarily in a market-centric society. These theories continue to be important and contain critical concepts that will be applicable throughout this book. But these theories do not go far enough. From a public policy perspective, as pointed out in chapter 1, it is important to know what nonprofits do, for whom they do it, and why they do it. From a public policy perspective the impact of nonprofits on policy, on government, and on the markets are important. Analyzing the roles they play in the public policy process and framing these for universal analysis and application become useful analytic, managerial, and policy challenges.

Consequently, a substantial part of this chapter has been dedicated to showing how nonprofits impact the markets (beyond the consequence of failure), and how they may impact or substitute for government beyond the concept of government failure. To make the point meaningful, a deliberate attempt was made to use examples that are large, determinative, and that occupy a significant part of what markets and governments do, that is, trading of securities, peace and tranquility, and regulations. These functions contain big public policy issues that affect the rich and the poor across the globe; and in each of these functions, the nonprofit is a prominent player.

To understand and to analyze the relationship between the nonprofit and the public, we need to go forward and incorporate a larger paradigm that focuses on the ingredients of a relationship, its substance (i.e., policy), and on the players or participants. In the public policy and political processes, the nonprofit as a player and participant can be viewed as both a social capital asset and an agent of the public. But it is not enough to make this assertion. The objective of the next few chapters is to articulate the nature of the relationship in a principal-agent framework.

Part II

Nonprofits as Social Capital Assets and Agents of the Public

In their essence, nonprofits are social capital assets. This is so because they meet the conditions we expect of any long-term capital and because the word "social" is more than sociological. Social refers, in this context, to property rights over the stock of assets (the organization) and the benefits that flow from these assets. In today's world of bidding, where virtually every area in which nonprofits operate is penetrable by for-profit firms, where firms and nonprofits compete for the same government contracts, the comparative advantage of nonprofits rests in the discovery of its intrinsic value in terms of the costs, expectations, and reliability of performance relative to its competitors bidding for the same contract. Why, then, would the government prefer a nonprofit over a firm for a particular public policy contract? How did the nonprofit penetrate the pool of contractors potentially available to the public? Who empowers nonprofits to represent the public as its agents? Why is the concept of social capital (used in a disciplined economic or business sense) so central? Why is the concept of social capital used in a particular sociological sense, such as a contribution?

Chapter 3

The Nonprofits as Social Assets and Agents of Public Policy

The purpose of this chapter is to lay out foundation concepts that are critical to our discussion and to the principal-agent paradigm as it applies to the theme: the nonprofit as a social capital asset and an agent of public policy. These concepts include (a) the nonprofit as a social capital asset and an agent of the public; (b) social capital—not a review of the literature on this subject, but precisely how it fits into our paradigm; (c) the substitution of nonprofits for governments as agents of public policy; and (d) the distinction between two types of agency relationships that a nonprofit may have when functioning as an agent of public policy—if it is under contract and if it is not. In the next chapter we see how these concepts fit into an application of the principal-agent paradigm.

The Legal Foundation for Our Argument

The concepts of the nonprofit organization as a public asset and agent have their foundation in law. The nonprofit is an institutional mode of organizing the acquisition, accumulation, and disposition of assets for the exclusive benefit of a group, a collectivity, a community, and ultimately for the public or society at large. Thus, the legal charter under which every nonprofit is formed and operates has words similar to the following, drawn from the Internal Revenue Service (IRS) model articles of incorporation required to obtain tax-exempt status under Section 501 (c) (3) of the Code:

> Said corporation is organized exclusively for charitable, religious, educational, and scientific purposes. . . .
>
> No part of the net earnings of the corporation shall inure to the benefit of, or be distributable to its members, trustees, officers, or other private persons, except that the corporation shall be authorized and empowered to pay reasonable compensation for services rendered.
>
> Upon the dissolution of the corporation, the Board of Trustees shall, after paying or making provision for the payment of all of the liabilities of the corporation, dispose of all of the assets of the corporation exclusively for the

> purposes of the corporation in such manner, or to such organization or organizations organized and operated exclusively for charitable, educational, religious, or scientific purposes as shall at that time qualify as an exempt organization. . . . Any such assets not so disposed of shall be disposed of by the Court of Common Pleas of the county in which the principal office of the corporation is then located, exclusively for such purposes or to such organization or organizations, as said Court shall determine, which are organized and operated exclusively for such purposes.

Section 501 (c) (4) provides exemption from taxation for civic leagues or organizations not organized for profit, but operated exclusively for the promotion of social welfare.

Nonprofit organizations under Section 501 (c) (6) are business leagues. A business league is an association of persons having some common business interest that is to be promoted and not to engage in a regular business of a kind ordinarily carried on for profit. A business league's activities are directed to the improvement of business conditions for an industry or a community.

Section 527 are political organizations, a party, committee, association, fund, or other organization operated to influence the selection, nomination, election, or appointment of any individual to any Federal, State, or local public office or for an office in a political organization. A political action committee (PAC) is one of these. In short, the nonprofit is incorporated to serve a specific set of public purposes. Even if the organization terminates, these assets must be rededicated to these public purposes and not distributed to persons other than for compensation; that is, no dividends are allowed and benefits are not personal except as for clients and to cover the organization's debt and for compensation. The assets and the flow of benefits from them are the community's.

Thus, whether we are referring to religious, educational, charitable, scientific, literary, arts and cultural, health, welfare associations, or even certain political organizations, the basic presumption is that if they are nonprofit and tax exempt, they exist to advance group, community, or public welfare. Ultimately, this welfare can determine who is elected or appointed, what public policies are passed and repealed, and how they are implemented. The law, therefore, provides for nonprofits to operate along this continuum—from the beginning to the end of the public policy process.

The Assets

The assets these organizations acquire, accumulate, and use may be monetary or nonmonetary, tangible or intangible, real (land and improvements—real estate), or personal (assets other than real estate). The nonprofit as an asset can acquire or affiliate with others. Thus, the nonprofit is an asset greater than the sum of its parts. But is it social capital?

The Concept of Social or Community Asset as Applied to the Nonprofit

Capital is a long-term asset that is acquired through purposeful investment and that is held to produce a long-term flow of benefits that have economic value.

An airport or a road is a form of a community's tangible capital. Both result from investments by the community intended to produce a flow of community benefits over a long period. Notice that in these and other forms of capital the benefits may be monetary or nonmonetary, but they have economic value and result from purposeful investments. In the same vein, a nonprofit organization that is created by the investment effort of donors and tax exemption is social capital and the public owns both the social capital and the benefits that are expected to flow from them.

The concept of community ownership of the nonprofit assets and the benefits that flow from them is legal and precise even though not commonly appreciated. The logic is as follows: The nonprofit (regardless of what it is called) is created by gifts to the community directed to and for the purpose of operating the nonprofit. The community compensates for this through a tax deduction to donors and tax exemption to the organization. The nonprofit corporation "operates" the nonprofit. It does not own it. Thus, the law never refers to a Catholic hospital as one owned by the Catholic Church. It refers to it as one "operated" by the Catholic Church on behalf of the public. The same is true of all nonprofits. Thus, upon the dissolution of a nonprofit, the assets that do not belong to creditors or to individuals (such as compensation, or a loan such as art) must, by state and federal laws, be transferred to a similar nonprofit for the benefit of the public or to the state which in turn distributes these assets for a public purpose similar to that for which they were originally intended.

Nonprofits as Social Capital Assets in the Principal-Agent Paradigm

As Portes[1] notes in his historical review of the concept of social capital, the concept is used both to indicate an asset that produces a good result for individuals or for society, or a bad result for individuals or for society. It, according to him, is also used as a concept of social control, as a concept to explain intrafamily support, and as a concept to analyze sociability and networks outside the family. He notes that recent uses of the concept extend to communities and to nations; and, he warns, that untamed stretches threaten to destroy the heuristic use of the concept. He concludes that the time has come where the concept is used in so many diverse ways that it is likely to lose any distinct meaning.

In thinking of the nonprofit as an agent of public policy within the principal-agent paradigm, therefore, it is not sufficient to merely assert that it is social capital or to resort to the cognitive and noncognitive norms, networks, and institutions (formal or informal) commonly used to denote what social capital is. As Schuller, et al.[2] have written, some prominent economists such as Arrow[3] and Solow[4] express dissatisfaction with the concepts "social" and "capital."

Within the principal-agent paradigm, an agent cannot be a norm or a network or just any institution (formal or informal) that facilitates collective action. It has to be an identifiable person or institution that can be hired as an agent and held accountable for its performance.

In this book, therefore, a nonprofit is considered a social capital asset capable of being an agent because:

1. It is a composite of assets and is itself a long-lived asset—a capital asset that is a legal person capable of entering into a contract. It can function as an agent and is licensed to function as an agent of the public by both the state in which it is incorporated and the federal government. This is witnessed in its charter and in its receiving tax exemption.
2. All property rights over the organization and its assets, except in the case of lenders, are owned by a collectivity, a group, a community, or a society, to which all properties must be distributed if the organization terminates. In this sense, exclusive ownership of the assets by the society or community, the nonprofit is social.
3. It is a long-lived asset with an expected flow of benefits. Since the community owns the asset, it also owns the benefits that are expected to flow from it. Over its life, the asset and its benefits might grow, become obsolete, or diminish in quantity and in value.
4. The acquisition of the assets, and their maintenance, results from the investment by the community or group in the form of donations, tax deductions, and tax exemption. All of these represent costs, called tax expenditures, to the public. Therefore, they are indirect payments by the public.
5. Because of the above, the nonprofit is obliged to be accountable to the public in the same manner that a public firm is obliged to be accountable to its shareholders. Accordingly, both are obligated by law to report to the public annually. Agents are accountable to their principals.

The nonprofit is therefore a long-term asset capable of growth, obsolescence, and diminution (a capital asset), and is created by the community or group for its own long-term benefits (a social capital asset). The nonprofit is capable of entering into contracts (an agent) with and on behalf of the community (the principal) and its elected representatives (the government).

It can be compensated and it can be penalized for its failure to conform to the contract terms. It is also accountable to its principal—the public.

This operational definition is distinctly different from other available definitions[5] of social capital. The nonprofit is variously defined as a sum of human capital,[6] and a locus of norms, networks, interactions, trust, and reciprocity that facilitate collective action.[7] Indeed, these definitions will play a role in this book, but they do not define the nonprofit as social capital and agent. They distinguish one nonprofit from the other in their probable effectiveness, cohesiveness, level of trust, and even in the quality of human capital (their age, mobility, homeownership, skill, and willingness to invest in themselves.[8]

In the principal-agent paradigm as in the real world, an agent cannot be a norm, network, or system of interaction. An agent has to be a legal, identifiable, responsible and accountable entity capable of entering and performing a contract on behalf of a principal. To be social, its assets have to be acquired for and by a community, exclusively for the community's long-term benefits, and therefore the entity has to be accountable to the community. It is in this new sense that nonprofits are defined in this book as social capital assets that serve as agents of public policy. The next chapter will develop the concept of "agent" within the principal-agent paradigm; but first more on networks.

The Network Form of Social Capital and Its Relevance to the Nonprofit as an Agent of Public Policy

All social capital are not capable of being agents of public policy. A network is generally not the type of social capital capable of being an agent.

Take an example of three nonprofit organizations, A, B, and C. Each of the nonprofits is not only a social capital asset but, independently, is capable of being an agent of policy. Each can make a promise, discharge it, be awarded for it, and be penalized for its failure. Each is accountable and responsible on its own. But A, B, and C may choose to work together to perform a contract. Here are their options for working together as a network.

1. A, B, and C may form a network represented by the lines that connect them. The network, the connection or interaction, is the net in which the work is embedded to perform the contract. But the net cannot sign a contract or make an enforceable promise or be accountable for one. The individual components, A, B, and C, can. Therefore, A, B, C—not the lines that connect them into a network—are the social capital assets that can act as agents of public policy.
2. A, B, and C can form and incorporate a separate organization, D, to which each contributes its agreed-upon share of assets. D, being an

organization that has a charter and is a legal entity, with a tax-exempt status, and its own ability to sign, discharge, and be penalized for a contract failure, is a social capital asset, a nonprofit, and has the capacity to be an agent of public policy. In this case, D is a corporation that is the result of a partnership or a joint venture among A, B, and C, but it is legally distinct from them. A, B, and C are merely shareholders in D and may be the only directors. In nonprofit law, these may be classified as 509 (a) (3)s and are discussed along with various network possibilities in conformity with nonprofit law in Bryce.[9]

3. A, B, and C may decide not to form a separate organization but to remain independent for the purposes of a contract; they may form a network and hold each one jointly and severally responsible for the performance of the contract. That is to say, each organization, being itself an agent and recognizing that it needs the cooperation of the others to succeed, makes the promise to perform with the understanding that it will be culpable if any other fails. In that sense, the network is a social asset, but it is not an agent of public policy in itself (it cannot sign or make a promise). Rather, it is A, B, and C acting independently that jointly forms the agency relationship with the public.
4. A, B, and C could merge, or one could acquire the other two. In this case, only the surviving organization, whatever it is called, is the agent, now reorganized and composed of the others or the acquired.

Therefore, a network, while being a social capital, may not be always an agent. This is not to imply that networks are of secondary importance. Understanding how networks operate is intriguing and points to the efficacy of performance in a principal-agent paradigm. Within the principal-agent paradigm, networks enable transactions to occur with various levels of trust or confidence,[10] and they reduce the cost of transactions.[11] For example, a supply chain reduces the cost of the agent contractor and ensures it that what it needs will be on time, but the chain is not an entity; rather each member of the chain is an entity and therefore the members, not the chain, are agents of each other. The chain merely makes it possible for the agents to function and to do so efficiently.

Kranton and Minehart[12] find that buyers and sellers seek out the most efficient networks to carry out their transactions. In the context of this book, agents and principals constantly seek the most efficient networks; thus, networks may not be fixed or be stable.[13] This concept implies that the networks to which a nonprofit belongs and operates are fluid partly because in a competitive environment it behooves the nonprofit to seek the most efficient network to carry out a specific task.

Networks also facilitate exchange. Based on an empirical study, DiMaggio and Louch[14] find that given asymmetric information or uncertainty about a product or service, buyers prefer to buy from sellers who are part of their noncommercial network, believing, in part, that information would travel about the product or service through the network and that, supposedly, this larger sanction would curtail cheating on the part of the seller. This is especially true where the goods are purchased infrequently (consumer durables) or the purchase is of a specially tailored or prepared consumer good. Sellers, on the other hand, prefer to sell to those who are outside of this larger network for the same reasons. Again, networks are important and will play a significant role, including this type of logic, in chapters 5 through 8 of this book.

Network membership may also be a determinant of the public's choice of a nonprofit as an agent of a specific policy. Podolny[15] distinguishes between networks that are "pipes" through which "stuff" flows, and networks as signals. Being a member of a network signals to the public that the nonprofit as a potential agent may have the right connections to get the job done. This is relevant to our discussion of state and federal contracting with nonprofit organizations for social and community development services.

The complete network of an organization is a composite of the relationship of the members of that organization to each other and to the group and the group to other groups and their individual members and to other individuals who may not be members.[16] Sociologists Linton Freeman, Murray Sunshine, and Thomas Fararo among others have mapped mathematically these types of networks. All networks are not formal and the motives for forming or joining a network vary. As well, networks are dynamic as members, the types of linkages among them, their aims, the norms that govern them, and the loci of specific transactions or loci of interaction may change. This concept of networks is important in appreciating the role of nonprofits as agents of policy formulation (lobbying) and in policy implementation and dissemination.

Katz, et al.[17] and Cook, et al.[18] have summarized and categorized much of network theory. Of particular interest to this book is exchange theory (sometimes called dependency theory). This theory sees a network as motivated by levels of exchange or dependency among the parties in the network. The objective for being in a network according to this theory is not always to maximize the probability that one would get what one wants, but to maximize the dependence of others on what one has to offer, which, in the case of a nonprofit as agent of public policy, would be its service. Therefore, being in a network may be a win-win situation for the nonprofit as an agent of public policy especially since most networks are voluntary and accommodate different levels of participation, including the discretion as to when and how much to participate.

The Cognitive Form of Social Capital, Its Properties, and Its Relevance

In the view of both Putnam[19] (who emphasizes the structural form of organizations or networks operating horizontally or cooperatively on an equal plain) and Coleman[20] (who emphasizes the cognitive form and a hierarchical network of associations where one leads the other), social capital refers to the enhanced capacity of a community (regardless of size) to take collective action in furtherance of a social good.

When social capital is used in its cognitive form in this book, it is used consistently but not synonymously with Fukiyama.[21] He sees social capital as the shared norms and values that promote cooperation among individuals. Fukiyama implies that there are an infinite number of shared values or norms. But the ones that are social capital are the ones that contribute to collective action. Stone[22] and other political scientists demonstrate the policy utility of this focus on cognitive social capital. In the study of educational reform, they find that the lack of civic capacity—the inability of the community to come to a common and coherent conclusion of what they want from the educational system—was a deterrent to their making a collective decision about what to do. In this book, the concept of cognitive social capital applies to those sociological factors such as shared norms and values, interactions and networks of interaction that enable an organization to decide on a common public policy position (to take collective action), to promote it, and to implement it—to produce results that promote public welfare that are consistent with the shared norms and values.

Accordingly, the U.S. Chamber of Commerce is an association where the members share values and norms, but only the shared values and norms that bind them in this particular association and motivate or facilitate a common collective action that benefits them as a group (i.e., a core norm, value, or mission such as to enhance the business environment); this is the cognitive social capital of primary interest in this principal-agent framework—not the other norms or values that the members may share but that do not motivate their collective behavior in the particular organization as opposed to all others. For example, the Democratic and Republican parties are made up of Americans with common American values, but they form different parties based on different philosophies. It is the philosophy of each that binds the party, motivates its collective action, and signals policy expectations when in office. Accordingly, the philosophies, not the American values, are the operative cognitive social capital in an agency relationship. Thus, each association represents a different cognitive social capital. Put otherwise, when used in this book, we see cognitive social capital as the core values or norms (i.e., purposes) for which a particular group is formed and maintained.

For the purposes of the theme of this book, nonprofits as social capital assets and agents of policy within a principal-agent paradigm, the concept of cognitive social capital assets have the following properties:

1. They are intangibles embodied in the product, process, or service of the organization.
2. They are sociological—the interaction among human actors or entities and those sociological factors such as norms, culture, regulations, and trust that govern these interactions.

3. They are accessible to all members of the collectivity or group to which they pertain and not subject to individual property rights. The group owns them.
4. They add economic and/or social value and can reduce contract costs—production and/or transaction.
5. They are identifiable and therefore can be taken into specific consideration by those who wish to engage, join, or hire the group.

The Nonprofits as Pervasive Players in the Public Policy Process

As will be demonstrated in the next section, nonprofits are active players throughout the public policy process. Often overlooked, as we focus on the nonprofit as an implementer of public policy, is the active participation of nonprofits in the determination of who will be the policymakers. Yet, perhaps the deepest and most extensive way in which nonprofits influence public policy is through their influence in the nomination and election of politicians; through these elected officials, they impact the choice of all persons who will subsequently be appointed and confirmed to write the rules, to oversee, to administer, and to contract with nonprofits or firms to implement the public's policies written by the politicians.

At the base, this pervasive power is exercised principally through political action committees (PACs) and through political parties—both are nonprofit, tax-exempt organizations under Section 527 of the Internal Revenue Code; and, hence their name, Section 527 organizations. The role of the political parties is obvious. But what do PACs do, for whom, and how?

PACs influence the public policy process by making monetary contributions to individual candidates, to other PACs, and to political parties. In general, corporations and labor unions can set up PACs to receive the voluntary contributions of their employees or members, but corporations and labor unions cannot contribute monies from their own treasuries to PACs. PACs need not be incorporated, and if they are, they are incorporated as nonprofit organizations. PACs such as those formed by individuals may be free-standing, and others may be affiliated with firms, unions, and associations.

Leadership PACs are formed by politicians—particularly members of the U.S. Congress. These are formed by individual congressional members and allow a member to curry favor with other members—particularly those in leadership positions—by making contributions to the latter's campaign. But there is another way in which nonprofits affect political candidacy and public policy, and that is by providing thinking and research in support of political parties or candidates under the guise of objective policy research. Thus, in Washington, D.C., there are the "liberal" and the "conservative" think tanks.

In chapter 9, we shall revisit the role of PACs that are affiliated with another nonprofit, associations. These PACs provide the association with an efficient vehicle for directly intruding into the political and public policy process. Associations can hone their messages to directly reflect the views of their membership and target the specific candidates on the state, federal, and local levels who are most important to the goals of the association and its members, regardless of that person's political party, location, or the level of office to which that person aspires.

PACs are also tax efficient since contributions to them that are to be used by them strictly for political purposes are not taxed. In general, 501 (c) (3) organizations are prohibited from engaging in political activities and may be severely penalized and taxed for breaking this rule. Associations and labor unions may make political expenditures from their treasuries, in which case the organization is taxed; or, associations and labor unions can avoid these taxes by making political expenditures from a PAC.

PACs influence public policy by influencing the voter's choice of political candidates through propaganda. For a PAC to be tax exempt its exclusive purpose must be for the victory or defeat of political candidates; therefore, any communication by the PAC is tax exempt only if it exclusively serves this unequivocal and clear political purpose. Accordingly, Revenue Ruling 2004–6 (26 CFR 1.527–2) states that a PAC's communication should:

1. Identify a candidate for public office.
2. Coincide with a political campaign.
3. Target voters in a particular election.
4. Identify the candidate's position on the public policy issue that is the subject of the communication.
5. Show that the candidate's position on the issue is different from that of other candidates.
6. Show that the communication is not part of an ongoing series of substantially similar communications by the organization on the same issue.

Thus, the distinguishing feature of associations and unions in the public policy process is their ability to directly choose who the policymakers will be. They do so either through their own treasuries (but at the expense of paying taxes) or through segregated funds known as PACs—the exclusive purpose of which is to unequivocally (see the six rules above) influence who is chosen in an election be it national, state, or local. Otherwise, associations and unions are like other nonprofits; that is, they can all influence policy formulation, funding, implementation, and evaluation. But only PACs (formed independently by citizens as a nonprofit organization, or formed by unions and associations as separate or segregated funds) can, without a tax penalty, directly and purposefully influence the choice of who will write, interpret, fund, and implement public policy.

Obviously, PACs are social capital agents of policy. They are formed by citizens or by organizations of citizens bounded and motivated by a narrow, single, cognitive value, and they facilitate collective action—the election of candidates who support or will at least not obstruct the expression of these values or objectives in the formulation and implementation of public policy. Unlike other nonprofits, they may be created without a sense of perpetuity, but their impact through the actions of those they support or oppose may be long-lasting.

Other nonprofits, particularly 501 (c) (3)s, influence the political process by being nonpartisan. These organizations may conduct voter education and registration drives as long as they do not advocate a political person, party, or philosophy. As William Raspberry of the *Washington Post* notes, these public participation drives are often disingenuously disguised since the public policy disposition of the organization often drives its involvement and this disposition is often well known by those it urges to the polls.[23]

Types of Collective Action, Nonprofits, and the Public Policy Process

Table 3.1 shows the types of collective actions that cognitive social capital facilitates at each stage in the public policy process.

Cognitive social capital is important to the theme, the nonprofit as a social capital asset and agent of public policy, because it points to the themes of public policy an organization may have been formed to carry out, the degree of its cohesion in doing so, and therefore its effectiveness. Cognitive social capital therefore differentiates among nonprofits even if they have identical missions. They affect public expectations about what is embodied in the process, product, or service of the organization. "It is a Catholic school . . . therefore we expect a Catholic religious orientation to be part of their curriculum and embodied in the training the student will get."

To illustrate, this concept of social norms or values that bind is consistent with the psychologist's concept of balanced theory. As Byrne and Nelson[24] explain, balanced theory (or the law of attraction) in social psychology states that people prefer to interact with those with whom they have things in common. The relationship between cognitively related parties increases the ability of one to be an agent (called an embodied conversational agent) of influence over the other. "They think alike." "They have the same values." Thus when people form groups of like kind, this likeness becomes a basis of social cohesion, and the influence of members of that group over each other is strong.

Nonprofit associations or membership groups are voluntary groups or congregations (including religious ones) of people who share one or more common interests. To sociologists, structural social capital may be a group, an association, an organization, or a network of people or organizations—a

Table 3.1
Public Policy Participation and Collective Action

Type of Public Policy Involvement	*Collective Action Required*
Selection of policymakers	Spending in support of or in opposition to political candidates or the manner in which they are chosen
Initial policy formulation	Information gathering, group formation, discussion, taking of group position, cooperative action, lobbying, commenting, information dissemination, influencing legislative drafting and voting
Implementation	Financing, facilitating, and carrying out policy
Monitoring and evaluation	Information gathering (research) and sharing
Experimentation and innovation	Information gathering (research) influencing and advancing new policy initiatives
Policy revision	Information gathering, discussion, advocacy, lobbying, commenting, information dissemination influencing legislative drafting and voting

structure. To sociologists, cognitive social capital are the norms, values, beliefs, and common outlooks that bind the members of the association or network, fostering a common trust that induces cooperation and therefore collective action. Clearly, trust varies by group[25] and clearly the amount of cohesiveness may be weak or strong[26] dependent in part on the formality and density of interaction among the members.[27] The point is that not all nonprofits are equally efficacious in bringing about cohesion or collective action; and again this distinguishes their readiness to be agents of different public policies.

Bowles and Gintis[28] argue that the usual assumptions of social capital (trust, a person's concerns for others, and a willingness to live by community norms) are repugnant to economic theory. Economic theory assumes individualism and selfishness. Bowles and Gintis introduce the concept of community governance to refer to that form of small-group organization distinguishable from the selfishness of the market and from the public character of the state, which specializes in problems where individual behavior cannot be regulated by complete contracts or by an external force and there is limited conflict among the individuals in the group.

In sum, cognitive social capital (the norms and shared values), which binds a nonprofit organization and facilitates its collective action and efficiencies, distinguishes one nonprofit from another as social capital assets and as agents of policy. Cognitive social capital points to a quality of the organization as an agent and to the type of public policies for which each organization is best suited. Cognitive social capital describes the organization's capacity in sociological terms. In chapters 5–10 we shall see how significant this is to our theme.

Cognitive social capital differs from structural social capital principally because the former is intangible and behavioral, and therefore cannot sign a contract. It can, however, influence a principal to choose the organization as its agent because the principal hopes to capture the cognitive social capital in the good or service it orders. The networks to which the nonprofit belongs that facilitate and lower its costs are considered cognitive social capital because they (a) fulfill the criteria enumerated earlier; (b) add value to the organization, and signal to the public the sociological assets the organization can bring to bear on a public policy issue, and for which the public may elect to hire the organization; and (c) facilitate the organization's performance throughout the policy process. Much will be made of this logic in chapter 5.

Distinguishing between Norms, Beliefs, Practices, and Other Forms of Cognitive Capital When in Society and When Embedded in an Organization

There are significant differences between norms, beliefs, and other factors that facilitate and motivate collective action when these factors are embedded in an organization and when they are in the society as whole. Let us demonstrate this point by using the belief in monotheism.

When commonly shared norms, beliefs, and other facilitators of collective action are embedded in an organization, the organization may (a) tweak and shape them in particular, differentiating forms; for example, the commonly shared belief in monotheism is expressed within different canonical and liturgical traditions; (b) a religious organization, a composite of specific beliefs and traditions consistent with monotheism, continuously invests in the development, dissemination, and indoctrination in its brand so as to deepen, retain, expand, and perpetuate membership; (c) like other investments, therefore, there is an expectation of a flow of benefits expressed as a better, perpetual life, or salvation for the believers; and (d) the religious organization may be motivated to be successful in exercising virtual property rights over these norms, beliefs, or practices, retaining the rights exclusively for its members.

How does (d) occur in religion? There are four ways that come immediately to mind. First, organized religious groups do take legal actions against groups that break away. They may not only expel the members that join the breakaway group but prohibit them from the use of certain group properties, and prohibit them from the participation in certain rites. Elsewhere I have described an example of an Episcopal Church in Detroit and the supporting court decision. Second, the larger group may have property rights making the reproduction of materials a challengeable action. Third, the larger group may seek a cease and desist action or make claims of misleading conduct that require, at the very least, a full disclosure.

Third, the more successful the differentiation, the greater the voluntary resistance to adopt certain identifying cognitive social capital. "Oh, we believe in the same god, but that is too Catholic for me." "The Jews believe in one god, but it is not Jesus." "We do not believe in the sacredness of mice or cattle; so we kill the former and eat the latter." "We won't use the Book of Common Prayers or the Koran in our services—they don't express our beliefs." "We believe in monogamy so, even though we believe in the same god, we'll do with one wife at a time." "We dress revealingly, we are not Amish or Mennonites."

When we refer to cognitive social capital in the context of this book, the general form of the cognitive social capital may be shared by society, but the specific form for which the organization is a public policy agent—for which it is hired to facilitate collective action to achieve what the society needs—is the operative concept. Put otherwise, an organization plucks a general norm from society, shapes and tweaks it to gain a competitive edge and distinction, and becomes an agent in which its variation of the general norm is embodied and may even be copyrighten.[29]

The Number of Nonprofits as Social Capital Matters to the Public Policy Capability of the Society

The number of nonprofits in society matters to the public policy process because:

1. The number of nonprofits affects the probability that varying public policies can be conducted through private, voluntary, nongovernmental

agencies with different public policy specializations, capacities, and commitments.

2. The number of nonprofits affects the probability of diversity of public policy views and the effectiveness of expression through organizations, and the competition in the public policy arena.
3. The number of nonprofits increases the probability that each person will be connected to a group in which he or she may elect levels of participation, receive information, and express his or her opinions on public policy.
4. The more nonprofits there are working effectively, the more nongovernmental and noncommercial energy is dedicated to advancing the public and the less reliance on government as the instrument of public policy.
5. The larger the number of nonprofits, the larger the pool from which society may choose to perform specific contracts, and this gives rise to the question of chapter 5: On what basis does the government choose a nonprofit over an equally competent firm?

Cognitive Social Capital, Asymmetric Information, and Public Expectations

Given an infinitely large number of nonprofits agents, how do we tell one from the other? When information about an organization is incomplete, its cognitive social capital signals certain expectations. The principal, by virtue of known and identifiable social capital of an organization, can evaluate the importance of the cognitive social capital when it is embodied in a process, product, or service that the principal wants and, as a consequence, is willing to choose and compensate the organization that contains it, even at premium prices. "We do not have complete knowledge of the school, but because it is a Catholic school we can expect . . . " The word "Catholic" tells it all by what it connotes or conjures. Since all signals do not elicit a positive reaction to all persons, cognitive social capital as a signal in an asymmetric situation could also lead to indifference or avoidance. "It is a Catholic school . . . and as atheists we wouldn't send our children there."

From a marketing perspective, cognitive social capital is treatable as a characteristic for both branding the organization and its performance. "We expect that children attending a Catholic school to . . . " Thus, cognitive social capital is important on both sides of a contract—to the principal (by setting certain expectations) and to the agent (by facilitating and differentiating its performance). This expectation-forming concept of cognitive social capital plays a significant role in chapters 4 and 5 in explaining the choice of nonprofits as agents of public policy.

When seen in this expectation-forming way, cognitive social capital is a long-term asset attached to an organization and warrants investments for maintenance, growth, and public awareness (advertising). As a long-term asset it can be depleted, destroyed, or made obsolete; and, in this vein, may be more difficult to restore or replace than other assets, such as machinery, the technology the latter may contain production methods, or organizational structure used by the nonprofit to do its work.

The Flow of Benefits from the Nonprofit as Social Capital

The community invests in social capital with the expectation of receiving a long-term flow of benefits. Some of these benefits flow directly to the community. But, how do the benefits of social capital also flow indirectly to make the nonprofit organization an effective agent of public policy? One set of benefits is internal. Putnam[30] states that these benefits may include greater reciprocity of treatment among members, greater trust, sharing of information, and ease of collective action. In this sense, social capital strengthens the internal capacity of the organization and therefore the organization's capacity to be an agent of public policy.

But social capital also yields benefits to the individual members. Therefore, as an agent of public policy the organization is able to develop and to transmit norms, values, ideas, methods, beliefs, goals, and policy information to and from its members and the public at large. Coleman[31] illustrates the relationship of educational achievement of a child to the child's relationship to a supporting group. These benefits may have spillover effects to the community as a whole. As a matter of fact, Coleman defines social capital as a public good because the benefits of social capital are available to all and are not necessarily diminished by use.

Social capital also connects organizations. Thus, Putnam describes bridging effects as connecting groups together. Therefore social capital is accretive, leading to a complex network of organizations bound in one or more ways to each other while remaining different from each other. Hence, we may conclude that the various nonprofits with distinctly different missions and public purposes, being part of and embodying social capital, form a network dedicated to the advancement of a common good—the ultimate advancement of the public. In a principal-agent paradigm the networks have the uses described earlier and especially in chapters 4 and 5.

The World Bank and the International Perspective on Social Capital

The concept of social capital is important in international economic development policies and there is an extensive literature covering villages, cities, and countries. Krishna[32] reports various measures of social capital and finds it important in village development in India. In the United States, nonprofits may also be seen as social capital in mediating between the government and the poor and in bringing resources to the poor. Couto and Guthrie[33] studied 23 Appalachian nonprofit groups and showed them as mediating between governments and the local communities.

Brown and Ferris[34] use a moderately adjusted multiple index approach constructed by Putnam and others at Harvard that includes the number of involvements of individuals in a group, whether the group is racially diverse, whether the individuals make philanthropic gifts, the level of educational attainment, the degree of trust in others, and so on to study social capital in Los Angeles. They find social capital so defined is less there than in the United States as a whole and in cities of comparable size.

Recognizing the utility of social capital, the World Bank launched a program called Social Capital Initiative to stimulate (if not create) and to capitalize on social capital in order to advance economic development within a democratic framework. World Bank affiliated economists, Grootaert and Bastelaer,[35] identify three ways in which social capital enhances economic development:

1. It facilitates transactions between individuals, groups, and networks through arrangements including credit and savings associations and various forms of information dissemination, including those on prices and crops.
2. It facilitates the management of assets, including sanitation and watershed assets where property rights are not fully developed and collective decision-making and cooperation are essential.
3. It inhibits opportunistic behavior of those individuals who would otherwise take selfish advantage of conditions at the expense of others in the community.

Grootaert and Bastelaer[36] also present the expansive research questionnaire the World Bank uses to assess social capital in various countries.

Social Capital and the Special Case of Religion

With respect to structured social capital, it is evident that every church or synagogue or mosque or other house of worship fits the five-point criteria set in the opening of this chapter. They are long-term investments made by the local congregation, which receive compensation in the form of tax exemption and deductibility of contributions, and are expected to provide a flow of religious benefits to the community. Throughout this book, reference will be made when necessary to religion as a special case. The federal government and all states have special laws exempting religious organizations from state intrusions, particularly in canonical matters.

In this book we shall distinguish between religion (an organization) as a corporate institution capable of signing and committing to a contract as they presently do and religion as a cognitive social capital upon which individuals may call to assist in collective action, as in the form described by James Coleman.[37] In chapter 4, we shall lay out the argument for the first and in chapters 5, 6, and 7 we shall see the role of the second.

There is no clear certainty when (if ever) the performance of faith-based organizations may be superior or different from non-faith based organizations in the public policy process. This must be at the center of our concern (aside from the constitutional arguments) because a principal-agent paradigm implies that the principal wants to choose the best agent for the job. Some studies imply very interesting questions about religion in that choice—aside from the constitutional question. Here is an initial sampling of such studies.

McVeigh and Smith[38] find that people who are regular church attendees are more likely to engage in protest movements than in other forms of institutionalized politics. They also find this to be true of people who have engaged in other forms of civic organization.

During the American Revolution and in the Civil Rights movement, churches were meeting grounds (often safe houses) for persons motivated by a common, and shared civic commitment. Williams[39] claims the Civil Rights movement had a religious foundation. But the movement also incorporated those who rejected that foundation (atheists), and those who interpreted it differently according to the doctrines of their denominations. Yet, all united to advocate a common public policy. Given any situation, cognitive social elements can be competing, collaborative, or subdued one by the other.

Kennedy and Wolfgang's[40] study of sectarian and faith-based job-training organizations found no significant differences in their rate of placement of trainees and their wages. In their meta-analysis of 60 studies on the relationship between religion and crime, Baier and Wright[41] found that at best there is a moderate mediating relationship between religion and crime. They concluded that the studies are varied, inconclusive, and provide no "persuasive" conclusion about the effect of religion on crime.

A study by Lee and Bartkowski[42] leads to the question as to whether religious and secular civic participation are equivalent in tempering interpersonal violence for certain age groups. Turner, O'Dell, and Weaver[43] found that about 25 percent of the women drug addicts in their study had sought help from a religious organization. About a third of these reported that they were helped by counseling and ministerial attention that included love, forgiveness, and understanding. If the ministerial attention is as described, is this not replicable in secular organizations? In a five-year followup study of over 430 drug addicts, Flynn, Joe, and Broome[44] found that those who remained in recovery attributed their success to a variety of factors, including personal motivation, job careers, religion, spirituality, family, and friends. This led the authors to the conclusion of the importance of "a network," not necessarily a religious one.

In short, does the religious form of social capital offer an advantage over the secular? Is there another advantage that matters other than the effectiveness of treatment? And if the religious form matters, is one religious doctrine or practice more efficacious than another? And if the government could determine which religion is more efficacious, would it not be inclined to contract with that religion over others, and wouldn't that open an unpleasant Pandora's box?

Chapter 5 in this book will develop five factors of confidence upon which contracting with nonprofits is advantageous that will all help avoid these questions. What the five factors indicate is that this problem of choice could be addressed partly because there are four other dimensions that could give a group (including a faith-based group) a competitive advantage without reference to a doctrine. These are illustrated in chapters 5–7.

What unique value has religion anyway? The Christian Research Association (CRA) in Melbourne, Australia[45] states that the word "religion" comes from the Latin "religare," meaning "to bind" (CRA). CRA argues that all religions are based on stories about the relationship of human beings to the world, to each other, to themselves, and to success and failure. CRA also argues that doctrinal groups differ in these orientations. Moreover, they argue, that secular reasoning and philosophy are sometimes substituted for religious ones.

In this book, we are not concerned with the content of the doctrine, but with its utility as an asset that differentiates agents in facilitating collective action and the economic value yielded. This will play an important role in chapter 5 in explaining the economic rationale behind contracting with faith-based organizations. It is the property of religiosity rather than its content—to the extent that the two are separable (and they often are not)—that matters in this book.

Nonprofits as Social Capital and Aid, or as Alternative to Government

Chapter 2 focuses on the properties of nonprofits in economic markets and transactions and in remediating government failures. Nonprofits are also important in civic governance. Again, the conceptual contribution of social capital as assets and agents is not just theoretical, it is policy in practice.

Nonprofits as Miniature Government: The Governance of Common Pool Resources

One form of nonprofit governance is that over common pool resources. These are resources that Ostrom[46] describes as available for anyone's use but, unlike public goods, they will diminish the more they are used. A bay, a pond, and a lake are examples. The lake may be used by anyone, but its resources (fish) and quality can diminish the more it is used. Some common pool resources can be replenished. Others cannot, or can be replenished only at extreme costs.

An issue that has fascinated social scientists about common pool resources is how to govern them and their use without invoking the weight of government. The problem lies in what is called the "tragedy of the commons," the origin and essence of which is discussed by Ostrom.[47] This tragedy occurs when people with unrestrained access to a resource, motivated by their own present self-interest, do not appreciate its diminishing future value to them and to the community as a result of their excessive use. These people are unlikely to act to preserve or enhance the value of the common pool resource. The tragedy is that by not preserving it, they act to their own future detriment. Soon there will be no fish in the pond.

This observation about common pool resources has sparked a considerable amount of intellectual exploration among political scientists such as Hardin[48] and Ostrom,[49] and philosophers such as McMahon,[50] about alternative norms and institutional forms (including nonprofits and collectivities) that may supply effective governance (not necessarily ownership) of these resources. An important part of the calculus is how, through what factors, and under what conditions individuals can be induced to act in a manner that is best for the group or collectivity even as each member considers his or her own self-interest.

Berkes,[51] Young,[52] and McCay[53] present many instances in which the governance of common pool resources have been successfully shifted out of government into nongovernmental organizations (NGOs). To them, the key ingredients of the NGO are the organization's inherent powers to organize principal users; to instill cooperation, trust, self-monitoring, and communication among member-users; and to tie individual self-interest to that of an identifiable common good. In these instances, nonprofit associations, cooperatives, and even some 501 (c) (3)s, such as the Chesapeake Bay Foundation, discussed in chapter 8, may be alternatives to government for managing common pool resources.

Nonprofits Absorbing Policy Responsibilities through Decentralization and Privatization

Nonprofits (as social capital) play a role in answering the demand for greater efficiency in the delivery of services. This occurs through the processes of decentralization of government functions to lower levels of governments. They, in turn, may contract with nonprofits including neighborhood organizations or through privatization by the upper level of government that turns over these functions to the private and nonprofit sectors. Wolpert[54] found the nonprofit sector is highly localized, with nonprofits providing services to their own local donor base but with unequal resources. Merget[55] described these processes as potentially resulting in not only less cost, but more local responsiveness to diverse needs. Other social scientists such as Donahue,[56] Schmidt,[57] Sherlfer andVishnay,[58] et al., have described the categories of goods best suited for transfer into the nonprofit sector.

But Oates[59] warns that decentralization risks concentrating control in a local elite. In the context of this book, that elite may be a community, clique, a nonprofit organization, or those who operate it. Ostrander[60] has described this capturing of dominance by elites within nonprofit social service industries. De Mello[61] finds that social capital in the form of greater associative behavior among local persons can be built by decentralization of responsibilities. Therefore, to the extent that greater associative behavior reduces poverty, decentralization can contribute to poverty reduction. A risk he acknowledges, is that decentralization could lead to control by local elites and increase the risk of corruption.

Government Contracting of Nonprofits as Agents of Policy: Protecting the Public Interest

The government can de facto privatize a function by closing it down as a government-produced or government-financed activity. This means that the function is not performed within government and government contracts with outside sources for that function are terminated, leaving it to private firms or nonprofits to pick it up as they see fit.

Alternatively, government can enter into a specific written contract with a firm or an entity to provide a good or service. Here the theorists point accurately to the need to consider transaction costs—the cost of gathering information and selecting the proper entity, of negotiating and monitoring the contract and the residual cost if the benefits are less than the cost of the deal. More will be said about this cost in chapter 5.

In this second case, the firm or the nonprofit is a contractor to the government. In the first case neither the firm nor the nonprofit is a contractor to the government. The implications are significant. When the nonprofit is a contractor, it has a specific contract that tells it what is expected of it, when it is to be delivered, how it is to be delivered, to whom it is to be delivered, and when and how much the government will pay. When the nonprofit is not a contractor it has no such guidance.

The government can call for an audit whenever it chooses, even if the nonprofit is not one of its contractors. Yet, in both cases, the nonprofit is expected to be performing a public service. All housing agencies that are tax exempt do not have government contracts, but all housing agencies that are tax exempt are by definition conducting a mission of public interest dealing with housing. The distinction between the nonprofit as an agent of policy when acting as a contractor and when not, is important to this book. Hence, in chapter 5 we confront the question: Why would the government select a nonprofit over a firm to be its contractor?

When the government contracts with the nonprofit for privatization, competitive performance, or any other reason, it has certain defenses it can use to protect itself—even when asymmetric information places it at a disadvantage. It can and usually does one or all of the following—none of which is available when the nonprofit organization is not under specific contract as a government contractor. Anyone who has written, negotiated, or signed a government (especially a federal government) contract will recognize these defensive strategies the government uses:

1. There may be conditions precedent: Terms that must be met before the contract goes into effect.
2. There may be nullification or revocation of contract if certain hidden facts are discovered.
3. There may be nullification of contract if certain events occur within a specific time after signing.
4. The party with the relevant asymmetric information may be required to disclose it: "full disclosure."
5. The rule of estoppel may apply to the party with asymmetric information—meaning that that party will not be allowed to make certain claims to deny or to relinquish certain liabilities because of it.
6. There may be a waiting period or investigative period before the contract kicks in.
7. There may be a period set after the contract for audit and redress.
8. There may be conditions antecedent: protective actions that must be taken once the contract is signed.
9. There may be an arrangement as to where and how contract disputes are to be settled.
10. There may be cost-sharing either in the front end or the back end of the contract; for example, research to back the application and loss limits at which time the government may stop its losses.
11. Performance, personal, legal, and financial histories may be required.
12. Warranties and representations may be required: "Vouch for it."
13. Performance and evaluation milestones (targets) may be set.
14. Periodic audits and unannounced inspections may be required.
15. Insurance may be required against certain event risks—things that may occur and adversely injure the ability of the organization to perform (performance or surety bond, for example).

The ultimate protection the government has and does exercise is the right to unilaterally stop contracts without paying a penalty. This right was frequently exercised during the first Reagan years and it, along with the above provisions, allows governments to contract with firms and nonprofits alike even when contracts are incomplete and unspecific. This unilateral penalty-free right to abort a contract is an unusual power of government. It can exit by merely paying all qualified earned fees and reimbursing all qualified costs.

The government, to protect itself in contracts with for-profit firms as well as nonprofit organizations, uses the strategies discussed above. The form of the contract has less to do with the profit incentive of the contractor than it has to do with what is at risk if the contractor fails. How much the government will seek to collect if the contractor fails will depend upon whether the government shares responsibility for the failure, as it might because of the contract requirements it imposed or changed. Also taken into account is the probability that the government may not collect, given the cost of collection and the insufficiency of the contractor's assets. There are no separate schedules for for-profit and nonprofit contractors.

The Nonprofit as an Agent Not Under Contract and the Principal-Agent Paradigm

In the above paragraphs the discussion surrounds instances where the government enters into a specific written contract with the nonprofit. All nonprofits are not under government contract and yet they perform as agents of policy by virtue of their government certification, as chapter 4 will explain. This certification is exactly what occurs when the government certifies the charter of the organization (the mission of which must always by law be public advancement directly or indirectly through members) and when it grants the organization tax-exempt status. When the organization is under contract the government monitors the contract to see that the nonprofit is complying with the contract terms.

When the organization is not a contractor, how does the government know if the nonprofit organization has failed to perform and what can it do about it? These questions are part of this book. We must distinguish between the nonprofit operating as an agent of policy when it is not under direct contract with the government and therefore the above strategies are not available, and when it is operating under contract and they are. In the former case, when a contract is absent, the government may still exercise the ultimate power of dissolving the nonprofit for failure to perform in accordance with the organization's mission.

At any given time, only a very small percentage of nonprofits are under contract with the government. To be meaningful, therefore, we must focus on the bigger picture, the nonprofit as an agent of public policy—not simply as government contractors or dealing with market or government failures. Rather the focus here is on the inherent nature of the principal-agent relationship that empowers the nonprofit as an agent of public policy and all that it implies about performance, expectations, evaluation, control, and feedback through political and legislative advocacy.

Therefore, the objective of the remainder of this book is not to explain the purpose of nonprofits from either a government or market-centric approach, or to explain the motivation for their formation. The objective is to explore the concept of the nonprofit as an agent of public policy within a principal-agent framework and in an interdisciplinary manner.

Issues in the Application of the Paradigm

Because this book views the nonprofit within the principal-agent paradigm certain issues are highlighted:

1. The mission as a contractual promise and the breadth of implied and inherent powers
2. Tax exemption as certification and indirect payment for a specific class of performance
3. The need to match performance with public expectations
4. The conflict between public expectations and organizational survival
5. Discretion as a necessary condition of agency and source of dispute
6. Asymmetric information as a basis of dispute, value to principals, and the rise of countervailing organizations
7. The exercise of self-interest as a benefit to the public
8. The meaning and power of goodwill and calculating the cost of the failure of trust
9. The advantage of leverage in nonprofit bidding
10. Some positive and perverse consequences of public control over the agent through controlling its raising of funds.

Social Capital as Agents and Other Institutions

The concept of social capital in this book, as compared to other acceptable uses, is not synonymous with formal or informal institutions. Informal institutions, regardless of their sociological or organizational structure and importance, cannot serve as agents for they have no legal capacity to perform, to be compensated, and to be penalized. This is the case of networks as discussed earlier. In the same vein, some formal institutions even though they have the capacity to contract as agents are not social capital assets within the meaning of this paradigm. This is so principally because they are not "social" in terms of who owns the property rights over their assets and the benefits that flow from them. Firms are highly structured social organizations; i.e., institutions capable of being agents. But they cannot be social capital in the context of the principal-agent paradigm because the property rights over all of their assets and the benefits that they yield are owned—not by the community or society—but by individual shareholders. This is not true of nonprofits by virtue of their legal definition and purpose. Their assets, benefits, and purposes are all publicly owned and directed. Therefore, they are public agents—existing in service of the public. Thus, "social" is used to connote a combination of property rights over the fixed asset (the organization and its properties) and those benefits that flow from them. "Who owns and controls what for whose benefits?"

The concept "agent" refers to the capacity and authority to make an enforceable promise to perform on behalf of the interest of another for compensation. Thus, an informal institution cannot be an agent; but neither can a formal institution that is not vested with such powers. The firm is a formal institution but not an agent of the public. It is an agent of its investor-owners because it is vested with the power to make profits on their behalf. But it can be vested (through a specific contract) to operate on the public's behalf as well; that is, a firm contracted to operate a prison for the community for profits for its shareholders. A nonprofit, whether or not under contract, is an agent of the public because all nonprofits are chartered exclusively to do a public good whether or not under a specific contract. In one case, the power is inherent and in the other it is acquired for specific purposes.

The concept "capital" is used in an investment and economic sense. It is a long-lived investment (a capital asset) from which a long-term flow of identifiable benefits are expected. With a nonprofit, the initial investment, the assets, and the long-term flows of benefits are all the public's. The next several chapters will explore the combination of these concepts (itemized in the five properties discussed earlier in this chapter) to the theme: nonprofits as social capital assets and agents of the public. The principal-agent paradigm is the framework in which this function is performed.

Summary and Preview

This chapter distinguished between social structured capital and social cognitive capital, but does so in a strikingly differently way than Woodcock.[62] It set criteria that each type of capital must meet to conform to the theme of this book, and it demonstrated the applicability of each type of capital to the theme. Accordingly, this chapter defined what is meant by the nonprofit as a social capital asset—given the criteria that must be met for an entity to meet that definition from a contractual and an economic perspective. The usual definitions (such as norms, shared values, and networks) do not work because in the principal-agent paradigm, the agent (the nonprofit) has to be a legal person or entity capable of making a promise, entering into a contract, discharging that contract, and being rewarded or penalized for its performance.

But, the chapter argued, these cognitive social capital (including religion) are significant as branding agents, as facilitators of transactions, as factors in the determination of both transaction and production costs, and as signaling devices in asymmetric markets, and can be shown to have economic value. Cognitive social capital also adds to the diversity of nonprofits available to the public as agents. In terms of contracts, this chapter closed with a discussion of the remedies available to the government when the nonprofit is under contract and fails to perform. The next chapter will look at the remedies the government has when the nonprofit does not have a government contract.

Chapter 4

Nonprofits as Agents of Public Policy

A Paradigm of Principals and Agents

The previous chapter explained why nonprofit organizations are viewed as social capital assets. This chapter lays out the principal-agent paradigm. The paradigm is the framework through which the nonprofit as a social capital asset becomes an agent. The chapter ends with a brief discussion of some nonprofits as bearers of society's risks.

An agent works for other persons or entities. The school is a socialization agent on behalf of society. The prison is a control agent on behalf of society. A nonprofit research and scientific lab is an agent of discovery and innovation on behalf of society. In the same vein, all nonprofits are agents of public policy, not just in social services and in markets, as discussed in chapter 2, or in community development as in chapter 6, but even in the advancement of science or in foreign policy.

The American Association for the Advancement of Science (AAAS) is a nonprofit organization established in 1848 and is the publisher of the magazine *Science*. AAAS describes itself as serving some 10 million individuals throughout the world. According to its website,[1] the AAAS seeks to "advance science and innovation throughout the world for the benefit of all people." Its goals are to:

- Foster communication among scientists, engineers, and the public;
- Enhance international cooperation in science and its applications;
- Promote the responsible conduct and use of science and technology;
- Foster education in science and technology for everyone;
- Enhance the science and technology workforce and infrastructure;
- Increase public understanding and appreciation of science and technology; and
- Strengthen support for the science and technology enterprise.

The Carnegie Endowment for International Peace is a nonprofit organization started in 1910. It publishes the prestigious journal *Foreign Policy*. The principal objective of the endowment is to stimulate cross-country cooperation, and to increase the involvement of the United States in world affairs. It does this partly through its cultivation of country capacities and networks, including the former Soviet Union. It also accomplishes its objectives through conferences, research, and publications that stretch across 120 countries. The Foreign Policy Association was founded in 1918 and its objective is to stimulate citizen involvement and awareness of public policy issues across the globe. It operates the World Leadership Forum, which convenes investors, foreign policy makers, and leaders of other countries where global trends affecting investments are discussed. The Atlantic Council, formed in 1961, promotes U.S. leadership and involvement in world affairs based on the principles of the North Atlantic Treaty countries, better known as NATO. The Council is a nonprofit organization that works through exchanges of ideas and promotion of policies, and stimulates the involvement of citizens in support of positions consistent with maintaining a strong U.S. transatlantic involvement. Other nonprofit organizations carry out U.S. foreign policy by providing direct services to communities in need. These cover medicine, educational programs at all levels, the building of civil society, governance capacity, health-related matters, and agriculture. Nonprofits stretch the full range of foreign policy involvement.

As described in the previous chapter, each nonprofit embodies and is part of the social capital of its community. This relationship between the nonprofit and the public makes the principal-agent framework a useful approach for viewing nonprofits in the public policy arena. It emphasizes the character, the risks, the seeds of dispute, the promise and expectations in the relationship between a nonprofit organization and the public it serves. A mission statement such as the above tends to place boundaries on the expectations. But this does not avoid disputes such as when the AAAS convenes to discuss, as it has, the origins of life.

Agency relationships are replete with managerial, operational, and decision-making problems, even in hard science, where things are supposedly quantifiable and objective. Guston[2] argues that scientists and the scientific community are agents of the government to carry out scientific research on the public's behalf. He then goes on to describe the agency problems and tensions between the agent and principal—the former being inventive and seeking scientific freedom, and the latter seeking accountability. But both seek productivity and integrity (scientific integrity on one hand, and integrity in the nature of the information used to formulate public policy on the other). Cooperation and conflict are both parts of every meaningful agency relationship, and will be made much of in chapters 5, 6 and 7.

The Universality of the Principal-Agent Paradigm

Chapter 1 discussed the advantages of employing a principal-agent paradigm. One of these is the universality of its application. A major advantage of the principal-agent paradigm is that it is universally applicable to all nonprofit organizations and gives a common framework for understanding their relationship to the society of which they are a part. This is true even of religious organizations. The previous chapter discussed why nonprofits are social capital assets. Now, why are they also agents of public policy? First, why, notwithstanding the separation of state and religion, are religious institutions agents of public policy? They are on one or more of the following levels.

1. *General.* Religious organizations advance the religious welfare of the public. They are also an expression of the public policy to defend freedom of worship, expression, and association without regard to the beliefs, doctrines, and rituals so long as these are not contrary to public policy. For example, the ritual sacrifice of children is contrary to public policy and hence prohibited, but not the religious sacrifice of chickens, as in Santaria.[3] At this general level, the religious doctrine is not public policy; but the freedom to choose forms of worship, expression, and association is public policy deeply rooted in the First Amendment. Thus, except for small churches, religious organizations, even if they operate solely on this general level, do obtain certification by the government as they apply either individually or through a group for tax exemption under Section 501 (c) (3) of the U.S. tax code as other organizations do. Their agency mission, therefore, is to carry out the public policy of allowing freedom of worship, expression, and association within the full discretion of their doctrines.
2. *Specific noncontractual.* Some religious organizations as a matter of their own policies will not solicit or accept a government contract. Religious organizations may elect to feed the poor, house the homeless, care for the sick, educate children, and perform other social welfare activities, but they are not under contract by the government to do so. These things they must nevertheless do within the codes set by governments. For example, a religious day care center, no matter how sacred, must meet local zoning codes, as do all sectarian edifices.
3. *Specific contractual.* Religious organizations or their affiliates may be under contract with the government to produce specific goods or services at home or abroad and for a fee. Here, tax exemption is for the performance of a public service function that is not in essence different from those performed by secular groups. Therefore, because the principal-agent paradigm may be used to describe nonprofit organizations regardless of type, this chapter applies to religious organizations too.

Core of the Principal-Agent Paradigm and Its Applicability

The key relationship in the principal-agent paradigm is: A person wishes to have something done for which he or she hires or contracts with another with the intent that this other will do as agreed for a fee. It does not matter if this other is an employee or an independent contractor, an individual person or an individual organization. The first person is called the principal, and the second, the agent. The principal is faced with obvious issues: How does the principal insure that the agent will act in the interest of the principal rather than in the agent's and at the principal's expense? This hazard is always present because the agent will have information the principal does not. What are the expectations of the principal, and how does it empower, reward, penalize, and protect itself against a self-serving agent?

Source of Organizational Empowerment to Be an Agent of the Public

In its deed of trust or in its charter and in its application for exemption the organization must state its intended mission.[4] All missions that qualify under Section 501 (c) (3) are to promote public (sometimes called community) welfare. Missions that qualify under all other sections of the code, such as those mentioned in the opening of chapter 3, are to promote the good of an identifiable group of persons with the ultimate beneficiary being the general public. In both cases, the public's welfare is to be promoted. In the first, it is done directly and in the second, indirectly. Thus, all tax-exempt nonprofits are certified and empowered to be agents of the public—to work on its behalf.

Associations are further empowered by their members. Their members can vote to dissolve them or to change their directions. Most 501 (c) (3)s, with the exception of religious organizations (which are technically associations), are not subject to this. The empowerment of organizations by government is basically analogous to a license issued by the state. A university does not need to be empowered by its students or professors in order to function. But it does need a license. The government represents the public and issues a license certifying the authority of the university to function. Similarly, the state seal on the charter of the organization gives proof of a license to operate as an agent of the public.

Donors, clients, founders, or organizers and clients do not empower the organization to be an agent of public policy. Their power is manifested in whether the organization is financially supported, it survives or remains relevant, or whether the organization can say it represents them and acts on their behalf when such declaration is requested, that is, in the case of associations that lobby on behalf of their members. A community development corporation does not have to prove that it has community approval to get a grant to work in the community or on behalf of it; but strong community opposition could cause it to be denied the grant. Why? Solely because the kind of product or service it is likely to be negotiating may require community acceptance or participation to be successful.

That the nonprofit is empowered by the government to serve as an agent of policy and that this empowerment is certified in the nonprofit's charter is tantamount to saying that the government has given the nonprofit a license to practice its agency role everywhere and anywhere that that power of government is recognized. The charter has no geographic restriction, although the nonprofit may elect to include such a restriction in its mission or bylaws.

Further it implies that a nonprofit may be a social capital asset of a community, but it may just as easily serve other communities. To be an agent of policy does not restrict where that agency function may be performed and does not require additional approval by the community that is served by the organization. It does require that the public policy purpose of the agency be stated as advancing the community's welfare through, health, housing, education, religion, science, and so on.

In short, as chapter 3 describes, the community owns the assets of the nonprofit. It also owns the benefits that flow from the assets. But, notwithstanding this ownership, community approval is not necessary for the nonprofit to operate in the community or on its behalf. This is determined by the state, representing a larger public. Why is this so? Because the agency functions carried out by a nonprofit are all characterized as having a public interest—a spillover that may be beyond the boundaries of the individual or the community where the organization operates or is located.

Key Relationships in the Principal-Agent Theory and Its Application to Nonprofits as Public Policy Agents

In this section we describe some of the key concepts and relationships in principal-agent theory and ask how they apply to our theme: nonprofits as agents of policy. Figure 4.1 shows the simplicity of the principal-agent paradigm.

The Principal and Beneficiaries

In the principal-agent relationship depicted in figure 4.1, the public is the principal and the government an agent accountable to the public and acting on its behalf. One of the functions of the government is to select other agents (such as the nonprofits), to contract with them and to oversee their operations on behalf of the public. In a principal-agent framework, a person playing the role of the government is often called a managing or general agent. The government exists to serve the public and to manage its affairs as delegated. The government is not the principal, the public is.

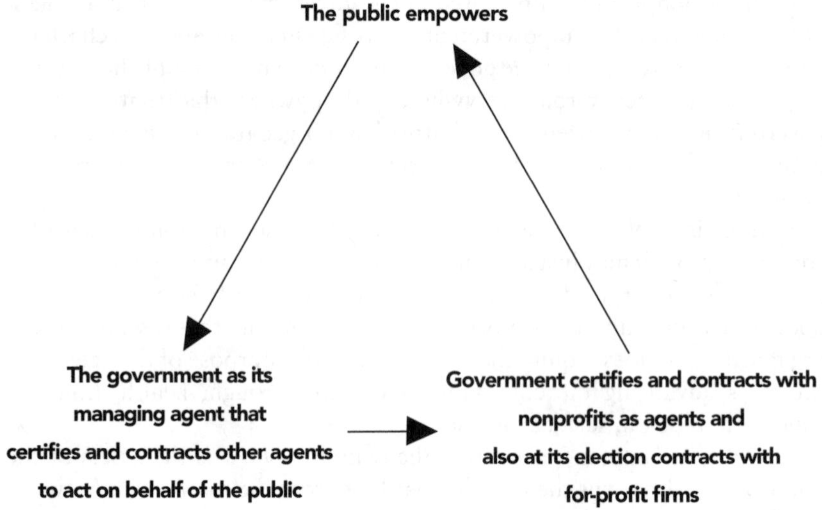
The public empowers
The government as its managing agent that certifies and contracts other agents to act on behalf of the public
Government certifies and contracts with nonprofits as agents and also at its election contracts with for-profit firms

Figure 4.1 The triangulation of the principal agent paradigm of nonprofits as agents of public policy accountable to the public

In a public policy "the public" as principal may be different from the "public" as direct beneficiary and there may be considerable spillover, externalities, or second-order effects beyond the direct beneficiary. The direct public beneficiary may be a neighborhood, but the public as principal may be the country, the state, or locality that hires the organization. The direct beneficiaries of the assistance provided by a U.S. nonprofit in a foreign village are those who live in the village; but the principal is the American people. The principal hires the agent or has its managing agent hire the agent. Thus, a local county may hire a nonprofit to do work for a specific group of residents, but the benefits spillover to the remainder of the county.

A program within a policy may contain several direct and indirect (spillover) beneficiaries. The Hispanic Serving Institutions Assisting Communities Program of the U.S. Department of Housing and Urban Development (HUD) contracts with two- to four-year college institutions. This specific program requires that the college or university enrollment be at least 25 percent Hispanic, at least half of whom must be from low-income families. According to HUD, some 200 institutions qualify under these terms. The program enables the institutions' faculty and students, in partnership with other local organizations, including religious ones, to build, acquire, and rehabilitate day care centers and senior citizen homes, to do housing and community revitalization, to assist in business development and to do job training, including computer literacy and placement in the community.

There are many beneficiaries in this program—not all individuals. They are the institutions of higher learning, Hispanics, students and faculty who may or may not be Hispanic, the community, a smaller group such as senior citizens, the individual as consumer or business person or employee. The agreement is not between the managing agent and the beneficiaries, but between the agent and the principal. In this case, the agents are the nonprofits, primarily the universities, and the principal is the U.S. public. The direct beneficiaries are the various "communities."

The Managing Agent: The Government

According to Young,[5] the government may have a complementary, supplementary, or adversarial relationship with nonprofits; it may also finance the works of nonprofits or partner with them in other ways (Salamon[6]). In the principal-agent paradigm, the relationship that is universally defining is the one derived from the classic democratic principle that the government is an agent of the people (the public) and that acting on behalf of the public it certifies, recognizes, and may contract with the nonprofit as an agent to act on behalf of the public. The ultimate principal is the public and the government is an intervening or facilitating agent. In principal-agent theory the government is a managing agent. It manages and monitors the nonprofit agency relationship to and on behalf of the public—the principal.

Moe[7] (1984) writes of government acting on behalf of the people, its principal. Therefore, within this principal-agent framework it acts as a managing agent preserving the status of principal to the people or public (a) by certifying nonprofits as agents of public policy, and/or (b) by electing to enter into a specific contract with one or more nonprofits having been certified into this club of agents according to law[8] that specifically allows exemption for the advancing of public welfare and providing assistance to governments in its responsibility to do the same.

Specifically, as managing agent, the government performs the following functions:

1. Empowers nonprofits to work on behalf of the public.
2. Serves as facilitator and controller that recognizes a general community need and then facilitates the creating and functioning of agents to satisfy those needs.
3. Continuously certifies the agents' competence and readiness to serve those needs through annual reporting and licensing, for example, and controls the agent's abuse of its agency powers by enforcing laws. We shall see this in chapter 9.
4. Signs contracts in the name of the public with nonprofit agents to conduct specific activities for which the nonprofits are empowered.
5. Facilitates that the public needs can be met by the nonprofits by providing grants, contracts, and tax exemption.

Contracting or certifying nonprofits as agents does not free the government from liability and responsibility for public welfare as constitutionally determined. The government's agency arrangement with the public is nondelegable, meaning that it may delegate performance but not its ultimate responsibility for getting the work done. Moreover, the government cannot delegate certain powers, such as the power of eminent domain. It does not deputize the correctional nonprofit but gives it custodial powers over prisoners.

The Nonprofit as Agent, Not Servant, and the Risk of Moral Hazard

As an agent of public policy a nonprofit may perform one or more of the following functions at the same time: It may be involved in policy investigation and development, policy formulation and advocacy, and/or policy implementation and evaluation.

Regardless of the function, agents must be vested with certain characteristics that allow them to operate. One of these is an identity. The charter of the nonprofit gives its identity—its given name, date of birth or incorporation, place of birth, parents or organizers, a personal identification number (analogous to the social security number), and its seal or birthmark. Identity and reputation have value and allow some nonprofits to be more effective agents than others and enable competition among nonprofits for agency jobs.

An agent must also express a willingness and promise to perform a specific function. This is the mission statement appearing in the charter and in the tax-exempt application. The agent must also be vested with the powers necessary to perform these functions. These include the power to engage in certain types of activities and programs; to buy, accumulate, sell, or otherwise dispose of assets; to borrow and raise funds; to make certain types of expenditures; to hire and fire personnel; and to form and empower a board of directors and officers to conduct the affairs of the organization and to commit the organization to certain contractual relationships. These officers, "the management," are operating agents of the organization.

When the government empowers the organization as described at the outset of this chapter, it also explicitly gives it specific powers that appear in the organization's charter. These powers enable the organization to operate as an agent. These include the power to raise and expend funds, to acquire other assets, to sign and discharge contracts, to hire employees, and to sue and be sued.

An agent that is an organization must also have its own agents authorized to act in its name. For the nonprofits these are the managers and the boards of directors authorized to negotiate and to commit the organization and to sign on its behalf. But they, too, are agents of the public in that they have custodial powers over the assets of the organization, which is a social capital asset of the community, and therefore the managers are accountable to the public for how these assets are used.

An agent must also have the authority to act on behalf of another in designated ways. For nonprofits the authority and specific topical areas such as health, education, welfare, civic activities, culture and arts, and certain sport activities are described in a set of laws, rulings, and court cases. The government certifies the authority that an organization has to act as an agent of public policy by conferring corporate and tax-exempt status. All of the ways that the agent may operate are not designated—some may be implied. Certain health-related functions are implied in being a hospital. Implied functions are important because they allow the agent to grow in its service faster than the community could conceivably designate it to do. Implied as well as inherent powers make it possible for the organization to deal with the unforeseeable, to grow, and to make future adjustments necessary to carry out their missions effectively.

Agents are not servants, therefore they do not await the direction of the principal. They have considerable latitude in their discretion as long as it is consistent with their agency role. This discretion, as we shall see in chapter 6 and 7, where the issue is on implementation, is often the cause of serious dispute. A servant works for, is controlled and directed by, its principal. The principal may hire, fire, assign, allocate, train, or otherwise decide on the performance of the servant. The various departments of the government are in a master-servant relationship to it. As an agent, the nonprofit is free to make all those decisions about its employees and other assets even when performing for the public. It does not need government direction.

A key distinction, therefore, between the servant and the agent is that the latter has autonomy and discretion. The unilateral use of discretion can be a topic of negotiation and the source of dispute. But discretion cannot be totally taken away without the agent being made a servant. The nonprofit as an agent, therefore, comes with managerial discretion and initiatives. The wider the scope of this discretion, the greater the possibilities for dispute. Discretion, and therefore the possibilities for dispute, is inherent in every principal-agent relationship.

Discretion has its advantages. Gains from the exercise of discretion can come from the exercise of creativity, innovation, choices of technology, improved processing and scheduling, cost sharing, flexibility and rapidity of tailored response, and reduced managerial costs over all assets. The government's savings from outsourcing to nonprofits are partly due to the greater discretion that the latter has. It is not infrequent that the principal-agent relationship is established precisely to capture the benefits of discretion.

Discretion and Moral Hazard

When an agent uses its discretion, the motive might be to promote or advance its own interest or those of its management at the expense of the interests of the principal. Thus, the public in a principal-agent relationship is always exposed to a conflict of interests—moral hazard. This hazard increases as the asymmetry of information between the principal and agent increases and speaks for greater accountability and transparency. But it is always present. The following is an example of all that has been said to this point in the field of science, although not in social services, demonstrating the range of applicability of the argument of this book.

An Example in Science of the Interaction among Managing Agent, Principal and Agent, and the Utility of Discretion

Argonne Laboratory is a science-related example of the nexus between (a) the nonprofit as an agent, (b) the government as an intermediary or general or managing agent, (c) the public at-large as the principal, (d) a subset of the public as the immediate or proximate beneficiary, (e) the custodial powers of the nonprofit, (f) the discretion of the nonprofit as an asset the government is leasing from the nonprofit, and (g) the empowerment of the nonprofit to exercise its discretionary and custodial powers through a contractual relationship with the federal government. Argonne Laboratory[9] is operated by the University of Chicago (the agent) for the U.S. Department of Energy (the managing or general agent) on behalf of the people of the United States (the principal). It is U.S. government property—therefore, it belongs to the American people. It is also the laboratory where Enrico Fermi and his colleagues carried out the first controlled chain nuclear reaction in the Manhattan Project that led to the atomic bomb. The discretion of the scientists and of the University of Chicago is essential to the success of the laboratory, which specializes in basic science, the development of nuclear reactors for peaceful purposes, environmental management, and educational programs. Argonne Laboratory is a structured social capital asset that meets the criteria in chapter 3, and its relationship with the university exposes it to all of the latter‘s social, intellectual, and other capital.

The Contract: The Mission

Every nonprofit organization that is tax exempt has a mission statement in its charter or deed of trust and in its letter of application. That statement is repeated in its annual report to the state and to the federal government, including what activities were performed as evidence that the mission was honored. In a sense, then, the contractual promise to carryout a specific class of agency functions (the mission) is reaffirmed every year.

My previous book[10] identifies five properties that characterize every mission statement. These will prove to be very important in the next chapter in discussing the question: Why for some contracts does the government, in its role as managing agent for the public, choose a nonprofit over an equally competent for-profit for some contracts?

1. *It is a social contract:* It is a promise that in exchange for its license or power to operate (charter) and its tax-exempt status, the organization

will perform only a specified and stated scope of functions that benefit society; for example, health care.

2. *It is a permanent commitment:* The nonprofit cannot abandon this promise without filing an amendment and risking losing its tax-exempt, nonprofit status, and having its assets seized by state governments if it strays too far afield from its principal purpose or fails to perform it.
3. *It is clear:* Mission statements of nonprofits are simple statements. Moreover, the range of interpretation and acceptability is set in law. If there is any room for a misunderstanding of the class of performance being agreed to with reasonable expectations of what is implied or inherent, the nonprofit and tax-exempt statuses are denied.
4. *It must be approved:* The signed mission is approved by the organizers of the organization and the government as part of the application for nonprofit and separately for tax-exempt status. Amendments are also subject to such approval and signatures.
5. *The performance of the mission is provable or verifiable:* The operating managers and directors of the organization are required to annually show the government (Form 990) that the organization is operating according to the agreement.

Accordingly, the tax-exempt nonprofit's mission is a running contractual agreement between itself and the public that it promises to perform a specific class of public welfare functions such as health care, education, arts and culture, or one of the other qualified classes in an annually verifiable manner. The principal-agent relationship between the nonprofit and the public is connected by contract—the mission as a permanent promise and agreement to perform specific public policy activities on the public's behalf.

The Mission as a Bounded Class of Performance Expectations

A promise that is offered and accepted creates expectations. A promise that is in the form of a contract as described above reinforces those expectations and gives the principal the power to make demands on the agent. Thus, the mission tells what performance may be expected or demanded from the nonprofit as an agent of the public.

Oster[11] speaks of the mission as a boundary statement and this is correct because the mission gives the boundaries of performance that may be expected from the organization as an agent of public policy. But what defines the boundary? And is the concept of a boundary consistent with the principal-agent paradigm: the nonprofits as agents of public policy?

The boundary of expectations is the specific class of public welfare to which the organization is committed—health care, education, civic, sports, arts, culture and so on. But principal-agent theory as it is employed in law and as viewed by March and Simon[12] in the concept of bounded rationality are offsetting. One expands the scope of expectations and the other narrows it as explained in the next paragraphs.

The concept of a promise in law would be the statement as well as what it implies. Thus, a promise to do health care implies that certain health-care-related things will be done in addition to those stated. An organization that has as its promise to be an acute care hospital implies that it will provide a variety of health care services whether or not they are stated. We shall see in chapter 7 how important this is in the evaluation by the IRS of whether a hospital is fulfilling its mission.

The statement of a promise also implies that there are some apparent aspects and some inherent aspects to the promise. An organization that labels itself a school can be expected to teach—that is obvious. But to teach means that it has to hire teachers and some of these teachers may be public hazards. Therefore, the hiring of the teacher is an inherent part of the performance of a school as is the risk that some of the teachers may be public hazards. Therefore, we shall expect not only that the school will teach, but that it will also hire teachers and be exposed to certain risks. The latter two performances are inherent.

In the situations described, the expectations from the performance of the organization are expanded beyond the direct words in the mission statement. This expansion is not limitless. In law "reasonableness" places a limit. In psychology, as March and Simon argued[13] the expectations are rationally bounded by our ability to see or to think or to imagine. Our expectations, they claimed, are cognitively bounded. The mission is greater than its words and bounded by what it reasonably implies, which is in turn bounded by our cognitive powers, which change with time and circumstances. But just because a concept is within one's bounded rationality does not mean that it would be accepted by all parties as understood, implied, inherent, or authorized. Disputes may ensue.

The Mission as a Dynamic, Broadly Stated Promise

Bounded rationality is both time and place sensitive and so is "reasonableness." Over time and space, learning takes place, needs change, expectations change, discoveries add to the list of what is reasonable. Therefore, the mission statement as a promise must allow for the dynamics of change. This allows the organization to make a promise and still be able to adapt while staying within the very same wording of the promise. If such wording is no longer satisfactory, the mission can be amended, but must stay within the promise.

For these reasons, the missions of nonprofits are broadly stated but can be presented in the form of a pyramid. At the top of the pyramid, the mission is defined as advancing public or community welfare. On the second level is the class of activity, and on the third a further breakdown of the type of acceptable tasks under that class. For example,

Advance Public Welfare

Litigation and Local Activities

Public interest litigation activities; other litigation or support of litigation; legal aid to indigents; bail

Hence, the organization certified under the above Internal Revenue Code (IRC) description advances the public welfare through litigation and local activities such as public interest law and legal aid to the poor. Excluded are all other forms of law such as entertainment law and legal aid to the financially capable.

The contract that nonprofits have with society is purposefully unspecified, incomplete, and written in broad terms. It allows the nonprofit to adjust to needs that differ over time, space, and groups. But, giving discretion, it is also a source of dispute about specific expectations.

The Mission as Cognitive Social Capital

As discussed in chapter 3, the mission is a form of cognitive social capital. Specifically, the mission is a shared value or shared commitment that induces people to act cooperatively and facilitates collective action. The mission of a housing agency may be to build homes for the poor. This, in turn, is a shared vision or value of those who work voluntarily through that organization to accomplish that mission. It makes it easier for them to take collective action with respect to housing the poor. They are not, as they say, "conflicted" about the policy: provide housing for the poor.

"Voluntarily" is used because a paid contractor need not be committed to the mission, only to the work and its financial rewards. Similarly a donor is distinguished from a lender. Two organizations may have exactly the same mission but differ in the way that mission is to be accomplished and therefore, while being the same in one aspect, the social cognitive capital may be distinctly different in the details of how it is to be achieved.

The Mission as a Source of Dispute and Government Retaliation

Contracts are subject to disputes. The more unspecified or incomplete the contract, the more are the possibilities for disagreements and disputes. When the nonprofit is a government contractor under a specific contract, the government may exercise any of the powers listed in chapter 2. When the nonprofit is not a contractor, the government can:

1. Sanction and impose monetary penalties on the organization and its management,
2. Revoke the tax-exempt privilege of the organization,
3. Dissolve the organization—close it down and seize its assets. Dissolution is the ultimate form of terminating the power of the organization to act as an agent of the public.

Sources of Rational Expectations

The mission is a major, but not the only, source of what the public may reasonably expect from a nonprofit. Table 4.1 below shows other sources. By contemplating the entries in Table 4.1, it is evident that the breadth of rational expectations can cause disputes between the nonprofit as agent and others, including the government, other nonprofits, and the public. Chapter 7 will demonstrate the real-world consequences of these conflicts in the case of nonprofit acute care hospitals. The maintenance of tax-exempt status by these hospitals depends upon their ability to meet these expectations—especially the regulatory ones and how they are interpreted.

Cognitive social capital is not the unfounded imagination of the public but a consequence of how the organization advertises, presents, and positions itself, and implies what it has to offer. Viewed in this way, the nonprofit has the power to influence the boundaries of expectations. Its power varies. To illustrate, whether or not it is highly ranked depends upon what other hospitals do and how the public regards them. But the hospital can elect how and if it advertises its cognitive social capital. An organization may choose to trade on its being faith-based or secular.

Expectations derived from different sources or logic may be in conflict. The school as an agent of policy is not merely about coherence and disseminating values and norms—a static socialization process. In those cases where the public preference is for dynamism, development, and change, the school must often be about changing cherished norms and beliefs to give way to modernization, human advancement in all spheres, experimentation, and innovation. These can be inherently discomforting and cause disputes. The dispute about stem cell research is partly a dispute about the appropriate public policy mission of science.

Nonexclusive and Noncompeting Contracts and the Proliferation of Nonprofits as Policy Agents

This section discusses two key characteristics of the contracts the government, acting on behalf of the public, enters into with nonprofit organizations. These characteristics lend to diversity and multiplicity of nonprofits as agents of public policy.

Nonexclusivity of Agency Contracts

A nonexclusive contract is one that allows the principal to contract with numerous agents for the same services. Thus, the contract that the public has with a nonprofit is nonexclusive because the public may enter into similar if not identical contracts with an infinite number of organizations. The fact that the contracts are nonexclusive gives the government as managing agent

Table 4.1
Selected Sources of Rational Expectations

Sources	*Expectations*
Mission	The stated mission and what is implied, inherent, and apparent
Cognitive social capital	Sociological factors, methods and descriptors by which an organization presents itself either directly, indirectly, or by implication to the public
Legal	Legal and regulatory rules such as truth in advertising, laws governing the operation of and solicitation by nonprofits, and the expectations that they will be obeyed and enforced
Ethical and operating norms	Ethical codes and norms of industry operation
Past performance	The assumption that the past presages the future
Capacity	Known or presumed tangible or intangible, monetary or non-monetary, human or non-human organizational capacity and what may be inherent, apparent, or implied about an organization's performance
Class membership	Organizational reputation, network, ranking, size, wealth, and other content-neutral descriptors not revealing an organization's culture
Public preferences or goals	Public preferences, needs, or goals and the urgency of them
Culture	The local, national, or ethnic culture in which an organization is embedded

choices. How the government chooses contractors is the subject of the next chapter.

Nonexclusivity creates the opportunity for an infinite number of potential nonprofit agents, working competitively, complimentarily, and independently to carry out a full spectrum of public policy functions on behalf of the public. There are no statutory limits, for example, on the number of nonprofits that may enter the housing, health care, arts, or educational business on behalf of the public and there is no limit to how many of these the government may contract. Consequently, principal barriers to entry into the club of agents are the entrepreneurial imagination of organizers and organizations, their creativity, their resource capacities, and their ability to perform.

Nonexclusivity allows the government to sign the same contract with any number of similar agents. This allows the government to respond to the same problem-type with various similar agents providing for diversification in treatment or methods, in location or place, in time, and even deliberately provide for duplication or redundancy. Redundancy may be needed where the principal has limited confidence in the agent's motives and faces the risk of failure or the moral hazard that may be related to that agent.[14] But it also serves the experimental purpose of learning where the mode or circumstance of operation may be different, stimulating competition, and bringing in a diversity of views.

Noncompeting Contracts

A noncompeting contract limits the number of principals for which an agent can work. A noncompeting contract prohibits the agent from entering into a similar arrangement with another principal for very much the same type of product or service within a specified period of time or a geographical area. If the contract a nonprofit day care agency has with the government is noncompeting, it may be barred from serving all other clients and from expanding to other localities to perform similar day care functions.

The fact that the contract is not noncompeting means that each agent could reproduce the specific promise it makes to the national government with each state, and therefore each jurisdiction in each state, and each and every community in each and every state. In short, the principal-agent relationship is not restricting the number of agency relationships the nonprofit has within the boundaries of its mission, expressed, implied, apparent, or inherent. Again, the principal limits are the entrepreneurial imagination, financial and other resources, the need of the public, and the ability of the organization to perform.

Tax Exemption as Compensation

In the principal-agent framework, an agent makes and keeps a promise based on its consideration of the compensation to be received. The nonprofit agrees to be an agent to the public based on some compensation it will receive. What is this compensation—especially when the nonprofit is not under contract to the government?

A contract between an agent and a principal is binding only when there is compensation. The agent made the promise in expectation or consideration that it will be paid. This compensation need not be in money and it need not be direct. When the nonprofit is a contractor to the government it receives compensation in money but it also receives compensation just because it is an agent of public policy. Tax exemption (revenues foregone by the government) is received by all tax-exempt nonprofits whether or not they are under contract to the government.

Tax exemption merely means that the government forgoes collecting a check and paying out the same amount to the nonprofit for what the nonprofit promises to do in the public's behalf. In this vein, tax exemption is compensation for expected performance. Therefore, any nonprofit that does not perform in conjunction with the terms of its mission can, as the IRS has done, be charged retroactively for the taxes from which the organization was exempt.

In the principal-agent framework, therefore, tax exemption is not a right. It is not awarded because the organization is a nonprofit or charitable. It is to compensate the organization or (in similar principal-agent language) to induce the organization to carry out an agreed upon mission on behalf of the public, one that is consistent with public welfare. There is one exception to this argument. As Zelinsky[15] concludes after a review of Supreme Court decisions, religious organizations are exempt on the principle that they are sovereign and to preserve their autonomy guaranteed by the First Amendment—but this must be only so when the religious organization is acting in its religious capacity.

But to what does exemption apply? Tax exemption applies specifically to revenues earned through the fulfillment of the mission. The exemption applies only to the activities consistent with the promise to advance a specific class of public purpose. Income unrelated to this promise is taxed. The fact that a nonprofit is tax exempt does not mean that it pays no taxes. It merely means that it pays no taxes on activities that are consistent with its contract with the public.

Moreover, the amount of exemption the organization gets depends upon whether the organization serves the public welfare directly or indirectly. A donation to a nonprofit that is a 501 (c) (3), such as a charity, or a health and welfare or arts and educational institution, is tax deductible to the donor and tax exempt as revenues to the organization. Donations to all other nonprofit groups (except veterans and some fire volunteer groups) are not tax deductible at all. These other groups include a range of civic, labor, and professional associations. But related earnings of these other groups are also exempt. In all cases, with some exceptions, earnings unrelated to the mission of the organization are fully taxed.[16] Thus, an exemption is compensation calibrated to how directly or intimately the organization is involved in the advancement of public welfare.

In sum, tax exemption is a payment for current performance consistent with the agreement (mission) and a down payment (economists call it a reservation price) for specific future performance—nor merely a subsidy.

The Moral Hazard of Government and the Agency of the Nonprofit

The principal-agent paradigm does not imply that the nonprofit is an agent of the right or best public policy. The principal-agent paradigm is a positive, not a normative, description of reality. The policies may be wrong, biased, inferior, and driven by narrow self-interest, and the word "public" may be a misnomer as in the theory of the first, second, and third best choices or in the theory of public choice, which are discussed below.

Public Choice Theory and the Purpose and Content of Policy

Public choice theory, the study of collective decision-making in the public policy arena, argues that legislators may be well intended. Through taxes, they have the power to finance their decisions and make them real. However, legislators do not personally benefit from any efficiency they may gain from the policies they enact and finance. But the constituents on whose support the legislator depends do benefit and consequently organize and lobby the legislators.

Several studies[17] have shown the types of outcomes we may expect from legislative lobbying (see chapter 8). Helpman and Persson[18] for example, show that the effects can vary depending upon the form of government and that support tends to favor those legislators who are agenda setters. Bronars and Lott[19] have shown that organizations such as associations tend to choose legislators whose views are compatible with theirs.

But, public choice theory continues, the decisions that the legislators make are not subject to easy monitoring by the electorate. These factors, when put together, can lead to inefficient decision-making. A favorite example of public choice theorists is logrolling. Two legislators exchange votes for each other's proposal. Both proposals pass. The constituency of each is satisfied with what it got, but is unaware that the price paid for what it got may be another project about which it is not enthusiastic; consequently, the total cost of its program should include the cost of other programs or projects.

Another form of the public choice problem is called rent seeking, or the use of lobbying powers to achieve private gains at the expense of the public. Tullock[20] gives the example of getting a tariff imposed on foreign imports to sustain or to improve the profitability of domestic firms, but at the expense of the public, which gets to pay an artificially high price for the import. But a core concept of public choice theory is that government bureaucrats and legislators are motivated by self-interest and are motivated to maximize the public's interest to the extent that their self-interest is served.

Economic Theories of the First, Second, and Third Best and the Distortion Created by Policy

Public choice theory reminds us that the government, composed of politicians and administrators, is not free of their moral hazards. Government officials are subject to lobbying and political pressures and are influenced by their own desire to survive. The economic theory of first, second, and third best choice takes us in another direction.

The theory of the first best implies that things would be okay if there were no resource constraints. But resources are constrained so that choices, often imperfect, have to be made. The theory of the second best choice says that things would be okay if there were not market imperfections such as monopoly and asymmetric information. But there are, and as a consequence, choices have to be made and they are often imperfect. The theory of third best warns that in trying to resolve these issues due to the imperfections of resource constraints and market imperfections, government policy is not always benevolent, or informed, and may introduce its own imperfections and distortions.[21]

For example, in Afghanistan farmers were paid to stop growing poppies. Cultivation fell. But cultivation began to rise because farmers wanted to be paid again and even more. In addition, the food that was distributed by nongovernmental organizations (nonprofits) meant that farmers no longer needed the fields to grow food and they began to use them to grow even more poppies. They have done so because poppies pay so well that farmers can hire help away from legitimate farming, creating a labor shortage precisely in the growing of crops, which the policy had encouraged. Now the poppy crop has returned to a level higher than it ever was.[22]

Therefore, being an agent for public policy might mean being an agent of market distortion or of a policy that is less than motivated by the general public good. The principal-agent paradigm is not a prism through which the policy content can be evaluated for its worthiness, but it is a prism through which the policy can be evaluated for its fit to the nonprofit as its agent. The following section and the entire next chapter engage that question: When is a policy appropriate for a nonprofit to be its agent? Here, again, the concern is with fit—not with content.

Adverse Selection and the Need for Nonprofits as Agents

There are common types of social problems for which the nonprofit organization is a natural fit and they are revealed by the principal-agent paradigm. These are problems of adverse selection.

Adverse selection occurs when individuals who would impose above-average cost or represent abnormally high risks disproportionately elect (or are left behind by the exodus of those of lower risks) to participate in an offer or event. The event is left packed with high-cost, high-risk individuals who may be unable to pay the full cost of their own services. To the extent that that event is privately financed, so that the cost that these high-risk individuals impose is greater than either the amount they pay or the amount that can be recovered from others to cover the difference, they eventually cause the event (or organization) to collapse as costs exceed revenues. Ghettos, slums, low-income neighborhoods, dead cities, and old industrial cities are all examples of adverse selection in geographic space.

When the government contracts with a nonprofit to deal with the poor, it transfers its risks to the organization. The transfer of risks is a deliberate and recognizable form of risk management and it is unrelated to the government's failure. The government has simply chosen a risk management strategy: Hire an organization well-suited and interested in dealing with the adverse condition and its associated risks.

An activity with heavy adverse selection can survive if at least the amount by which its costs exceed its revenues is subsidized or paid for by other persons. These others making up the difference may be those who pay above their average cost and thus provide a subsidy. Hospitals do this by charging third-party payers more to cover lower payments by poorer patients. Nonprofits can also rely on donors and a secured "payment" in the form of tax exemption. Public hospitals, urban schools, and prisons are examples of adverse selection in institutional space.

One way in which firms and individuals deal with adverse selection is to avoid it—often by forming nonprofit associations to enable them to do so. Gated communities, associations, private schools, and clubs are examples. Firms also avoid the consequences of adverse selection. Examples are redlining or refusing to insure individuals in a poor neighborhood. Family or firm migration to other areas is an example of risk avoidance. All these measures exacerbate adverse selection. They cause a compaction of those adversely effected. But the public cannot cut loose and walk away. This is especially true if the affected group is (a) visible, large, vocal, and draws public sympathy or is influentially represented, or (b) if there is a serious spillover or external cost including opportunity cost to the larger community if the situation went unattended. Nonprofits (community organizations) may also be formed to deal with these adverse conditions.

In a principal-agent context, a nonprofit organization allows the public to share and spread the costs of this above-average cost population by: (a) collecting tax deductible donations from a wide range of the entire public; (b) from foundations or other funding agencies; (c) charging a fee and earning other income where applicable; and (d) from direct government contracts or grants. The market mechanism fails and in distressed communities the nonprofit may be an alternative to government (or hired by government as in a contract) as an agent of change.

Dealing with adverse selection can also occur on a more micro level or with a subsector of the community. The Grameen Bank of Bangladesh in its microlending program illustrates these points. Anthony[23] describes the group as an alternative mechanism for screening, selecting, monitoring, and enforcing a credit contract. The amount available to the group in credit is fixed and decreases by the amount of outstanding loans any member has. The group may be liable for a member's default. Only a fixed number of loans are made per period. Thus, every member not having received a loan has a strong incentive to be sure those who have, pay. Further, as Cook and Hardin[24] note, in the Grameen Bank of Bangladesh program of lending to the poor, the need for trust among the members is reduced by the use of informal monitoring, sanctions, and normative social control.

Nonprofit Agency as the Bearer of Risks

The Grameen Bank case above serves as a reminder that the principal-agent paradigm serves to emphasize the characteristics of the nexus between the nonprofit and the public. The framework emphasizes, however, that the agency relationships do not necessarily eradicate agency problems between the firm and the public, yet it makes certain transactions possible. In the Grameen framework, the firm shifts risks from itself to the nonprofit group. This makes a market transaction that is beneficial to all possible. But the nonprofit group acquires risks of adverse selection, moral hazard, the need for trust, and the exposure to the aggravation of these problems through asymmetric information and free ridership. In short, part of the role of the nonprofit as an agent of public policy is not merely to implement the policy, but to be the bearer of certain risks. A charity hospital absorbs the risks of adverse selection of patients on behalf of society!

Sometimes this risk is transferred, as in the Grameen case; other times it is merely transformed and shared. H. Naci Mocan[25] found that parents, when choosing and using nonprofit day care centers, do not use all of the information available and often interpret signals of quality incorrectly. In the case of nonprofit day care centers, a clean reception room often misled parents about the true quality of the centers.

Summary and Preview

All nonprofit organizations by virtue of their charter and the granting of their tax-exempt status establish an agency relationship with the public. Therefore, each nonprofit neatly fits into a principal-agent relationship with the public. This relationship has many features. These include specifying the role of the principal, the agent, the contract terms, the agency to be performed, the risks of moral hazard attendant to asymmetric information, the risks of adverse selection, and the freedom to compete and to create other multiple agency relationships.

This principal-agent relationship is, by itself, a sufficient focal point of analysis and exploration; that is, the way in which the organization connects to and interacts with the public it serves. The primary focus of the principal-agent paradigm is to connect all organizations in a utilitarian and a standardized way to the remainder of the society and to focus on the expectations, risks, and benefits of that interaction. As a result of this connection and as a result of the standardized nature of agencies, certain potential problems arise across organizations. One of these is a paradox of discretion, where the society benefits from the inherent powers of discretion in an agency, but is placed at risk when that discretion is exercised. From a public policy perspective, faith-based organizations are no different legally or functionally.

Finally, a significant part of what nonprofit organizations do as agents of public policy is to absorb certain of society's risks as they carry out a public policy. Often the absorption of that risk frees government as well as market providers. Contracting is a formal process through which that risk is transferred. But how does the government choose a contractor? Why would it choose a nonprofit over a firm when it is free to choose either? What are the factors that may give the nonprofit a competitive edge in a bidding contest? Those are the types of questions to which the next chapter is directed.

Chapter 5

The Choice of Nonprofits as Agents of Public Policy

The previous chapter describes the principal-agent relationship and how in general it is established. This chapter describes how a specific contractual relationship is established through the government contracting process and why the nonprofit may be the chosen contractor. When the government signs a contract or makes a grant to an entity, it has selected that entity to be an agent to perform functions specified in that contract on behalf of the public the government represents. Governments at all levels and throughout the world enter into these contracts every day, selecting from a pool of qualified agents that are either firms or nonprofits. The basic questions of this chapter are: How does the government do this? Why would it select a nonprofit over an equally qualified firm?

In a good empirical study that this author recommends to the reader, Ferris and Grady argue that local governments try to minimize the weighted sum of production and transaction costs of providing a government service through contracting; that is, its objective is to minimize total cost, recognizing that for any contract, one cost may carry more weight than the other. Thus, even if a firm has a production cost advantage, it can, depending upon the contract, be overcome by a nonprofit with a transaction (particularly monitoring) lower cost.[1]

This book takes a different approach. It focuses on matching core characteristics that run through both production and transaction costs that, given the laws and practices under which federal, state, and local governments contract with firms and nonprofits, could give nonprofits a competitive edge. These are within the powers of all nonprofits to cultivate for competitive purposes. It then demonstrates the operation of the characteristics under various circumstances. Thus, what are the underlying characteristics that give an advantage to nonprofits to be contracted by the government in the furtherance of a public policy? The chapter begins with a walking through of government contracting objectives, procedures, and practices as derived from government operating regulations and empirical findings duly cited.

The Government Incentive to Contract with Firms and Nonprofits

The Federal Activities Inventory Reform Act (FAIR) (PUBLIC LAW 270) and OMB A-76 Performance of Commercial Activity require that by June 30 of each year, each federal agency must prepare an inventory of all of its activities and submit it to OMB. The activities must be divided into those that are inherently governmental and therefore not subject to contracting and those that are commercial (basically all others) that may be contracted out to commercial vendors—firms or nonprofits. Activities that are considered inherently governmental are those that involve the exercise of the government's discretionary powers and authority, that commit the government to a course of action, or are of broad public interest and impact. These are not delegable and cannot be contracted to others. Negotiating and signing treaties, criminal prosecution, and the selection of policies the government should follow are examples of inherent government functions.

Activities that are considered not to be inherently governmental are "ministerial" activities, which are basically operational, housekeeping, and management support functions, including the making of studies and recommendations, informational technology, and providing products and services in support of the government's responsibilities. The express purpose of this annual inventory is for the agencies to select the provider, whether that be the government, a firm, or a nonprofit, that would provide the "best value for the taxpayer dollar." The agencies are instructed to choose the provider based on total cost considerations in accordance with OMB comparative cost calculation procedures but without sacrificing quality, risking operational failure, or losing the ability to improve the product or service.[2]

Many states and local governments have adopted a similar policy. For example, the California Welfare and Institution Code Section 12301.6 requires the State Department of Social Services to report annually on the efforts of counties to contract with a public authority or a nonprofit consortium in the provision of in-home supportive services. The public authority is created by the local government as a separate, and independent nonprofit, nongovernmental corporation. Authorities will be discussed in the next chapter.

A Foreseeable Trend: The Rising Success of the Large Corporate Competitor

A foreseeable trend in education, job training, health, and social service contracting on all levels of government is toward larger corporations winning bids, and corporations working across jurisdictions. EDS, a large multinational firm, has a multi-year renewable contract to administer the Medicaid program in Arizona. The actual provision of services to the over

600,000 patients in that state is left to private providers, firms, and nonprofits that are left to absorb both the risk and costs of adverse selection as discussed. As is evident by what a competitor chooses to do, as in the Arizona case, creaming (the process of selecting only the best, easiest, and least costly) is often not the creaming of clients but the creaming of activities.

Bear in mind that large corporations have advantages of the following nature:

1. They are likely to be players in many markets and for many agencies across the country so they bring experience, history, a record, transferable capacity, a decentralized management and the willingness to use these not only to perform but to bid on contracts.
2. They are also likely to have greater information for the contracting officer from annual corporate filings and through corporate offices dedicated to government liaison.
3. Consequently, they are also likely to be better known.
4. They can buy or lease trust, or other social capital, by partnering or subcontracting with nonprofit organizations when necessary.

These are formidable advantages. In an entrepreneurial and dynamic society, market or government failure may offer only temporary strategic advantages, awaiting the discovery by firms of ways to penetrate those markets profitably. This has happened in higher education (for-profit universities offering college degrees), and it has happened across the social services. When this occurs, these firms become formidable competitors because they are unconstrained by the contractual nature of their mission or the bounded expectations about what their duties are. They have no defined agency function with the public.

To illustrate, as this book goes to press, several states have announced actions against nonprofit hospitals, claiming that they use aggressive collection and pricing techniques against uninsured indigent patients. To this point, one state, Illinois, has removed the tax-exempt status of a faith-based hospital for that reason. But in no state has it been shown that this technique per se is illegal and unacceptable as a business practice by hospitals that are for-profit. Expectations, as we shall see in this chapter, arise from various sources and threaten the tax-exempt status of many nonprofits—especially hospitals, as chapter 7 will illustrate.

On all levels of government, contracting has become competitive among the government, firms, and nonprofits. In a study of 433 cities, Ferris[3] finds that the percentage of publicly provided services that is contracted out increases (1) the greater the expected cost savings, (2) the more stringent fiscal conditions, and (3) the less powerful are public service constituency groups. The question that this study generates is, given these conditions, why would the city choose a nonprofit over an equally qualified firm to provide these services? Comparing Philadelphia and Houston, Wolpert and

Reiner[4] find that Houston has three times as many service contracts as Philadelphia. Why does the government choose a nonprofit over an equally qualified firm? This question relates to two parts of policy: (a) the budgetary cost of choice; and (b) the consequent fiscal capacity of nonprofits to discharge their promise to serve the public. But this leads to the backdrop question: What would be the budgetary or capacity advantages of a nonprofit? Again, what gives rise to the government's choice of a nonprofit over an equally qualified firm?

Common Answers to Why Governments Contract with Nonprofits

Common answers are because of greater trust, because the cost (particularly the monitoring cost) of transacting business with the nonprofit is lower than it is with the firm, and because of the inability of the government to adequately specify the terms of a contract. The government, according to this line of thinking, must, therefore, depend upon its trust in the nonprofit contractor. These responses may work well when the question is about why the government may choose to contract out rather than to produce a good or service internally. When the issue is a about making a choice between the firm and the nonprofit as required by current practices, as will be described factually in this chapter, these responses beg a question such as: Why and on what credible basis would the government have greater trust in a nonprofit than in an equally competent firm?

What does trust mean and what is the genesis of this trust if the government does not know the nonprofit or the firm other than by due diligence and what is reported in their bids? Or even if it does know one more intimately than the other through personal contact, is it not prohibited by contracting rules from choosing on that basis? This occurs, for example, when an employee leaves the government and goes to work for a competing firm. According to the Government Accounting Office (GAO), about 25 percent of the state-level managers who leave a government child welfare agency that has contracted out its functions go to work as executives in a for-profit or nonprofit provider of those services. But the GAO finds that there is no evidence that the providers for whom they work get the winning contract from those states any more frequently than those where they do not work.[5]

On what basis could the transactions cost (particularly the cost of monitoring a contract) be higher for the government when dealing with a firm as compared with a nonprofit of equal size and competence? How does this occur? This question is particularly germane because studies cited above of the actual monitoring costs by the GAO indicate that the principal monitoring cost is in the form of information technology, not because of the lack of trust (as we may presume). The study also finds that the principal type of monitoring that is done is over compliance with regulations, not over outcome or performance. Roper,[6] in a study of social service contracting in New Jersey, found that because nonprofits lacked the capacity to collect and process information, they had problems in monitoring their contract performance.

Johnson and Romzek[7] provide the same findings as the GAO and Roper and gave even more detailed information on monitoring in their Pricewaterhouse study of social services contracting in Kansas. They found that the costs of monitoring these contracts were related to: (a) the subcontracting of parts of the contracts by primary contractors, making it difficulty to trace and to assign direct responsibility for performance; (b) the compensation method because the type of reimbursement or compensation scheme affects provider accounting and performance incentives; (c) the nature of the information-gathering and reporting system; (d) the training of monitors in the techniques of monitoring a specific service; (e) the contracting out of monitoring by the agency to a third party not equally driven as, supposedly, the government; and (f) the objective of minimizing the total contract cost to the government that reduces the quality of monitoring. They concluded that often reporting was good with nonprofit organizations that had both "the experience" with the program and an "incentive" to report.

Another common answer is that the profit motive drives firms into service-compromising or even dishonest performance. For example, the record of for-profit chains and their illegal accounting with Medicare and Medicaid patients is that the for-profit hospital may be more inclined to cheat in order to show greater profitability, allow executives greater compensation, satisfy shareholder expectations, and increase the firm's access to capital as its performance expectations attract investors. But isn't the cost and frequency of inspecting, reporting, and auditing (monitoring) not roughly the same for both firms and nonprofits since both are required to fulfill these on equivalent schedules, given that neither the Federal Procurement Policy Act (41 U.S.C) nor the Federal Acquisition Regulation (48 CFR, Chapter 1) gives special concessions to nonprofits? Don't nonprofit managers also have an incentive to cheat and to do so for some of the same self-serving reasons? Recall that the United Way of the D.C. metropolitan area was accused of raising performance in fundraising by deliberately double counting to attract more donors and that its executive later pleaded guilty to inflated compensation and diversion of funds. Finally, isn't it the same profit motive that could lead to greater efficiency under the same fixed cost contract, and isn't efficiency one of the motives for contracting?

In at least one state, Georgia, the state has placed an additional burden on nonprofit bidders, declaring that the state has a duty to be assured that public funds are used as intended. Accordingly, through an Executive Order A-11–0005-May 1997 by the governor of Georgia and state law 5–20-1 (Senate Bill 474 Chapter 20), any state agency contemplating entering into a contract with a nonprofit shall require audited financial statements from the nonprofit, including its sources of other finances and a disclosure on whether it has used funds for such purposes as politics. The agency must also inform the state auditor of its intent to enter into such a contract and the state auditor is required to report to the legal authorities any irregularities in the nonprofit operations prior to letting the contract.

An unspecified contract is one in which the terms cannot be fully specified. This means, for example, that the inputs or outputs cannot be easily measured, the date of delivery cannot be certain, or even that the configuration of the output is not easily determinable—that is, the government is not even sure what the final output would look like. Even the final cost may not be fully determinable at the outset. This means the principal must trust that the agent will do the job—a reason given for contracting with nonprofits because they can be trusted. If the lack of specificity of the contract were so determinative of the government's choice, why, to take an extreme example, are weapons contracts (the most severely under specified in the government's arsenal of contracts) not given to nonprofits rather than to firms, even after the latter have cheated over and over again? Indefinite quantity contracts are strategies the government uses when it cannot foresee or specify its future needs. It also, as Kelman[8] notes in his study of government procurement of computer services, provides the contractor with a comfort level for developing ideas and solutions—especially when the government may have been unable to specify in the "specs." In short, the government has both a strategy and a habit of dealing with unspecified contracts with firms—not just nonprofits.

A purpose of this chapter is to explore these backdrop responses (which clearly beg deeper questions) by looking at the specific steps taken by the government to enter into a contract. Where in this process does the nonprofit have an advantage, and on what is that advantage based if the competitor is technically equally competent? We must first establish who is competent to bid on a government contract, and the basis that the nonprofit and the government would have a mutual interest as implied in the contract. After all, the basis of any contract and the principal-agent relationship is that one party is driven by the incentive to get something done, which another party is equally driven to accept—at the right price.

The Qualified Nonprofit or Firm

In order to compete for a federal contract, the Federal procurement policy law, 41 U.SC. Section 405, states that a qualified or responsible bidder is one who: (1) has adequate financial resources to perform the contract or the ability to obtain such resources; (2) is able to comply with the required or proposed delivery or performance schedule, taking into consideration all existing commercial and government business commitments; (3) has a satisfactory performance record; (4) has a satisfactory record of integrity and business ethics; (5) has the necessary organization, experience, accounting and operational controls, and technical skills, or the ability to obtain such organization, experience, controls, and skills; (6) has the necessary production, construction, and technical equipment and facilities, or the ability to obtain such equipment and facilities; and (7) is otherwise qualified and eligible to receive an award under applicable laws and regulations.

The Convergence of Interest between the Government and Qualified Bidders

The most fundamental requirement of a successful contractual choice is that there is a good fit between the agent and the principal. The agent can do what the principal wants, when, where, and how the principal wants it done, and the principal trusts that the agent will get it done as agreed.

In every principal-agent relationship there are two costs that the principal or its managing agent must consider. One is the cost of establishing and entering the relationship, of maintaining it, and of closing it. These are costs of managing the relationship (transaction costs). The second cost is the cost of actually producing what is wanted (the cost of production). If the firm and the nonprofit are equally competent, then the latter cost is about the same for both of them. In that event, the choice would be based on the costs of managing the relationship (the transaction costs). "They may be just as good but it is too much of a hassle to deal with them."

It may, for example, be relatively too expensive to be sure that they maintain all the criteria, such as having proper licenses; writing up the contract and negotiating it with them; monitoring their performance; getting them to make modifications; getting them to report on a timely basis; getting them to keep auditable records; and getting them to close or to extend the contract as circumstances change. These are all hassle and nuisance costs that must be taken into account in choosing between two equally competent contractors.

The Assumption that the Choice Is between Two Equally Technically Competent Bidders

That the choice is between two technically competent parties is not unreasonable. Empirical studies don't point to any difference in efficiency in nonprofit organizations over firms of the same size and in the same business. After reviewing the works of other scholars and his own work, Sloan[9] concludes that there is no difference in the efficiency of for-profit and nonprofit hospitals and the evidence shows that the rates of return on assets of nonprofit and for-profit hospitals[10] are similar and ditto for nonprofit and for-profit HMOs.[11] Therefore, that the choice would be based on the differences in nuisance or hassle or what is known as transaction costs is not unreasonable. Therefore, we explore that cost.

Transaction Cost in Establishing a Pool of Agents

The competent and interested agents must be drawn from a pool. Given the arguments of the previous chapters, the government has two sets of transaction costs when dealing with nonprofits. The first is trivial but must be dealt with before setting it aside. These are the costs to approve the charter and to award an appropriate tax-exempt status to the nonprofit—allowing it to be part of the pool or club of agents from which the government may choose. These initial organizing costs, as with a firm, are borne principally by the founders of the organization. The government is paid an application fee.

Thus, the government and the public get a pool of potential agents at low if not zero cost to either. The government does have a cost of monitoring these organizations through their annual reports (Form 990) to the IRS, to be sure that even though they may not be under direct contract with the government, they are operating according to rules and in conformity with their mission to the public. This transaction cost to the government has only to do with the creation of a pool or club of nonprofit agents. But our question is: Why does the government choose one from this pool over an equally competent firm for a specific contract? The issue is not about the creation of either pool of agents, but selecting from them.

The Decision-Making Process that Leads to Contract Choice

To answer this question, we must begin with the process that leads to transaction costs in the government's making a choice of contractors. The following are some of the key elements in how the government operates in its bidding process and incurs transaction costs—the cost to have a relationship with a contractor. To the extent the cost of any of these is higher for a nonprofit than for a firm, the nonprofit is disadvantaged on that dimension.

Request for Proposal (RFP) Preparation

At this stage the government agency deliberates and decides on the content of the RFP—what it wants, when, and how much it expects to pay to have the contract fulfilled. When in doubt, the government agency may enter into a contract to help it with the technical and conceptual aspects of the proposal. For example, it may (as specifically authorized by FAIR) contract an architectural firm to help decide specifications for a construction RFP. This stage of RFP preparation is roughly the same whether the contract is won by a for-profit or a nonprofit. In either case, the government has to decide and to communicate what it wants, when it wants it, and how much it is willing to pay. This is, in effect, the first stages of FAIR.

Pre-qualification

The government often reduces its cost of screening by prequalifying bidders. Many states and localities require that social services be contracted only to agencies that are prequalified. See, for example, the *Minnesota Department of Social Services Manual: Grants and Purchase of Service Contracting (VII 9000)* especially Part 9550.0040 Subpart 3.E. This is done in part to assure that the organization or firm is qualified within the terms of state and local laws—for example, that a day care center meets all of the licensing requirements.

One way a government agency may prequalify is by stipulating that only a small disadvantaged business, a business owned by a female, on a business located in a designated development area is a qualified bidder. Federal procurement law, for example, requires the Small Business Administration to annually certify that government agencies have contributed their share to the federally established goal (currently about 25 percent) of all federal contracts going to such groups. There is no equivalent goal for nonprofits. The situation is the same in most states. Since nonprofits are not qualifiers in this pool, it cannot be argued, at least with reference to this pool, that nonprofits compete unfairly—as is often argued.

Why, then, is it that the federal as well as state and local government also stipulate that for some contracts only nonprofits may bid and for some, nonprofits may compete with for-profit firms? What is the incentive aside from the public policy objective of "fairness and opportunity"? Aside from the public policy or political objectives, prequalification reduces the government's cost of screening through a bunch of applications it knows are unlikely to be acceptable. What the government is seeking is to reduce its transaction costs by reducing the number of bidders it knows it won't consider for any number or combination of reasons stated under "The Qualified Nonprofit or Firm" section above.

Screening

Once the bidders are qualified through the prequalification process, screening among them may be based on criteria such as number of years of experience, size of the business, minority or female ownership, being nonprofit or for-profit, and location of operation. These screening criteria are usually written with the conjunction "and" so that prospective applicants must meet several criteria at the same time. Different scores may be assigned to each criterion so that even if a prospective applicant satisfies all of the criteria, its total score may not give it the winning bid.

The out-of-pocket cost of qualification is borne by the applicant—not the government. Some of these costs are fully reimbursed by the government to the winning contractor. The government reimburses only the winning bids. The setting of criteria causes contractors to screen themselves out—self-selection. In any pool of potential providers, the screening criteria work similarly for nonprofit and for-profit groups and should (unless excluded) allow both firms and nonprofits to be considered. Therefore, why would the government select a nonprofit over a for-profit firm from this pool if it utilizes the same procedure to ensure that it gets what it wants?

Selection Cost

This cost is determined by the number of bids that must be read, visits that must be made, and interviews that must be done by the government in its exercise of all of the diligence needed to make the best selection. There is nothing inherently less costly in this stage for selecting a nonprofit than for selecting a firm. The cost of due diligence is more related to the production complexity of the product being requested and the extent to which the government wishes to reduce the risk of failure by the provider. The government selects nonprofits in the same way it selects firms for the same types of contracts.

Negotiating the Winning Bid

At this stage, the government selects the entities, and the details of the contract must be negotiated. For most contracts, negotiation is not complex. First, much of the contract may be standard or boilerplate material. Second, by this stage each party has a strong interest in doing the deal and each party has been informed about what the issues are and what each must be prepared to resolve. Each party knows what it wants and what the other wants and can give. The difficulty of the negotiation is not dependent upon the organizational form (for-profit or not) but on the objective, requirements, and content of the contract and each side's ability or willingness to compromise.

Monitoring Time

The time that is needed for monitoring a contract is dependent on the history of the organization or firm, the nature of the production process, the quality of output, and the cost of error. In construction, the government may require daily monitoring. In other situations, the government may set milestones—dates at which specific phases of the project are to be completed, reported, and an assessment made. More importantly, it is also dependent upon the factors described by the GAO and particularly Johnson and Romzek, as discussed earlier in this chapter.

The government monitors for contract performance, but also for safety and other standards, and, as those studies show, mostly for compliance and for its own learning. It may assess penalties, accelerate and intensify monitoring, and terminate the contract depending upon what it learns from monitoring. This is true whether the organization is for-profit or not. Monitoring does, however, have to do with the question of trust. Presumably, one monitors more the less trustworthy the agent. But on what basis does the government trust the nonprofit more than the firm? Recall that both studies cited above point to the emphasis of government monitoring on regulatory compliance, not on performance, albeit that since the Government Performance and Results Act of 1993, an effort has been made to increase performance measures and monitoring. The GAO[12] finds no clear difference in the monitoring or performance between nonprofit and firms even on the state level as far as child care and other welfare contracting are concerned.

But one of the major problems in monitoring is cited in the report of the California Department of Social Services on the in-home supportive services alluded to above. It is the failure of the government itself to create either performance standards or monitoring standards.[13] The cost of monitoring is not attributable solely to the behavior of providers.

Post Contract Evaluation, Continuation, or Closing Costs

This part of the transaction costs involves a report and evaluation of outcomes. The process is the same for nonprofits and for-profit contractors. The decision is made whether to close the contract before or according to schedule, or to continue it even in a modified form or to reopen it for bid.

Summary Statement of the Process of Choice

The principal insight from this step-by-step procedure is that the government has the choice of setting the prequalification for bidders. It will announce whether or not a nonprofit may bid on the contract. If it thinks the nonprofit form is inappropriate it can always say no nonprofits can apply, if it feels that the nonprofit form is most appropriate it can say only nonprofits can apply, and if it is indifferent it may have both for-profit and nonprofit providers apply, or it may ask them to partner. If the government selects a nonprofit for a contract in which the nonprofit form is inappropriate it can expect its production or its transaction costs (for example, monitoring and closing the contract) to be higher than if it had correctly chosen a firm in the first place. Hence, we return to our basic question: Why would the government give the nonprofit a preference in a particular bidding? If the two organizations are equally competent, it must be because the nonprofit form is superior for that contract to the commercial. What is it about the nonprofit form? We shall systematically go through some ideas beginning with the concept of trust. Step by step we shall work our way to what this chapter describes as the five factors of contracting confidence that leads to this choice and what the concept of trust must mean since it appears nowhere under the topic "The Qualified Nonprofit or Firm," discussed earlier.

Empirical Results of State-Level Contracting Methods

A study of state government procurement criteria[14] found that the most common criterion upon which states make their selection of contractors is price (48 states); in addition, 47 used assurance of timely delivery, 47 assurance of quality, 45 quality of performance, and 43 record of performance. Now we will explore the methods they use to make their choices.

To keep our discussion in real context, and having described earlier the procedures that federal agencies use to determine qualification and award contracts from the pool of qualified bidders, let us look at the various methods empirical studies find that states use for selecting contractors. Using definitions and model contracts from the National Association of State Procurement Officers, Council of State Governments, the American Bar Association's Model Procurement for State and Local Governments, and drawing from a survey of nearly 2000 members of the National Institute of Government Purchasing and from the American Public Works Association, Qiao and Cummings[15] find three common methods states use to choose. Below, I describe these three and then impute the implications of each for the nonprofit competitor.

The Lowest Cost, Most Responsive and Responsible Bid Method

This is the most commonly used method by state agencies to select contractors. The bid goes to the lowest bidder demonstrating the financial and operational capability and history of performance and that is also satisfactorily responsive to the requirements and questions of the RFP. In this method, all sealed bids are opened at the same time, and the lowest bidder that is also responsive to the contract requirements, shows the greatest evidence to perform, and is financially sound is chosen. In general, in these types of contests, the most competent and trustworthy nonprofit wins only if it is also the lowest bidder. Among equals, cost matters.

Qualification-Based Bid Method

In this method qualification is the principal metric for grading bidders. Bidders are ranked according to the qualification criteria set out in the RFP and then eliminated in order one by one through the process of negotiation. In this method, the nonprofit wins, not by being the lowest cost bidder but by being the most qualified. Qualification trumps everything else.

The Best Value Method

In this method, contracts are selected based on the best and highest interest of the state being served. Therefore, the total return to the state or the "best value" criterion, not cost, is determinative. The highest cost bidder may be acceptable if the returns it is expected to offer are also highest. In this method, the nonprofit has the opportunity to show that it offers better value to the state and is more consistent with the state's interest than a firm. Value and return trump cost.

The reader is requested to keep these three methods in mind as the five factors of confidence with which the government is hypothesized in this chapter to elect a nonprofit over a firm are discussed. They dovetail nicely. We may deduce that in method one, the nonprofit wins if it produces the same product for less cost. It can do this in one or a combination of two ways: (a) have a lower cost of production, or (b) have the same cost of production and subsidize the difference through donations and volunteering, thus lowering the cost to the government.

It can win through method two if the "qualification" set by government is one that the firm cannot meet. Given two equally competent competitors, this is hardly likely to be a technical qualification. But it could be one such as "the bidder must demonstrate a history of community involvement and an ability to garner the involvement of the community so as to ensure the success of the project."

The nonprofit can win through method three if it can yield the public the greatest value. It can do this by (a) bringing more resources to bear to the problem—thus leveraging the rate of return to the government's investment, or (b) providing more benefits for every dollar the government spends. Since the federal government uses best value method, the argument that will follow will apply to state and to federal government contracting.

Now, the question is: How do the implications of these methods of selecting contractors comport with some of the concepts such as trust, mission, social capital—none of which appears in these methods? How do they lead to what will be referred to in this book as the five levels of confidence upon which government choice of a nonprofit as an agent of policy is made over an equally qualified firm? Two methods, the best value method and the qualification method, allow discretionary criteria other than cost that could favor nonprofits; but the nonprofit could compete on cost by subsidization of costs through volunteers or donations. Thus, all three methods are in play and the five factors should be generalizable across contracting methods, even though they may differ in relative weight from one method to the other. We begin with trust. What must it mean?

Trust and Its Impact on Government's Choice of Agents

Trust is a very credible rationale when referring to why an individual would choose a nonprofit over a firm. As Arrow[16] puts it, there is a convergence of expectations. As social capital theory puts it, this convergence occurs through common values, common goals, and so on. The same can be said of the government—that is, that it shares a common goal with a nonprofit more so than it shares a common goal with a firm. The firm's objective is profits, and providing housing may be a means toward making such profits. The government's and the nonprofit's objective is the housing to improve public welfare. The primary objective is the same. There is a convergence of interest.

The word "trust" may also mean confidence—a statement of reliability such as "I trust that it will be done." The less reliability or confidence the government has in a contractor, the greater its actual and prospective transaction costs. It needs to monitor, to develop, and to agree upon strict milestones and criteria, and it must expect to close down prematurely if the contractor fails. One reason for failure is what Williamson[17] refers to as contract maladaptation, that is, picking the wrong institution for the job. Among two equally qualified entities, the wrong choice may be the one that has the lower convergence of interest, and the ultimate cost of choosing incorrectly is the cost of failure.

The cost of failure is calculable and must be taken into account by the government. Even Williamson[18] in his debate with Carswell[19] admits that for business purposes trust must be calculable. It must be calculable if a legal remedy is to be available if the contractor is unable to perform specifically as required in the contract. It is the cost of starting over again minus any salvage value. But an important aspect of that cost is what Jensen and Meckling[20] refer to as the residual cost, which is the reduction in the economic welfare of the principal (in this case the community or public) due to the failure of the agent.[21]

Hence, we conclude that the word "trust," when explaining why the government will choose a nonprofit over a firm, must mean: "it trusts or has confidence that the work will be done aside from technical competence." The greatest source of such trust is that the nonprofit shares the same primary motive as the government—improving public welfare. When the motive of advancing public welfare matters in causing the agent to be reliable, the nonprofit is more trustworthy (reliable) than the firm; and the government is likely to choose the nonprofit to avoid the cost of failure or nonperformance of the firm. The most obvious example of this is when the government knows that the activity is not likely to produce the profits that a firm would want, and, therefore, the firm has no built-in motivation to perform as expected.

We have identified one root of trust. This is the convergence of commitment and purpose of the government and the nonprofit to an identified problem, and motivation by the same exclusive objective of improving public welfare. Thus, when the government's housing agency chooses a nonprofit housing organization in a city, it is choosing one that shares its commitment in search of the same general results for the same reasons—in this case better housing for advancing the welfare of the same community. Indeed, the commitment of the organization to the community (being formed by and located exclusively in that community for that community's purpose) may be greater than the government's.

In this sense, the government's contract has an important element of economic rent—a payment to the nonprofit for doing something it probably would have done anyway, providing that it could have raised the funds internally, or through donations. Thus a government contract is both a payment for specific services being bought by the government from the nonprofit and economic rent. It is a subsidy not by intent of the government but by virtue of its being used by the nonprofit to finance its mission activities.

This is an important conceptual distinction. The government subsidizes Amtrak by making an annual appropriation for it without a specific demand that it carry so many passengers—there is no specific quid pro quo. With a contract it demands specific performance. Within a principal-agent paradigm, trust is based on the expectations of a specific performance—granted that the degree of specificity may vary. One source of trust, when competitors are equivalent in skill, is the convergence of motives and commitment. "Are they so committed that even if we couldn't pay them or couldn't pay them enough, or can't pay them in the future they will carry on seeking other funding because they are committed?" Would they be committed to the job even if we, the government, did not hire them? "If they exist exclusively because of that commitment can we not trust them to be our agent?"

Cognitive Social Capital as a Factor in Choice

Cognitive social capital is another element of choice of the nonprofit organization as agent. The specific theory of social capital, discussed in chapter 3, applies here. The theory in its cognitive form states that individuals of common interest tend to interact frequently with each other and that they develop norms of behavior that facilitate their interaction among themselves. They also develop trust, commitments to common goals, and the cooperative behavior to accomplish them.

In its structural form, these individuals congregate into groups or associations such as nonprofit organizations. The net result of this trust, common outlook, cooperative behavior, and ease of communication (the cognitive form) is that these structural groups can more easily take collective action. In short, the transaction costs—specifically the costs of internal communication and persuasion, involvement and commitment, decision-making and monitoring—are lowered the more dense the social capital. An example is a faith-based organization compared to a loose, informal, and infrequent gathering to discuss great art or a book club.

A related group of sociologists, led by Granoveter,[22] argues that all transactions are embedded in the relationship that parties to the transaction have to each other. It is the nature of this relationship between the parties that determines transaction costs. They argue that it is the quality of that relationship (the trust and understanding) that allows contracts among them to be incomplete or unspecified and still be viable. "We understand each other." "We are family." "We want the same thing."

To paraphrase Zukin and DiMaggio,[23] embeddedness of social capital may result from structural relationships such as family, fraternity, or friendship; it may result from cultural relationships such as a common belief or value system or country of citizenship; it may result from cognitive similarities such as a common way of thinking, perhaps due to professional training or common experiences; it may be due to common political or economic incentives, such as the orientation to profit-making. In all these cases two parties can proclaim: "Oh, we can get along, we think alike, we dig each other." It is the application of the same "logic" to a problem that allows one to trust and to predict better the reaction of the other. Where does all this lead?

This leads to a suggestion. To the extent that transactions are embedded in strong social capital, the transaction costs are less because the group monitors and controls behavior and because communication is easier. It can be argued therefore that when the government contracts with a nonprofit it seeks to gain from this embedded relationship. Thus contracting with a nonprofit organization makes the government and ultimately the public the beneficiaries of these inter- and intra-organizational attributes. "They can get the word out." "They stimulate community involvement and cooperation." "This project will empower the community." "We can't succeed without the involvement of the family or the church." "It will motivate them to produce and finance their own projects."

The logic of the above argument links nicely to the market-centric argument. The market-centric argument is that nonprofits are formed by individuals who trust the nonprofit form of organization more than the market form, at least for certain goods and services. Therefore, the current argument goes, the government, recognizing this trust within nonprofit organizations, and recognizing that it offers an opportunity to reduce the cost to the government of a contract, leads the latter to contract with the nonprofit organization as long as there is trust—specifically reliability and confidence that it can perform. The greater the degree of social capital, defined as those networks as discussed in chapter 3, norms and values that facilitate cohesion and collective action, the greater the trust (confidence grown of reliability) that the group will be able to police itself and keep its commitments. As stated in chapter 3, cognitive social capital contributes to the production or implementation of public policy consistent with the shared values and norms of the group. Therefore, social capital is the sociological framework in which the public policy position of an organization is framed and is produced. As shall be argued later, this can be proprietary and unique and therefore has contractual value that can be "cheated."

The Mission, Incomplete Contracts, and Expectations in Choice

Contracts are often incompletely specified. This, it will be argued, gives rise to the need for trust rooted in the bounded nature of a mission as a contractual promise. This is different from trust rooted in a common purpose as discussed earlier. The less specific the contract offer of the government, the greater are the possibilities for misunderstanding and dispute. This is not a new observation. Some economic sociologists draw from Emile Durkheim and his observation over a hundred years ago that contracts are always incomplete if only because human beings cannot fully foresee all that may happen to affect a contract. But governments sign incomplete contracts with firms as well as with nonprofits. An indefinite quantity contract is an extreme example of this. The government contracts with a for-profit or a nonprofit organization for a certain dollar amount, but not a specific project. The intent is to reserve the organization (and the money) for a quick response to future unspecified need with payment made when such need is identified and satisfied. See the earlier discussion about an indefinite quantity contract.

The one advantage that a nonprofit has over a firm when the contract is incomplete is that the mission of the nonprofit places boundaries on what can be expected from it and accountability lends to insuring that expectation. See the discussion in chapter 4. A contract to a nonprofit to provide housing implies a contract to provide low and moderate-income housing. This is not the same with a private developer. Here, it is not the incompleteness of the contract or the "trust" in the organization that matters, but the bounding of expectations in a mission statement that is legally binding. "The government knows what it is buying."

But the mission does more than that which makes it a strong basis upon which to choose a nonprofit over a firm. It has been argued that every nonprofit mission has the following properties,[24] which bind the organization permanently to the policy theme that it has submitted a voluntary promise to perform. These are not momentary or opportunistic promises, but firm and permanent ones. " We can be confident that they can't walk away without risking losing their exemptions or being involuntarily dissolved." "They won't take that chance."

1. *It is a social contract:* It is a promise that in exchange for its power to operate (charter) and its tax-exempt status, the organization will perform only a specified and stated set of functions that benefit society. These functions are stated in its charter.
2. *It is a permanent commitment:* It cannot abandon this promise without filing such an amendment and seeking governmental approval at risk of losing its tax exemption and nonprofit status, and

having its assets seized by state governments and heavy penalties on its management.

3. *It is clear:* Mission statements of nonprofits are simple statements (even in the grammatical sense). Moreover, the range of interpretation and acceptability is set in law. There is very little if any room for misunderstanding of what kind of performance is being agreed to and therefore expected.
4. *It must be approved:* The written and signed mission and the commitment to it is approved by the organizers of the organization and the government in the application for nonprofit and separately for tax-exempt status. So, too, are any amendments that future managers may conceive.
5. *The performance of the mission is provable:* The operating managers and directors of the organization agree to prove annually in a format and in a time frame set by the government (Form 990) that it is operating the organization according to the agreement made above. Failure to do this or to do it accurately can lead (at the government's choice) to removal of tax-exempt status and/or fines—in some cases against the management itself.

Thus, the mission is a voluntary but permanent contractual commitment to conduct a core business for the benefit of the public and to demonstrate that this is being done annually in a clear and direct form as chosen by the government acting on behalf of the public. What stronger basis does the government need upon which to establish its trust? Firms agree to no such thing in their charters and may legally deviate with relative ease. The government not only knows what it is buying, but it also knows that the nonprofit cannot change course the way a for-profit firm can without first informing the federal and state governments through its annual report and getting "approval" to the extent that neither government disapproves.

Goodwill and the Contractual Value of Nonprofits

Another reason the government may choose a nonprofit over an equally competent firm is because it seeks to benefit from the goodwill of the organization. As used here, goodwill is not social capital; it is technically distinguishable from social capital. Goodwill is used here in the business sense. It is identifiable, salable, and separable from the organization or its cognitive social capital.

Goodwill is an intangible asset such as credibility, reputation, contacts, quality of product and staff, performance history, the extent of communication and marketing channels, familiarity, name recognition, location, connections, brand acceptance, loyalty of members, a "halo" effect, and so. Clearly some aspects of goodwill, for example reputation, are sources of trust. But it is also obvious from the above list that goodwill goes well beyond and includes clients, channels of communication, and marketing.

Goodwill as used in business and in this text denotes intangible assets acquired by long-term financial investment. Goodwill is not only intangible but it may also be inanimate and unrelated to behavior; for these reasons, it is distinguished in this context from social capital. Location, market share, a list of clients, copyright are all important elements of goodwill in business and to many nonprofits ranging from hospitals (location, expertise, and clientele) to universities and museums (copyrights, patents, and other property rights). To universities, for example, this includes the licensing of its names for shirts, hats, pens, pencils, mugs, and other items. Any item that is considered goodwill in business has a calculable monetary value and is private (not social) property. The property rights over a license a university holds belongs to the university, and only indirectly to the society. Goodwill is identifiable private property that can be sold, leased, depreciated, and disposed of by the organization.

These intangible, nonbehavioral, and nonsociological assets have value in use. When the federal government used the American Red Cross to collect contributions for the September 11 tragedy, it was employing the organization's goodwill—a combination of the factors listed above for the benefit of the victims. These factors included reputation as source of trust or trustworthiness, and also reputation as an intangible asset, meaning recognition. It was also employing the organization's channels of collection and communication, its experience, and its capacity in an emergency public appeal. These are elements of goodwill.

Goodwill as an asset does not only have one use or one user. Thus, the nonprofit may lease its goodwill to any number of users simultaneously and for a wide variety of reasons. This is not to say that aspects of goodwill have unbounded utility. The reputation of the nonprofit organization may be very localized, as is the case of the community development corporation. But this is site specificity and not specificity with respect to the government or any single potential user. Thus the organization may lease its goodwill to any number of users simultaneously.

When a for-profit firm contracts with the American Heart Association for its seal of approval, it is buying the organization's reputation (credibility). When a credit card company uses a nonprofit's name on its card, it is not buying trust. It is buying "affinity" into the university's list and it is using that list as a screening device for prequalified customers. In every case it pays the nonprofit. Goodwill has a price. It is an asset accounted for in the balance sheets of businesses. It is priced when a nonprofit is converted to a for-profit firm or when it is selling a part of its operation.

Goodwill is not to be confused with asset specificity. Williamson[25] describes asset specificity as the value an asset derives because of its value for a specific purpose or use—and only that purpose or user. A technological firm may acquire or develop a specific part that fits only one make of car. It has no value otherwise. Asset specificity according to Williamson may derive from location, the physical characteristics of an asset, the specific training of a person, brand names, dedicated assets, or temporal or temporary specificity. One of Williamson's concerns about asset specificity is that it increases the mutual dependence between the owner of the asset and those who need it and, as we shall discuss later in this chapter, creates the opportunity that one would abuse the other.

Goodwill does not in general suffer from this. The key difference between goodwill and asset specificity is that goodwill is usable in a number of ways, by any number of users all at the same time or at their choosing, and the use by any one does not (unless abused) diminish its use by others. Thus, an organization may lease its name and mailing list to any number of users. The names of universities are on shirts, mugs, pencils, watches, credit cards. Goodwill has value to an infinite number of entities that may hire the organization or lease its goodwill. Contracting with any one does not prohibit contracting with others.

Governments may choose a nonprofit over a firm because of goodwill. The nonprofit has a halo effect; it connotes goodness and community spirit; it improves acceptability. But goodwill is also a productive asset. Therefore, it connotes a lower cost. The nonprofit as a brand is different than the for-profit as a brand. The government may choose a nonprofit over a firm when the nonprofit as a brand has a decided advantage in marketing, in outreach, in cost relative to the benefits the government desires.

Leverage, Augmentation of the Benefit-Cost Ratio, and the Choice of Nonprofit Contractor

Thus far we have argued that if the competence is the same, then such contracting is based on (a) a concept of trust as reliability or confidence due to shared motivation or common purpose to advance the public welfare; (b) limited guessing as the result of bounded expectations by the contractual, clear, permanent, agreed, and verifiable mission statement of the organization; (c) the ability to exploit the social capital of the organization, which facilitates collective action and cooperation, which can be translated to reduce costs; and (d) goodwill that improves the feasibility, acceptability, and reach of the project being financed. In this section, we turn to one other factor—the ability of the nonprofit to leverage.

Leveraging occurs when a dollar attracts other dollars and resources to the same cause. Put another way, how does the government get more benefits from an identical contract cost to a nonprofit than to a firm? How does leveraging occur within a nonprofit? What are the implications of the following empirical and theoretical studies for this book? Leverage increases the benefit-cost ratio without the necessity of the nonprofit to demonstrate that it produces secondary benefits—even those that the government did not intend and often are not part of the contract, and therefore, under the rules of a cost reimbursement contract, are not billable to the government.

Fama and Jansen,[26] using a principal-agent framework, argue that donors make unrestricted donations to nonprofit hospitals because they have confidence that their donations will not leak to the pockets of residual claimants—stockholders who have claims on the assets of the organizations. Nonprofits cannot pay dividends, so the profits or surpluses they earn plus the donations that they receive are retained to finance the hospital's mission, as Hansmann[27] asserts in the nondistributional constraint—the law that prohibits nonprofits from issuing dividends whether in cash or in kind. Wolf and Weisbrod[28] find that volunteers are more drawn to nonprofit than to for-profit hospitals.

Sloan[29] and Eggleston and Zeckhauser[30] found that the efficiencies between nonprofit and for-profit hospitals are not significantly different. But as stated in the previous paragraph, the dollar and its earnings will remain in the nonprofit hospital and not be paid out in dividends. Also as stated in the previous paragraph, in the nonprofit hospital the dollar will attract more volunteers and charitable donations in cash and other in-kind gifts and contributions because these are deductible to donors who give to nonprofit hospitals and not deductible if given to a for-profit hospital. The combined effect is greater leverage.

The implication is this: The dollar spent in the nonprofit tax-exempt hospital attracts significantly more dollars than that spent in a for-profit hospital, given that the efficiencies are similar. Moreover, these additional dollars can only be used for the public purpose stated in the mission, thus increasing the capacity of the organization to be an agent of public policy. This kind of leveraging effect can be presumed to be similar across all nonprofits because it is based on the normative (legally required) way of operating a nonprofit—the organizational form.

In short, a dollar spent on a nonprofit tax-exempt organization is likely to yield more than a dollar spent on a for-profit one because the former can leverage more than the latter. In social services this is especially important since these services are always underfinanced by the government relative to their known needs. It is to the advantage of the government and the public to seek as a partner an agent that can leverage.

For the nonprofit organization, leverage arises from the influence of one or a combination of the following factors, as discussed above, once the government contract is let to the organization:

1. The attraction of cash, in-kind, and human resource donations
2. The absence of outside claims on earnings or asset except in the cases of leases and debt-reducing leakage
3. The nondistribution constraints on dividends whether cash or non-cash, also reducing leakage
4. The benefit to the contract from the exclusive focus of all other organizational expenditures and resources to a mission of which the

contract is but a small part—the spillovers from all other organizational activities

5. The exclusive use of tax-exempt earnings (which may differ among organizations) for the common purpose to which the contract is related.

None of these things is true of a firm. Yet, those who are familiar with social service and community development contracting know that ever since the Kennedy years government contracts have implied or required some measure or indication of cost-benefit and leverage.

Choosing Nonprofit Contractors Based on Five Factors of Confidence

When the choice is between two equally competent entities, one for-profit and the other nonprofit, the above arguments point to five factors of confidence upon which the choice of a nonprofit contractor may be made. They are:

1. *Trust Derived from a Convergence of Interest—Shared Motivation for Being:* Trust is established due to the convergence of motives between the government and the nonprofit organization. Both exist to advance the public's welfare and to conduct the public's policies. The firm's motive is to make profits and the contract is a means to making that profit. The public purpose of the contract is not the motivating factor to the firm. Therefore, absent the possibilities of profits or other incentives, but sharing a common interest in an adversely selected or impacted population or place as described in this and the previous chapter, the government may rely on the convergence of a similar interest with a nonprofit as a motivating factor. "They both want to do the same thing for the same people for the same reasons."
2. *Trust Derived from the Bounded and Contractual Nature of the Mission:* Not only can't the nonprofit abandon its mission without consequences, but the mission defines the boundary of expectations. The government knows the outer limits. A nonprofit housing agency by definition deals with low- and moderate-income families. A for-profit housing agency is free to deal with whomever it pleases. The mission bounds what one may expect from a nonprofit and therefore places confidence in what it may (must) do. "The government knows that the nonprofit has long ago voluntarily elected to bound itself exclusively and legally to the objective the government now has in mind."
3. *Leverage as a Means of Sharing Financial Burdens:* Confidence that the government can get more than it paid for because of the non-

profit's ability to attract resources through donations of money and in-kind gifts including volunteer labor and the spillover benefits of related projects, and that all of these benefits or assets will be reinvested in the shared objective year after year. "The amount of money that will be applied to the objective will be more than the government has invested."

4. *Goodwill as a Branding Asset:* Confidence that the organization's intangible assets such as its location, its property rights, its list of contributors, and members, all can potentially add value in fulfilling the contract. The amount of goodwill a nonprofit has is not as powerful as the first three items, since they are more endemic to the nonprofit organizational form and goodwill depends more critically on managerial action. As an asset, goodwill is subject to destruction, depreciation, and obsolescence. Patents, for example, are subject to these; the name of an organization can also be ruined. The nonprofit has certain organizational and proprietary advantages that will make its performance superior. "It knows more, has greater contacts, reputation, loyalty, and recognition that would lend to greater success." Branding may apply to the product of the organization or to the organization itself. Writing about corporate branding, Aaker[31] notes that organizations (as distinguishable from their products) have brand identification. This identification signals certain expectations and confidence to potential consumers, and capabilities and conduct to contractors; distinguishes the organization from other organizations in the same line of business; and can be a basis of employee pride. He also notes, as does this book and others in business administration or marketing, that brand is an asset. It is subject to impairment and destruction and it is a consequence of long-term investment with an expectation of a flow of benefits. It is an intangible asset, but it is not a sociological one and therefore it is distinguishable from the cognitive social capital described next. The word "nonprofit" and the recognizable names of specific nonprofits connote a brand.
5. *Cognitive Social Capital for Diffusion and Cohesion:* Confidence that it can reduce certain internal transactions costs and therefore the contract cost; and, confidence that it can diffuse the benefits over a targeted population more efficiently than government or a firm and also gain internal cohesive behavior toward advancing the purpose of the contract. "It can pull the players together, make them work better together, and diffuse the benefits over a wider population." An organization may also brand itself by its social capital. In religion, for example, two congregations of the same denomination can brand themselves differently by the environment that they create for activities, including worship, to take place. The difference between branding by social capital and branding by goodwill is the latter is alienable and the former is not. Much more will be said about this in the next section.

Another comment about the fifth item above is in order. It is easy to misunderstand the importance of this factor if it is viewed purely as community action or involvement. The fact is that most activities that nonprofits are involved in require coproduction. This means that they require both provider and client inputs to be successful (schools are as good as their students, who are as good as their parents, who are as good as the community). Moreover, the objectives of what they do are ultimately served by diffusion (parents encouraging other parents who encourage their children). The cognitive social capital is sociopsychological in nature and is inseparable from the organization. One gets it by hiring the organization. With goodwill one may be able to get it by leasing it or leasing a product or service in which it is embodied. An organization's goodwill is in its name and its name can be placed on a cap without carrying the entire organization on the person's head.

Cheating Social Capital of Its Contracting Significance

Conceptual lumpiness in the social capital literature cheats the concept of cognitive social capital of its significance in contracting. It also fails to recognize that no two parties enter into a contract without reasonable specificity of what one wants from the other and a strategy to get it.

If an entity is motivated primarily by the goodwill of an organization, it has three contracting strategies available: (a) it might choose to contract the organization; (b) it might choose to lease the asset containing the element of the organization's goodwill it wants—the manufacturer leases the name of the university and puts it on shirts and another leases the same name and puts it on mugs; another leases the same name and puts it on writing pads; or (c) it might choose to require that the organization apply jointly with another—a small firm is required to joint venture with the nonprofit because the latter has more reliability, reputation, and intellectual property.

What allows strategies (b) and (c) is that goodwill is alienable. It can be completely, as in (b), or partially, as in (c), separated from the organization that owns it; therefore, to get it one does not have to hire the entire organization as in (a).

As used here, cognitive social capital is different. It is embodied in the organization and cannot be alienated. Therefore to get it, one has to hire the organization. To get the advantage of the university's social environment one has to be on the university's campus. The social dynamics are an asset; but they are physically, operationally, and conceptually inseparable from the organization. They are embodied or embedded. Social capital is the sociological and psychological context in which the production occurs. It is an asset. It is a differentiating characteristic that can be cultivated. But it is not alienable. It cannot be separated from the organization.

Cognitive social capital is like the trust derived from convergence of interests that is encapsulated in the mission. To get it, the government must hire the organization because it is inseparable. But cognitive social capital is different. It has no legal standing and it is not a contractual promise. It is dynamic and changes (grows, improves, or declines as every day passes). Cognitive social capital is not readable, although it may be described. A mission statement is readable and need not be described. "This is how we operate," as distinguished from, "This is what we shall do."

Cognitive social capital is also different from trust due to the bounded nature of the mission. With the mission statement, bounded rationality is more circumscribed and less dynamic. With cognitive social capital, the range is broader and subject to human, environmental, and other dynamics. "Come see the Pandas, but we make no promise that they will mate today."

Cognitive social capital is different to leverage. Cognitive social capital is an intangible asset. Leverage is tangible and quantifiable. "Give me five dollars and I shall turn it into ten." When the organization sells its cognitive social capital, it need make no assurance of what quantifiably it will produce. When it sells leverage it assures a multiple of what was invested and therefore a quantifiable measure of what it will produce and the assurance that what it will produce is more than what is invested. There is the ability to quantify and an assurance in leverage—and neither in cognitive social capital. "Come to this university and you will learn and mature." "Come to this university and your income will be doubled." These are very different statements.

The Five Factors of Confidence as They May Relate to Faith-Based Organizations

The five factors of confidence can go a long way to also explain why a faith-based organization may be the chosen contractor.

1. Leveraging, being able to attract other dollars for the purpose from affiliates as well as from direct donations, will decrease the true cost to the government for program results. Religious organizations receive the majority, 47 percent, of all donations, followed by human services with about 10 percent. Religious groups are also more able to attract volunteers.[32] The Independent Sector[33] finds that over a quarter of all volunteer hours go to religious organizations; Choi[34] finds that among older persons, religious involvement is a significant factor in their volunteering and Frank[35] finds the same significance of religious involvement in explaining volunteering by women physicians.[36] Gronbjerg and Never find that religion does make a difference in volunteering, but that its impact varies by activity.

   Campbell and Yonish,[37] using data from *Giving and Volunteering, 1989–1995*, find that people who participate in religion tend to volunteer more to both secular and religious causes. Most volunteers are churchgoers who volunteer mostly to religious causes, and "among volunteers, the more one attends church, the less likely one is to engage in non-church voluntary activity."[38] Similarly, Nemeth and Luidens[39] find that most donors are religious people who give more to religious organizations than to secular, but based on the empirical studies cited in this book, also give more to secular organizations than do nonreligious people. In either case, religion gets more in dollars and in volunteers, and as chapter 11 describes, this is a zero-sum game with managerial implications.

2. Goodwill are those nonsociological or nonbehavioral assets over which the faith-based organization has property rights. It owns, operates, controls, or can commit these assets. One of these is location, another is its membership list, and a very important one is its whole-owned subsidiaries or affiliates. Combined they may form an extensive network capable of pooling resources. In local economic development this is obvious. The church attends to its community. But it is also true in the conduct of U.S. foreign policy. Many of the faith-based organizations, Christians and Jewish, carryout their U.S.-financed humanitarian action abroad through their international affiliates or subsidiaries. The truth of the matter is that most local secular nonprofits cannot compete effectively with these mega-organizations outside of the local arena.[40]
3. Cognitive social capital (the religious-related aspect of the faith-based organization) not only lowers costs, but it can widen, deepen, and increase the staying or lasting power of a treatment. In crime or dropout rates, for example, the concern is whether the application lasted so that people did not drop out again or repeat a crime (recidivism). Moreover, some persons are especially amenable to the religious brand. Religiosity can deepen even a nonreligious treatment by attaching religious motives or incentives or its application in a religious environment. Thus, the process of learning to read is biologically the same in secular and religious schools, but the social capital of one attenuates learning differently to the other.

   This is evidenced by the former drug addict or alcoholic who attributes being sober with having found god. Alcoholics Anonymous has its roots in religion.[41] The choice of a faith-based organization is bolstered to the extent that these aspects of cognitive social capital are desired. But we are reminded by the work of the Christian Research Association, chapter 3, that secular stories sometimes substitute for religious ones as sources of motivation with similar effectiveness. This implies, as stated, that all policy situations are not amenable to one or only one approach.
4. The choice of a faith-based organization may rely upon trust derived from the convergence of interests as expressed in the mission. An evidence of this is the amount of contracting the Agency for Interna-

tional Development (AID) does with faith-based organizations to conduct charitable missions abroad. The charitable purposes are inherent in the religious mission of many faith-based organizations; thus, the television requests "support our mission by sending . . . " to feed or take care of this child, or to cure this illness, or to help this village, and so on. The humanitarian aspect of U.S. foreign policy converges with the mission of the faith-based organizations and that commitment in turn is inherent in the cognitive social capital of the organization (its beliefs).

5. The choice of a faith-based organization may be based on trust derived from the bounded nature of the mission of the faith-based organization. Herein lies the constitutional risk. As the previous chapter discusses, expectations or cognitive boundaries come from various sources with different degrees of reality, enforceability, or probability that actual behavior will conform to the expectation. The charitable purpose of the faith-based organization may be bounded (directly or indirectly) by its primary mission to propagate or preserve the faith. An objective of contract performance and monitoring is the assurance that this expectation is not realized. Therefore, while 1–4 are seen to be stronger reasons for contracting with faith-based organizations, reason number five may impose an additional transaction (monitoring) cost even if specified in the contract terms.

The weakness of number 5 can be appreciated in a simple example. The physician attends to a child who is critically ill as the parents watch, expecting death. The physician prays as he or she tries to save the life of the child. The child recovers. The parents wonder, didn't the prayer help? Was the prayer determinative? Why did the physician pray—if prayer were not helpful? Why don't we begin to pray? It may help us in the future. Should we not say thanks to god? And faith is propagated to one more family with evidence that it works.

The ranking of these factors will, of course, depend upon the specific facts and circumstances of the contract, the competition, and the religious organization. But leverage will almost always count in favor of faith-based over secular organizations and the latter over firms. When the government lets a contract it is interested in finding its lowest-cost or greatest value provider for what it wants. Leverage reduces the government's cost first by bringing additional required revenues from elsewhere (partnering). Second, it reduces cost because the cost of labor and some in-kind requirements are reduced by the amount of donations. The Independent Sector[42] estimates that the value of volunteer labor in 2001 was $17.60. Handy and Siriniavasn[43] estimates that for every dollar spent for a volunteer, a nonprofit on the average gains $6.00. This implies that the labor savings is between $6.00 to $17.00 per hour.

Religions, or congregations within religions, are not equal in what they can bring to the public policy process in terms of leverage. Jones,[44] using the

Statistics Canada's *Giving, Volunteering and Participating,* finds that the rate of volunteering and the capacity to increase volunteering differs among the major Christian groups. The capacity to give money may also vary by religion. Using the National Longitudinal Survey of Youth, a nationwide survey of about 4,950 persons, conducted by Ohio State University for the U.S. Bureau of Labor Statistics, Keister[45] finds that those who attend church often are more wealthy than those who do not, and that religious affiliation makes a difference. The median net worth of Jewish people was nearly seven times that of Baptists, Jehovah's Witnesses, Seventh Day Adventists, and Christian Scientists as a group, and about three and half times that of Methodists, Presbyterian, Lutherans, Unitarians, and Catholics as a group. Keister relates these differences not only to differences in the capacity to give, to family values and upbringing, but to differences in the life-orientation embedded in the religious teaching.

The Choice of Nonprofits for Social Services: The Five Levels of Confidence in an Alternative Form

Contracting allows the government to provide a wide range of social services to clients in disparate locations and with distinguishable needs. It also allows the government to provide these services with less internal staff and at the same time it allows the community to build social capital and to generate community participation. Partly as a consequence of contracting, more social services are provided through nonprofit and private firms than through the government itself. Contracting may be expensive, may cause variations in standards, in access, in quality, and in performance. Contractors may concentrate on the easiest and least expensive cases. This is a composite albeit cropped picture as drawn from the works of such scholars as Smith and Lipsky,[46] Gronbjerg,[47] Kahn and Kramerman,[48] Kettle,[49] and Salamon[50] with an excellent listing by Kramerman and Kahn of the pros and cons of these transactions.[51]

The question of this section is: Why do governments choose to contract with nonprofits specifically for social services? This question appears in many of the writings concerning nonprofits. The most common explanation emphasizes greater trust, lower transactions costs, the higher competence of nonprofits, and the unspecified nature of contracts. These have been discussed above. Frumkin[52] explains that nonprofits could experience a declining share of the market because of (a) limited size and scope of the organizations; (b) limited capital; (c) limited access to power; (d) a strong social mission and commitment to quality and to not cutting corners; and (e) inability to attract talent because of limits on compensation. This is true, but what determines the government's choice if a firm and a nonprofit are equally competent? Do the five factors of confidence help to explain, or at least offer reasonable hypotheses? Here is an application of the five factors based on the characteristics of the service, rather than on the organization, as previously has been done.

1. The rate of profitability in the actual provision of social services is low. With a price ceiling, firms may elect to cut corners that may reduce the level of performance expected by the community and the government. To protect against this performance-cutting risk motivated by higher profits and to simultaneously reduce its screening (transaction) cost, the government may prefer a nonprofit to a firm. The government wants an agent that it feels confident will do the work even when it is aware that the monetary rewards are not large. The most reasonable agent is one who has a long-term contractual and voluntary commitment to deal with the same adversely impacted population as the government; that is, the convergence of interest. "They and we are motivated by the same thing and the same reason; therefore, we can trust that our performances are aimed at the same purpose or objective." "They may want to do it more badly than we do."
2. Furthermore, because social services are generally underfunded by government relative to known financing needs, government is served by choosing a nonprofit rather than a firm because the former can leverage the government's investment with donations and volunteer work, capturing spillovers from projects the government is not paying for but that the organization is doing. Since the donations avoid residual claims, the amount of resources brought to the problem through donations is a multiple of what the government contributed; that is, confidence that its investment will be leveraged. "They will add to our investment." "We need them, our budget is not large enough."
3. Moreover, because the organization must stick to its mission and because of the permanent contractual character of the mission, the government may also have greater confidence that the work it paid for may be carried on well after its initial investment is made if it chooses a nonprofit over a firm; that is, confidence because of the contractual nature of the mission of the organization. "We know what they will do and they will be around to follow through."
4. Furthermore, social services work best when there is involvement of community, family, and other significant others. A drug program's success depends upon the willingness of the clients and those surrounding them to cooperate, as does the success of a school or hospital. "They can bring the parties together." Levels and quality of sociological interaction—cognitive social capital—are important to success.

   Recall that cognitive social capital is not alienable; therefore, to get it, the principal has to hire the organization. A network, for example, is defined as a cognitive social capital asset because what is important is the interaction between two or more entities. The network cannot be separated from the entities that make it. The entities themselves are social capital assets capable of being agents, but the interaction between or among them is sociological and there is no guarantee that if one or more of the entities is hired away or changed that the network will have the same results. The situation is analogous to a quarterback and his front line or receivers or the offensive coaching philosophy. Goodwill (item five below) is different. It is alienable.

5. The costs and outcome of many social services depend upon the reputation, the skill and commitment of the provider's staff. Staff can be hired away. It may also depend upon the provider's name. The name can be leased as in the case of shirts and hats with university names. If the goodwill is a secret formula, that too can be leased. Distributors of Coca Cola, for example, don't know the ingredients, but they can lease the rights to use the name and the product. This type of arrangement allows many universities to enter into leasing arrangements with pharmaceutical, medical device, and Internet companies. It may depend upon the provider's marketing channel. A mailing list can be leased. With goodwill assets, the principal may (a) lease, borrow, or hire it from the organization that has it; (b) ask the organization to "partner" or joint venture with another that doesn't; or, (c) contract with the organization. With cognitive social capital only option (c) is usually available. "One has to take the organization has a package."

Firms may compete with nonprofits in terms of goodwill or lease it from them or partner with them to get it. They may locate in the same place, develop the same technology, rent or lease their names, joint venture or partner with them. But they cannot do these with cognitive social capital without changing their essential sociological character or forming a subsidiary that mimics the nonprofit (a corporate foundation, a "nonprofit" marketing channel). Faced with this option, many firms would elect as they currently do to "lease" or joint venture with the source of the goodwill rather than try to create it. The situation is analogous to the rent or buy calculus familiar to every student in business and economics. Therefore, goodwill can be less powerful than cognitive social capital as the principal reason why a nonprofit of equal competence with a firm may be the chosen contractor. Goodwill is alienable.

Note from item 3, 4, and 5 above that the government, in contracting with a nonprofit, is the beneficiary of the lower transaction cost internal to the operation of the nonprofit. The lower the cost of the agent to communicate and to involve those with whom it must interact on behalf of the principal, the lower the cost to the principal of getting the job done (its contract cost). Therefore, the effects of 3, 4, and 5 are not merely in their sociological importance of cohesion and cooperation (as they may apply in the general social capital literature) but in their economic value in affecting the cost-effectiveness of the nonprofit as an agent of public policy.

The Risk of Dependency: A Contractor's Concern

To complete this chapter, we turn to a discussion of the dependency that may occur once a nonprofit becomes a contractor of the government. Borrowing from Williamson's presentation of mutual dependency, it can be argued that the nonprofit may become dependent upon the government (or its major foundation or corporate sponsor) if it fashions all of its assets toward satisfying that one. The advantage to the government includes a reduced cost of search, delay, monitoring, and even uncertainty about performance—all transaction costs. Ferry[53] and others have warned about the possible negative effects of this dependency. What are some of the risks to which the nonprofit as agent is exposed?

General Types of Risks of Dependency

Two types of risks are created for the nonprofit agent: (a) a de facto master-servant relationship, and (b) a resulting risk of opportunism. Both of these risks can have fatal consequences for the organization. Here are five types of consequences within a public policy context—the theme of this book:

1. The organization warps its performance to please its principal patron at the expense of the public; for example, providing untruthful or unsustainable results in a drug trial leading to increased use of the drug to the detriment of the public.
2. Collusion between the management of the nonprofit and the management of the principal patron for their personal benefits as well as the mutual but unethical benefit of the organizations (e.g., bribes for steering a contract or for obscuring cost overruns).
3. The nonprofit agent withholds essential information to hold the contracting principal sponsor hostage or to shield the latter from embarrassment.
4. The principal sponsor holds the nonprofit agent hostage by its constant threat to terminate the contract.
5. The nonprofit becomes an advocate or lobbyist for its patron, hoping to reap the indirect benefits of further contracts.

The ultimate financial risk for the nonprofit is that the patron (the government) can walk away, leaving the organization unable to carry on.

Opportunism

Opportunism means that the nonprofit agent, having committed itself and resources to pleasing and insuring a relationship with the principal, is exposed to the probability that the principal may (for any of the good or nefarious reasons Williamson[54] describes) terminate the contract and move to another agent. The risk is heightened the more that the specific assets that are acquired and cultivated can only be used to meet the specific needs of this one principal. The organization is left with assets it cannot otherwise use. The simple and ultimate managerial strategy for dealing with this is obviously organizational growth through diversification of revenue and customer basis.

Mutual Dependence of the Servant and Master

Resource dependence theory says that this dependence on external forces will cause changes in the organization.[55] Ferry and others argue that it will cause the organization to bend its activities to meet those external forces upon which it depends for resources.[56] Williamson is most concerned with the risk of opportunism—that the dependent party will be left exposed to the coercion, cheating, connivance, and termination of commitment by the other party and left with assets that have no value in another use or to other users. DiMaggio and Powell hypothesize that the nonprofit, among other possibilities, may change "to resemble" the organization that it depends upon and that this may come about because the former is coerced by the latter.[57] These are deleterious adjustments to the threat that the principal patron will step aside, cutting off funding.

But the principal-agent paradigm places a particular perspective on this problem. In this paradigm, both parties voluntarily enter into a contract that they have negotiated. Self-interest drives each. Therefore, unless the possibilities of dependency are unforeseen, the existence of a seemingly dependent relationship implies that one or both parties intended it or at least voluntarily acquiesced to it. In that case, the questions become: (a) What were the incentives? and (b) How is the risk of dependency being managed?

To illustrate, among the consistently large recipients of Defense Department money are elite research universities. In the case of the elite universities, this frequently means the financing of large-scale, highly expensive, and forward-looking scientific research that may not have another patron than the Pentagon. This research may require asset-specific equipment and instruments—being usable only for the specific contract work as long as the contract lasts. But the residual property rights over the physical assets, the intangible goodwill, including patents, may belong to the university or the researchers. The intellectual property rights of the Pentagon are limited because the researchers must be able to publish some significant part of the research. For the university, short-run mutual dependence leads to long-run benefits in its reputation and accomplishments, not to mention the physical capital the Pentagon leaves behind. These become part of the university's goodwill and social capital that it utilizes as an asset in future bids for contracts, students, faculty, and fundraising.

The point is that where there is mutual dependence, a managerial challenge is created to avoid the pitfalls of such dependence, but such dependence is neither rare nor in itself disadvantageous to either party. In addition to revenue diversification there are strategies for governing property rights so that there is at least a residual benefit to the organization. There is also the option of insulating the organization by operating the activity through a subsidiary, as some universities do with science research, or through a partnership, such as that described in the next chapter.

The Five Factors of Confidence under Regimes of Outsourcing, Competitive Contracting, and Privatization

The Federal Acquisition Council[58] characterizes privatization as a divestiture in which the government's property rights over assets and its governmental responsibility for a product or service are quitted. In the extreme, this does not require a formal contracting out; it is sufficient simply to stop actions, or abandon the assets, or encourage others to bid to take them over completely. In outsourcing, the government maintains its ownership of assets and responsibilities but the discharging of these functions is conducted by a private firm or nonprofit organization. In competitive bidding, the government, before concluding that a private firm or nonprofit would do the job, competes with them to determine which of the three would add more value to the citizens. The council reports that in only about a third of the cases does the government lose. What is important about these three instances, however, is that the government's concern for any criteria of choice and oversight may be least when the motive is privatization. When the motive is outsourcing or competitive bidding, the foreplay of these criteria prior to a decision is very strong.

The Five Factors of Confidence, Benefit/Cost Ratios, and the Soundness of the Government Contract as a Business Transaction

In this section we discuss contracting with the nonprofit as a business transaction—not as a subsidy or as charity. How do the five factors of confidence work to justify the government's choice of a nonprofit strictly as a business deal?

Lets begin with leverage. It implies that even though the production cost of a project or product may be the same for a firm and a nonprofit, the fact that the nonprofit can bring donations and other revenues to bear on the problem (a) lowers the out-of-pocket cost to the government for the end results, and (b) gives the government a higher rate of return on its expenditures for that program. This is true even if the secondary benefits are zero. If the secondary benefits—such as building community or social capacity—are added, the rate of return is higher yet. Couple this with the contractual commitment of the nonprofit (a source of trust), and the effects are (a) that the flow of benefits are likely to be sustained for a longer period of time, and (b) the risk of project abandonment or failure is lowered. Both of these give a higher present value for the project financed through a nonprofit as compared to a firm—a present value that is likely to exceed the government expenditure. This meets the principals of investment theory and the aim of government to get the highest value per dollar it spends.

Trust due to the boundary nature of the nonprofit's mission also contributes to lower risk (discount rate) and therefore an expected higher rate of return (benefits) or higher present value. This is so because the bounded nature of the mission reduces the expectations that the contract would not be met as intended. Finally, goodwill and social cognitive capital contribute to the lower production cost. For example, goodwill in the form of location reduces the transport and transference costs as well as the cost of the organization, building community confidence. Social cognitive capital reduces costs by allowing the organization to bring those sociological and behavioral factors, including its network, to bear on the problem. When operating costs are reduced, the net present value (the discounted flow of net benefits from the project) increases—making it more economically attractive.

The Five Factors of Confidence, Transaction Cost, and a Government Contract as a Business Transaction

Given tightening budgets (at federal, state, and local levels) and the increased competition between for-profit firms and nonprofit organizations—many of which have toiled in the field during good and bad times—it is appropriate to pursue the question: Why would the government contract with a nonprofit rather than an equally competent firm?

If one concludes, as many do, that it is because of the lower transaction cost, then one has to demonstrate how and why that cost is lower in a nonprofit than in a firm. What is the source of the lower transactions cost? If one concludes that the source is trust, then one has to demonstrate why the government would trust a nonprofit more than it trusts an equally competent firm that is equally (un)known to the government, and when there is no reason to believe that nonprofit managers are anymore trustworthy than the managers of firms. Public choice theory and history remind us that they (nonprofits and firms) are both managed by people often driven by self-interest. Good management, as discussed in this chapter, requires the organization to survive in order to provide a continuity of benefits, which is also a responsibility of the trustees. Short-range benefit may come at the expense of long-run capacity to grow as needs grow.

If one concludes that the government chooses a nonprofit because the contract is unspecified and imperfect, then one has to ask: Why does the government deal with for-profit firms for the most unspecified contracts—weapon systems? One would also have to argue that the traditional remedies (discussed in chapter 2) are inadequate because they are applied to both firms and nonprofits. Added to these remedies are two strategies. One is the finding by Corts and Singh[59] that when contracts are complex, repeated interaction between the parties is a frequently employed ameliorative strategy, as previously shown by Gulati,[60] and the findings by Schwartz and Watson[61] that when contracts are too expensive to be fully specified, parties will often choose to provide for renegotiation. In short, an imperfect contract when all contracts are imperfect and when they are both remedies and strategies applicable to all contractors does not seem a sufficient answer unless one argues that the probable transaction (contract) cost of these is higher for a firm than for a nonprofit. But this again begs the question, why?

An alternative argument presented in this chapter is that the government (per its own statements) seeks to minimize cost or to maximize the value (what the public gets) for every dollar spent on a contract. Transaction costs is only one cost. The cost of actually performing the contract is another. The alternative argument is that the explanation for why the government contracts with a nonprofit rather than an equally competent firm lies in five factors that the government has reasonable confidence (and it can verify) are more inherently true of nonprofits than of firms. All of these factors are based on the unique characteristics of nonprofits as economic and legal entities—independent loci of productive economic activity even though their purpose may be societal rather than individual inurement (benefit).

Note that the question "Why does the government choose a nonprofit over a for-profit firm for the same contract?" precludes the answer "contract failure," as described in chapter 2, because the two are competing for the identical contract. This is the case under the mandate of FAIR, which deliberately sets such competition.

"Contract failure" works as a possible answer when the firm or the nonprofit is precluded from bidding because of the nature of the contract. When bidding for the same contract, there must be another reason—therefore, the hypotheses of the five factors, which give one (the nonprofit) a competitive hedge over the firm, apply when both are competing for the same contract. As described earlier, FAIR and its counterparts in state and local governments seek the greatest value for the contract dollar.

"Market failure" does not work as an explanation either, since clearly the competition is between a market entity (the firm) and a non-market entity (the nonprofit). In FAIR and its progenies, "government failure" also fails as an explanation because the government is required to consider its own abilities before contracting. In these senses, "failure" can only mean that the nonprofit beats both of them in the competition, which is why understanding the five factors and how they enhance the competitiveness of the nonprofit should be important to nonprofit managers.

For managerial purposes, it does not help to lump the five factors into singular concepts such as social capital, trust, or even transaction cost if the source of that cost cannot be reasonably identified and traced for managerial manipulation and action; therefore, the five factors identified in this chapter. Within the meaning of these factors, even the concept of "trust" becomes a calculable estimate of risk of failure rather than one that implies having faith. These factors are readily extended to evaluate the competitiveness of secular and faith-based institutions.

This does not mean that transaction cost is immaterial. Take two equally competent nonprofit organizations with similar or offsetting five factors—the transaction cost may well lead to the choice of one over the other. One may be too much of a hassle. In addition, a history of past transaction with the government could lead to a (dis)advantage of a nonprofit organization over a new for-profit entry into the competition since the past history (assuming that it is favorable) may reduce transaction cost. Moreover, the transaction cost as stated in the text may also be determinative in a competition between a firm and a nonprofit if the cost of dealing with the nonprofit is so high that it washes out the advantages of the nonprofit accruing from the five factors of confidence.

Moreover, the five factors of confidence may also be construed as risk management strategies. The risk the government aims to minimize is the risk of failure of the contractor to perform (not that the contract fails, since the very same contract can be let to a similar for-profit or nonprofit as the entity that failed). Indeed, the costs of cleaning up and regenerating a new relationship with another contractor or contractors are principally transaction costs. Note, however, that in the initial letting of the contract, the transaction cost should be construed as an expected cost. It is associated with and varies up or down with the government's estimate of the probability of failure. It is not, in this sense, an actual cost that has occurred in the contracting process. In short, the government contracts with foresight. It minimizes prospective transaction costs by the way it selects contractors, beginning with the setting of prequalifying criteria. It uses the five factors of confidence to distinguish between firms and nonprofits when it opens the bid to both, as it does when it closes the bids to nonprofits only and chooses among them. Finally, note that the lower contract cost of contracting with a nonprofit reflects the lower internal transactions cost of the nonprofit given the objective of the government.

The lower internal transactions cost need not be related to reducing the government's cost of monitoring. In community development programs community participation is desirable not only for civic purposes but because of externalities (the upkeep of one house affects the price of the other) but also because of the involvement needed to maintain common pool resources (open space and other community facilities). The cost of inducing others to participate is a transaction cost; and the ability to reduce this cost depends upon the goodwill and the social capital of the community development corporation—a subject of the next chapter.

Summary and Preview

This chapter has been about answering and exploring the question: Why does the government choose a nonprofit organization when it has a choice of an equally competent firm for the same contract? Exploring the concepts of trust, transaction costs, social capital, goodwill, mission, and leverage, the chapter suggested and illustrated what it refers to as five levels of confidence upon which such choice is hypothesized to be made in favor of the nonprofit. On what basis does the government trust a nonprofit more than it trusts a firm that is equally unknown to it? On what basis do we conclude, a priori, that managers of nonprofits are more trustworthy than managers of firms? Are responses such as trust, contract or market failure, government failure, unspecified contracts, and high transaction cost sufficient? These reasons may be applicable when the question is about why the government contracts for rather than produces a good or service internally. But do they explain why the government would choose a nonprofit over a firm, which is the competitive reality required by federal and state laws as cited?

Walking step by step through the government contracting process, the chapter also raised the question: On what basis can we conclude that the transaction cost is greater with a firm of equal size and competence than it is with a nonprofit? Many of the common answers beg a deeper question. It turns out that the sociological concept of cognitive social capital offers a theoretically testable way of adding to the competitive advantage of nonprofits over firms of equal size and competence and also for explaining reduced transaction costs. The government benefits from the low transaction cost and leverage internal to the operation of the nonprofit organization.

The chapter also explored the consequences of being chosen repeatedly for the same contract so that a mutual dependence is developed between the government agency and the nonprofit. What are the risks and what are the strategies?

The next chapter begins an explication of the problems of implementing a principal-agent paradigm. But, drawing from this chapter's discussion of the possible advantages of a faith-based organization based on five factors of confidence in contracting, the next chapter will also touch on a question of choice between religious and sectarian organizations. As Seeley and Wolpert[62] have argued, the controversy over government funding of faith-based organizations would be simplified if each operated in a different niche market of social services; rather, they both tend to provide the same social services. Therefore, while we focused on the question of the choice between the nonprofit as an agent of policy and a firm in this chapter, there is now the need to explore why a religious nonprofit over an equally competent sectarian nonprofit. We shall visit that question in chapters 6, 7, and 11, based partly on the points made in this chapter.

Part III

Agency Powers, Performance, and Problems through the Prism of the Principal-Agent Paradigm

It is not sufficient to think of nonprofits as theoretical artifacts. They are legal entities capable of and charged with discharging public purposes. If all that has been said so far in this book merits credibility, they ought to be portrayed in examples in the real world—thereby revealing problems arising from conceptualizing nonprofits operating as social capital assets and agents of the public. Among these are problems of rational public expectations about the performance of the nonprofit on its behalf. "What have you done for me lately that I like and value?" becomes an appropriate question. The answer is grounded not only in accountability (which is a revelation of facts), but in reconciling public expectations with organizational capability, organizational and managerial selfishness, and the use of the discretionary use of organizational power and authority on behalf of the public. This potential source of dispute is inherent in every agency relationship. The engagement of an agent on behalf of a principal (the organization on behalf of the public) is always predicated on the expectation that the agent has some superior position, information, or capability, or disposition compared to the principal. The risk (called a moral hazard) that the organization would abuse this status is ever present; but the potential benefits are significant, as illustrated in community and housing development corporations, acute care hospitals, and business associations acting as agents of public policy. When the government contracts with a nonprofit it is simultaneously transferring all or some significant portion of a risk to it.

Chapter 6

Housing and Community Development

A Case Study of an Agency Function

Having discussed why the principal-agent paradigm is useful, having established its profile, and having demonstrated how it relates to the nonprofit as a social capital asset and agent of public policy, this chapter and the next are about perspectives gained in implementing the principal-agent paradigm. This chapter begins with a review of what is known about community development corporations and how they fit into the public policy picture as agents. It then presents a specific case in New York City, shows how the concepts of the previous chapters apply to performance, and then takes some of the same concepts and applies them to public authorities. These authorities lay the foundations for community development by providing the required infrastructure. This is illustrated by the New York–New Jersey Port Authority (a nonprofit organization). The chapter ends with a discussion of faith-based organizations and the applicability of the principal-agent paradigm to them in implementing community development policies.

America,[1] Clay,[2] Stone,[3] and Hula[4] have produced four of the several books that deal with community development and the role of nonprofits. Hecht's[5] book deals with the particular problem of affordable housing and Weber[6] with the problem of writing and meeting contract expectations when firms are subsidized for economic development projects. Taylor[7] looks at public policy and community development with some reference to initiatives to promote social capital. This chapter takes a different twist. Through specific examples it shows nonprofits engaged in their capacities as agents of public policy in the areas of housing and community development marked by adverse selection. It employs the principal-agent paradigm to do so and therefore represents a case example of the previous chapters. Special focus is placed on illustrating the concepts of public policy agency, adverse selection, network interaction, mission, leverage, and goodwill.

Community Development Corporations as Social Capital and Agents of Policy

According to Bratt and Rohe[8] the number of community development corporations (CDCs) has grown since 1970, but there have been failures, mergers, and downsizing within the ranks. The factors leading to success and to failure have been delineated by Gittel and Wilder[9] and by Cowan, Rohe, and Baku.[10] The first study points to political capital, mission, competence, and funding as causes of a CDC's success in enabling its residence to have access to economic, political, and other resources. The central purpose of this chapter, however, is not about success or failure but about the CDC as a social capital asset and as an agent of policy. Why is the CDC a structured social capital asset?

The CDC as a Social Capital Asset and Agent

A community development corporation or a housing organization is a social capital asset because it meets all five criteria discussed earlier:

1. It is a composite of assets and is itself a long-lived asset—a capital asset that is a legal person capable of entering into a contract. It can function as an agent and is licensed to function as an agent of the public by both the state in which it is incorporated and the federal government. This is witnessed in its charter and in its receiving tax exemption.
2. All property rights over the organization and its assets, except in the case of lenders, are owned by a collectivity, a group, a community, or a society, to which all properties must be distributed if the organization terminates. In this sense, exclusive ownership of the assets by the society or community, the nonprofit is social.
3. It is a long-lived asset with an expected flow of benefits. Since the community owns the asset, it also owns the benefits that are expected to flow from it. Over its life, the asset and its benefits might grow, become obsolete, or diminish in quantity and in value.
4. The acquisition of the assets, and their maintenance, results from investment by the community or group in the form of donations, tax deductions, and tax exemption. All of these represent costs, called tax expenditures, to the public. Therefore, they are indirect payments by the public.
5. Because of the above, the nonprofit is obliged to be accountable to the public in the same manner that a public firm is obliged to be accountable to its shareholders. Accordingly, both are obligated by law to report to the public annually. Agents are accountable to their principals.

Community development corporations are also agents of policy. As Clavel, Pitt, and Yin[11] argue, these nonprofits are alternatives to the delivery of community development directly by governments. Hence, the nonprofit is contracted by them to fulfill their nondelegable responsibilities as discussed in chapter 4 and as described with respect to housing by Schill[12] in Great

Britain and the United States. Their success may depend on factors identified by Chaskin and Garg[13] as legitimacy, representation, capacity connection, and long-term viability; and indeed as Hual, Jackson and Orr[14] suggest, the effectiveness of these nonprofits may turn on their ability to form linkages and affect the local political agenda. Thus, these nonprofit agencies may play the role of implementation and of policy formation.

Nonprofits carrying out housing and community development activities may be acting as agents of a policy of change. They may also be acting as agents for the conservation of the community's social capital. Accordingly, they are implementing a variety of public policies to improve the housing and community environment where adverse selection (the density of an above-average cost and at-risk population) is severe and where market forces are evidently unsuccessful in the prevailing environment. Since the results of community development is a shared result, these nonprofit organizations are building social capital at the same time that they are contributing to the private capital of individuals within the community. Smith[15] finds that in Indianapolis the value of housing increased faster in the areas with CDCs than in similar areas without them.

The CDC as a Social Capital and the Network Effect

Glickman and Sevon[16] identify resources, political outreach, organizational strength, programs, and networking among the capacities of over 200 CDCs they studied. As stated in chapter 3, networking is an important part of the social capital of nonprofit organizations and attention will be given to the networking capacity of CDCs. Silverman,[17] in a study of CDCs in Jackson, Mississippi, concludes that access to social capital by a CDC is limited by the environment in which it is embedded, that emphasis on social capital may overshadow the need for human and financial capital, which may be the limiting resources. Moreover, he concludes that networks tend to be parochial (local) and may even limit innovation and may be along a single dimension of work and may be tenuous. Fredericksen and London[18] argue that emphasis on localized social capital or networks as a basis of supporting CDCs may be based more on the currency of policy to localize development for any number of reasons, including as Saidel[19] noted, that CDCs may be better able to reach a specific clientele than government.

The CDC and Its Public Policy Charge

Community organizations represent both a potential positive and a negative to community governance and control. There is the benefit from the decentralization of planning, production, and distribution of housing and community development services according to community characteristics, needs, and capacities, and the potential for increased community participation and involvement. But there is also, as discussed in chapter 1, the potential that the nonprofit as an agent of the community seeks its own self-interest and those of its managers at the expense of the community and that elite control by the powerful persons in the nonprofit organization will result in their undue influence in the community.

What are the incentives to get the nonprofit agent to be responsive to the needs of its principal (the public or the local community in the case of the CDC)? How does the agency balance its self-interests (perpetuation, budgets, employment, status, power) against the interests of the public and the local population? Who and how should an agency be monitored? What are the appropriate measurements of success? When has the agency outlived its usefulness? In a principal-agent framework, planning must include devising mechanisms to achieve the optimal link of the principal to the agent so that the latter serves the former. This begins with the definition of a mission that is of public interest and for which the agency can be contracted.

Defining the Public Interest in Housing and Community Development

A principal-agent relationship to advance the public interest requires some specific definition of what is in the public interest and deserving of public compensation. Accordingly, housing and community development are carried on by nonprofits as public policy agents according to criteria set by the government as managing agent for the public (the principal). The specific housing and community developmental needs that qualify under current public law as being in the public interest appear in the two pyramids below. On the lowest level are the specific functions to be performed—and for which there is public compensation in the form of tax exemption. These pyramids are created from qualifications given in IRS Form 1023.[20]

I.

Advance Public Welfare

Housing Activities

Low-income housing; low and moderate income housing; housing for the aged; nursing or convalescent home; student housing; orphanage; instruction and guidance in housing; other housing activities

II.

Advance Public Welfare

Inner City or Community Activities

> Area development, redevelopment, and renewal; homeownership association; job training counseling and assistance; zoning and rezoning; attracting new industry or retaining industry in area; business loans and grants to minorities; day care center; ecology and conservation; crime prevention; consumer protection; community promotion; right to work; use of drugs, narcotics, and alcoholic beverages; anti-communism; capital punishment and criminal defendants

Putting these two lists together, it is obvious that within them are the powers for tax-exempt nonprofits to engage in the complete process of community development preservation and protection—all toward improving the welfare of an adversely impacted community. A nonprofit may specialize in one or any combination of these public welfare functions.

Sources of Financing Community Development Corporations—the Money Network

To finance the public policy stated above, CDCs may obtain funds through contracting with state, local, and the federal governments. The CDCs add (leverage) to funds from government contracts, loans, donations, investments, fees, and profitable activities and from foundations. But CDCs have one additional source of funding: The Local Initiative Support Corporation.

Financing: Local Initiative Support Corporation

The mission of the Local Initiative Support Corporation (LISC) is to provide financial and technical assistance to local community development corporations (nonprofits) throughout the country. LISC assists local community development corporations (CDCs) in creating affordable housing, commercial and industrial facilities, and jobs. It also helps them to forge alliances with other community nonprofits and with the local government and it helps them by advocating on their behalf on the local, state, and federal levels.

Formed in 1979, as of June 2003, LISC had raised over $4 billion from investors, donors, and lenders and used that to leverage another $11 billion from the public and private sectors in support of CDCs—demonstrating the power of leverage described in the previous chapter.

LISC operates four specialized funds to generate more investment capital for CDCs. One fund is set so that private investors can invest in providing affordable housing and get an investment tax credit in exchange. A second fund allows private investors to invest in community retail facilities. A third fund allows investors to invest in community development properties. The principal purpose of these funds is to raise capital to finance properties and development. These are properties and projects that do not qualify for commercial loans. The funds give the CDCs access to the capital market they would not otherwise have had and therefore provide them with additional capital to invest in distressed communities unable to attract private investors. Thus, LISC moves funds from donors and other investors into a community in which they may have had no interest or not otherwise have invested as individuals.

The Social Utility of CDCs

The LISC invests in the community through grants and loans to the community's nonprofit development corporation. A CDC is a corporation the mission of which is one or a combination of the tasks listed under both the housing and the community development pyramids presented earlier in this chapter; and it must pursue this mission for the benefit of the public—as an agent of public policy. Therefore, given its own mission, the LISC funding of CDCs makes a financial connection—a network based on a common objective: community development. One organization in the network provides the financing, and the other does the work.

The CDC can select among these functions in any combination, and within any combination, the priority or emphasis may vary from organization to organization. Because any function can be delivered in a variety of ways, the number and diversity of possible CDC offerings across the country is infinitely large. CDCs can tailor their programs to the needs of their individual communities—relieving or at least reducing the government's costs. Therefore, the LISC can take advantage of diversity across space and across community ethnic ties in which the CDCs are embedded.

Although working on behalf of communities, CDCs do not need community approval to function in a location. Yet, community acceptance may be crucial for program success. This is so because almost all CDC programs involve and impact the community. Thus, an advantage of working with a CDC is its community reach and ability to involve community members toward a common good. If all members of the community get involved in keeping it clean and upgrading their property, the value of all properties will rise to the benefit of the community. The CDCs can capture externalities for the benefit of the community.

Nonprofit tax-exempt CDCs such as the one to be described are organized by individual citizens. These CDCs may be encouraged by a local government that will often provide seed money. A government will seed these organizations so as to have an independent agent to do what the government may have had to do otherwise in these distressed neighborhoods. The advantages are (a) that the local government does not have to fully finance these nonprofits because they are expected to leverage the seed money by getting donations from foundations, corporations, and individuals; (b) that while exempt from local taxes, the CDCs are also exempt from state and federal taxes (a net gain) that must be plowed back into the community; and (c) that the CDCs have access to relatively inexpensive capital from organizations such as LISCs that are also brought into the community. They can do all this leveraging without creating additional claims on the local government or the community residents. The latter do not have to mortgage their properties.

New York City: A Case Presentation

This is a real case study followed by a specific analysis demonstrating the utility of the principal-agent paradigm and several of the concepts that in the last chapter we noted as distinguishing reasons for contracting with a nonprofit organization even when an equally competent for-profit may be available.

A New York City CDC Partnership

Here is an example of a CDC at the center of a public-private partnership to rebuild a distressed area. It is used to provide a basis to discuss the following: (1) some advantages of using a nonprofit agent to carry out this function; (2) how the agent may subcontract or share the function with other agents and improve the probability of success in carrying out its agency; (3) double (or multi) agency; (4) the use of tax exemption as an inducement or compensation; and (5) the concepts of adverse selection, leverage, goodwill, and trust.

New York City, the State of New York, Enterprise Foundation (a nonprofit), its subsidiary Social Investment Corporation (a for-profit), the Federal National Mortgage Association (a for-profit that was previously a nonprofit), a community development corporation (a nonprofit), and both its for-profit as well as its nonprofit subsidiaries created a partnership to deal with the housing problem in New York City.

The city agreed to provide 1,000 rental units from its inventory of abandoned homes. The units were vacant and unfit for rental tenants, being below occupancy code. The city was losing because taxes were not paid and also because there was no future tax flows to be expected from unoccupied units. Also, these properties were havens for crime and fire. These abandoned units were a distraction to every phase of neighborhood economic development, including both tourism and the lack of affordable housing in specific neighborhoods. As a consequence, their existence generated a high social and economic cost, placing unnecessary demands on health, fire, and police personnel.

The process of restoring these housing units began when a nonprofit with neighborhood or community development as its mission (a CDC) submitted a proposal to the city and the state to get the units rehabilitated and eventually occupied and managed. In response to this request, the city and the state made a loan at 1 percent interest for the start-up investment in the rehabilitation project. Because the loans provided that regular payments of the principal did not have to be made, the rents of the future tenants could be held comparatively low and yet provide a positive cash flow. Moreover, because these units were to be occupied by lower income individuals, some late payments had to be expected. With this flexibility in the loan agreement, late payments by the tenants were less likely to trigger default by the CDC, leading to bankruptcy.

With a fully developed proposal for neighborhood and unit rehabilitation in hand, the community development organization then submitted its proposal to Enterprise Foundation, a nonprofit, for evaluation. The purpose of the evaluation was to determine the degree to which the project could attract corporate investors. In those cases where the project evaluation suggested the potential of an economically viable investment by sophisticated private investors putting up tens of millions of dollars, it passed on the papers to Social Investment Corporation (a for-profit subsidiary of Enterprise) to sell interests in the partnership to these qualified investors.

In turn, the Social Investment Corporation sold equity or ownership interests in the project to for-profit corporations. Thus, the Federal National Mortgage Corporation (Fannie Mae) invested up to $28,000,000 through purchase of ownership interests in these properties. The proceeds from the sale of these interests to Fannie Mae by Social Investment Corporation provided the additional funds needed to cover the cost of rehabilitating the units and the immediately surrounding neighborhood and to increase property values.

Fannie Mae (as did other private investors) became a limited partner. The community development corporation created a for-profit subsidiary to be the general partner. The general partner's responsibility is to manage the project. By going this route rather than making itself, a nonprofit, the general partner, the CDC avoided financial disaster due to project failure. It also placed itself in a superior position to avoid mixing the daily trials and tribulations of running a nonprofit with those of running a hard and difficult property restoration and management business. The for-profit subsidiary was dedicated exclusively to running a profitable business and to help its nonprofit parent (and exclusive shareholder) carry out its mission to the community.

Being only limited partners, the large corporations (and various ones, including American Express and BP, a worldwide oil company, have participated in these transactions) that invest in these projects limit their liability exposure and avoid managerial involvement in a line of business (local economic development) in which they have no productive interest as a major segment of their business and in which their local knowledge is often zero. Being a partnership rather than a corporation allowed some of the gains and all of the early losses that are tax deductible to be passed on to the corporations.

Because the rehabilitation project was organized as a partnership rather than a corporation, all depreciation and losses could be distributed to the corporate partners, who could deduct them from their taxes. These deductions were not valuable to the nonprofit because it does not pay taxes. The gains, which could be allocated mostly to the nonprofits, were also not taxable because these nonprofits were tax exempt. The corporations would have had to pay taxes.

Furthermore, U.S. tax law provides for a tax credit to corporations that invest in these activities and that held that investment for nine years. Thus, in time, the corporate investors could get a positive rate of return without the rental being so high that the projects could not serve the mission of the nonprofit—community development in the form of affordable housing. These projects only attracted highly profitable firms with good cash flows because only they could use the tax credit. Firms with losses could not because they had no tax to pay against which the credit could be taken.

Notice in this example the level of interorganizational cooperation (social capital as a network) that is required not only between the government and the parent nonprofit and the investors, but also with the subsidiaries that made the deal work. To illustrate, because the firms had to hold their investment for nine years for them to get full credit, and since a cash flow is required to pay operating and other costs, the property manager as a wholly owned subsidiary of the nonprofit parent was key. The subsidiary (even if it were a nonprofit) existed solely to serve its parents. The requirement to stay and perform to meet a predetermined objective (community development that preserved the value of the investment) gave the investors confidence.[21] This is a convergence between the interest of the CDC and the interest of the financing firms and is derived from the confidence in the bounded nature of a mission as a permanent contractual promise.

What Do We See in This Example?

1. The neighborhood reflects adverse selection—the exodus of lower risk residents while high-risk residents are left behind. Clearly, under prevailing situations the market has failed. The profit motive provides no incentive in such a neighborhood where transaction costs, production costs, and rent ceilings do not provide for an adequate rate of return. The value of the individual home depends upon the collective decision to upgrade the neighborhood.
2. The public cannot walk away. There is a loss of revenues, an increase in crime, a deterioration of infrastructure. All of these have spillover effects and consequences to the public beyond the specific neighborhood.
3. The government, rather than undertake restoration itself, enters into a contract with a nonprofit CDC to work on behalf of the public as an agent of change—to carry out a public policy to rehabilitate the neighborhood.
4. What does this particular CDC bring to the effort? It brings goodwill as an intangible asset—its asymmetric knowledge of the community is one such asset. Since local development corporations usually include

the name of the community, such as Bedford Stuyvesant Community Development Corporation, the name signals a convergence of interests. "They are one of us, they must be working for us."

Location is another element of its goodwill. The CDC is always located in the neighborhood. Its promise or mission is another element of its goodwill. But unlike a for-profit contractor, the CDC cannot walk away from its promise or its neighborhood. It is immobile, and its and the neighborhood's failure or success cannot be separated.

These elements of goodwill allow wealthy investors to be limited partners. This means they do not participate in the management and are free to carry on their other responsibilities knowing the nonprofit CDC is bound by its location and singular purpose to advance the community. The CDC has a multiple agency—to itself, its community, its managers, the public, and the state.

5. The CDC can leverage each dollar from the small loan from the state and city tens of millions of times over without incurring any investor claims on any assets, whether the CDC's, the resident's, or the government's. On the basis of the original loan, it is able to attract foundations, donors, volunteers, and most of all tens of millions of dollars from private investors.
6. Deals such as the one described above are structured as partnerships. In this particular case it is a network for channeling money. Partnership agreements can specify which asset belongs to which partner and how benefits and losses are divided among partners. The net cash flow is not likely to be of any interest to wealthy investors. They would prefer to have it kept in the program so that the property remains in service. Therefore, they will exchange this cash flow for all of the tax depreciation, operating losses, and credits that are of no value to the nonprofit because they are tax exempt, but are of immense value to a wealthy investor. They would be fully entitled to these tax benefits since it is their capital, not the CDC's, that finances the project.
7. In this situation, the principal-agent relationship is extended horizontally, involving other organizations, and vertically, involving subsidiary organizations—a network for doing the work. The parent subsidiary has a principal-agent relationship with the public, in which case it is the agent. It is also the agent of the partners, since it manages their investments. It is also the agent of the state, the city, and the community. But the nonprofit CDC is the principal when it hires individuals or firms on the community development projects or when it involves its subsidiary.
8. Experienced corporations such as BP and American Express would not make such large investments based on trust. In the end, trust must mean more than faith; it must be based on reliability, that is, trust based on the contractual promise of the mission. "They'll be there."
9. The contract is incomplete not only as to output but as to procedure. How to get it done is not specified and what the units should look like

outside of the basic code and habilitation requirements is not specified, but the number of units is given. This gives flexibility but it is also a potential source of dispute.

10. With community development associations and other community-based organizations, including middle-class housing associations, there is site specificity in that they serve a specific area and the value of this goodwill is related principally, if not exclusively, to that site. The contributions of these local or neighborhood organizations to the creation and expansion of social capital is also principally, if not exclusively, related to that site. The mutual dependence with the site is voluntary. It is also contractual, and contributes not only to the value of the organization but also to the value of the community and its ability to attract people and firms.

    The dependency on the limited partner is of no concern. The limited partner has done all it can without jeopardizing becoming a general partner. As a general partner, it would be responsible for participating in the management of the entire project and assuming total liability for it. As a limited partner, the only amount that is at risk is the amount it invested. In this way, the management and daily responsibility is exclusively and solely the responsibility of the CDC. This emphasizes the trust based on the contractual promise of the mission and trust based on the bounded aspect of the mission. "They have to stay in the community and they have no other distraction." "This is what they do." "This the reason they were formed and granted tax exemption."
11. A CDC incorporates community members with diverse interests but with one overriding collective interest—community improvement. Therefore, every CDC has the potential of being a hub of a network of community organizations from churches to clubs. Networks facilitate communication, interorganizational cooperation, and volunteer recruitment. They also help each organization benefit from the spillover of efforts of the other.

Powell and Smith-Doerr[22] write:

> By definition, a network is composed of a set of relations, or ties, among actors (either individuals or organizations). A tie between actors has both content (the type of relation) and form (the strength of the relation). The content of ties can include information or resource flows, advice, or friendship, shared personnel or members of a board of directors; indeed any type of social relation can be mapped as a tie. Thus, organizations typically are embedded in multiple often overlapping networks.

12. Why does the public benefit from this deal? Community development produces a collective good. The upgrading of each home has a spillover benefit to all other homes, meaning that the collective benefit exceeds the sum of each owner's investment. A public malady is

resolved by spreading the cost and financial risk beyond the neighborhood boundaries since investors or donors can be drawn from anywhere. Furthermore, the government avoids the daily managerial problems but can take the political credit for success. Bringing together these observations, we see the power of community development organizations in the creation and maintenance of social capital, both in its structural and in its cognitive forms. It does this partly by utilizing its goodwill, mission, and leverage powers.

Pitfalls of Partnership with For-Profit Corporations

When a nonprofit participates in a partnership such as the one described above, there are certain rules it has to follow to avoid jeopardizing the organization's tax-exempt status or that of the deal. If exemption of the deal or the organization is lost, the organization's ability to leverage will be impeded because donor contributions would dry up either for the project or for the organization or for both. This is so because foundations would be prohibited from contributing and individuals and corporations would have lost the tax incentive for making contributions. The theory for the disqualification of the project or the CDC is that the deal serves private for-profit interests and not the public interest, as is required for exemption. Notice how these reinforce the five factors of confidence, especially how they maintain the nonprofit as a social capital asset committed to its mission even as it joins forces with firms to increase leverage.

The Rules When the Nonprofit Is an Agent or Co-Agent

Here are the basic rules:

1. The nonprofit cannot assume the risks or cover the costs of its for-profit partners.
2. The nonprofit cannot place the assets of the organization under the control of the nonprofit partner. This may occur in a number of ways, such as when the for-profit partner maintains the deciding votes on asset and mission-related issues.
3. The nonprofit must be able to withdraw from the partnership.
4. The partnership must be about organization's mission exclusively and necessary to its furtherance.
5. The nonprofit's fees should not vary with the profits of the partnership because this implies a profit-motive.

In short, the partnership must further the promise (mission) of the nonprofit without residual claims on its assets.

The Rules When the Nonprofit is the Principal

In some housing and community development arrangements, the nonprofit is the principal and a for-profit the agent. The nonprofit hires the for-profit. This is common, for example, when the CDC contracts with a private construction company. This issue also occurs when, for example, the university's hospital or its bookstore is managed by a firm.

The issue relates to who controls the assets being managed by the for-profit corporation. The issue of asset control has become one of increasing public policy concern as nonprofits enter into principal-agent relationships with for-profit organizations in the form of management contracts, joint ventures, partnerships, and other cooperative arrangements.

The cutting issue is not over administrative control. It is over property rights, the powers that that implies, and the beneficiary ownership that is implied by the exercise of certain powers over the assets, including disposition or sale and the use of the asset. Who is the principal beneficiary? Beneficiary ownership means that an asset while held in someone else's name really exists for the benefit of another: Are the assets being used for the benefit of the profit-maker even though they are held in the name of the nonprofit?

Thus, when a for-profit organization manages the assets of a nonprofit or enters into an agreement with the nonprofit and is allowed certain rights of decision-making that accrue benefits to the for-profit corporation (other than a reasonable fee), the asset is deemed to be operated for the benefit of the for-profit—that is, for the benefit of profit-making. With this motive, no tax exemption for nonprofit purposes is given.

Sounds so easy, but this is a particularly tricky and prominent problem, placing a heavy burden of proof based on facts and circumstances of each case. To avoid this loss of exemption, there are some IRS-set guidelines in Revenue Procedure 97–13.

1. At least 95 percent of the compensation to the for-profit manager must be fixed fees that are not related to profits but that may be periodically changed, as explained in the next condition.
2. Fees that are fixed but may be changed periodically for incentive or cost purposes (for example, according to the consumer price index) must be unrelated to net profits or net earnings of the enterprise. A productivity incentive can be stated in dollars, and can be calculated based on gross earnings or a reduction in gross expenses—but not on both or the difference between them, because that would be net profit.
3. No control of the assets is managed. An inherent power may be to change how the asset is used; but it does not include disposition of the asset or the use of the assets to further related interests of the contractor.
4. The term of the contract cannot exceed the lesser of 15 years or 80 percent of the expected life of the asset under management.

5. The nonprofit and its directors combined do not have a 20 percent or more interest in the for-profit manager and are not related to the manager. The purpose of this is to allow the nonprofit to act freely, even to cancel the contract.

For the reader who wishes to pursue this discussion, I discuss elsewhere the various state rules on how control is measured. (Bryce 2000). Let us return to the central theme of this chapter, the role of nonprofits as agents of public policy as illustrated in housing, economic, and community development.

Authorities as Agents of Public Policy: The Provider of Infrastructure

The authority is a social capital asset because it is characterized by the five factors in chapter 3. These are:

1. It is a composite of assets and itself a long-lived asset—a capital asset that is a legal person capable of entering into a contract. It can function as an agent and is licensed to function as an agent of the public by both the state in which it is incorporated and the federal government. This is witnessed in its charter and in its receiving tax exemption.
2. All property rights over the organization and its assets, except in the case of creditors, are owned by a collectivity, a group, a community, a society to which all properties must be distributed if the organization terminates. In this sense, exclusive ownership of the assets by the society or community, the nonprofit is social.
3. It is a long-lived asset with an expected flow of benefits. Since the community owns the asset, it also owns the benefits that are expected to flow from it. Over its life, the asset and its benefits might grow, become obsolete, or diminish in quantity and in value.
4. The acquisition of the assets, and their maintenance, result from the investment by the community or group in the form of donations, tax deductions, and tax exemption. All of these represent costs, called tax expenditures, to the public. Therefore, they are indirect payments by the public.
5. Because of the above, the nonprofit is obliged to be accountable to the public in the same manner that a public firm is obliged to be accountable to its shareholders. Accordingly, both are obligated by law to report to the public annually. Agents are accountable to their principals.

The authority and other nonprofits' social capital assets, such as the CDC, as agents of policy are different due to (a) the authority is formed by governments, not citizens acting voluntarily; and (b) the citizenry does not make direct investments to the authority in the form of donations but does so through tax exemption and fees. The U.S. Census of Governments reports over 32,000 public authorities in the United States.

Governments form authorities when the agency function is so technically complex and yet crucial to the community that governments create nonprofits to discharge these functions. In the case of the CDCs, the government merely supports the efforts of a few entrepreneurial citizens. In the case of public authorities, the government takes the first step and all other initiating steps to create the organization having "authority" in its name. The authority, too, is an agent of public policy. It specializes in large infrastructure projects. The authority is a public nonprofit in the sense that its formation is created by the public sector while other nonprofits are private—created by individuals.

It, too, removes certain critical public functions from a potentially destabilizing public budgetary process, releases the government from managerial burdens, provides leverage, and has the valuable intangible asset called goodwill. Because authorities deal with large, specialized activities, they are excellent devices to finance projects that can be shared across communities, and across jurisdictions, while removing operational details from any one jurisdiction. Authorities have their own staff and their mission is advancing the common good, just like other nonprofits. With respect to leverage, the authority is more like a firm. It does not get donations like the other nonprofits involved in housing and economic development, but, unlike a firm, its finances remain dedicated to a specific class of public purpose in a specific area defined by its mission. A for-profit firm may export capital to other places and may diversify into any segment of business it chooses and, unlike authorities, may pay dividends to their shareholders.

Authorities have been created to provide a range of public benefits including housing, highways and bridges, subways and airports, seaports, sports arenas, cemeteries, lotteries, water and sewer systems, hospitals, major industrial and commercial developments, university dormitories, and prisons. The Organization for Economic Co-Operation and Development[23] (OECD) observes that in several countries there is a growing trend of assigning government functions to agencies outside of the government bureaucracies. Among these agencies are authorities and other nonprofits, the principal purpose of which is to relieve government and to gain greater efficiency. The OECD refers to this as "distributive governance."

Authorities Differ in Levels of Agency

While authorities may be described as social capital assets, they differ not only in function and how they are financed but in the extent to which they are quasi-government agencies and therefore a social capital asset distinguishable from government. Here are some models. In chapter 5, reference was made to the California legislation that allows counties to contract out in-home support services to authorities; these authorities, while created by local government, are not government agencies and operate with their own liabilities that do not extend to the government.

In the Philippines, the Board of the National Economic Development Authority is comprised of the president of the country, 15 cabinet secretaries, and the heads of other agencies, including science and technology, labor, agrarian reform, health, foreign affairs, agriculture, office of management and budgets, socio-economic planning, and transportation. It has an independent staff and staff director. The staff coordinates economic development planning, financing, and budgeting throughout the country and oversees the implementation of related projects, laws, and rules. They also make budget recommendations to the president. They are required to involve private sector and local communities in their deliberations.

In Great Britain, a National Park Authority administers each national park. The directors are appointed by various levels of government. The Peak District Authority, for example, has 38 members—10 of whom are appointed strictly because of their knowledge and involvement in park preservation. Their duty is to oversee the planning and management of the park for the public benefit and to oversee the officers (the day-to-day managers) in achieving the best results. There are some 16 of these park authorities and all are required to be publicly accountable and to seek public involvement. They are assisted by the Council of National Park authorities, a registered charity, which not only coordinates the work of these 16 publicly appointed bodies but of nearly 50 groups and raises funds and lobbies on behalf of the preservation of these parks and those that deserve this status in both Great Britain and Wales.

In the case of the Port Authority of New York and New Jersey, which will be described below, the governor of each state appoints six persons to the board. These are private persons who serve as public officials for a six-year term without pay and who continue their private professional work (e.g., as principals in real estate, engineering, and law firms). Each governor may veto the actions of those whom that governor has appointed. But the Port Authority of New York and New Jersey is clearly a distinguishable social capital asset.

According to the American Port Authorities Association, in the United States there are about 100 authorities that are port authorities. These public nonprofit bodies manage ports to facilitate import, export, and intermodal transfers (e.g., between ships and rails, ships and trucks, and ships and other sea vessels, and the transport of passengers). Port authorities may also include airports, bridges, tunnels, commuter rail systems, inland river or shallow draft barge terminals, industrial parks, foreign trade zones, world trade centers, terminal or short-line railroads, shipyards, dredging, marinas, and other public recreational facilities.

The events of September 11 brought one such authority into more popular prominence.[24] In 1921, the states of New Jersey and New York entered into an agreement that created the Port Authority of New York and

New Jersey, which is the second-oldest public authority, preceded only by the Port of London. The New York and New Jersey Port Authority, a public nonprofit, is responsible for the financing, construction, and maintenance of much of the infrastructure (bridges, tunnels, subways, airports, industrial and business parks, bus and train facilities, and land, including the location of the World Trade Center) that makes New York City and the New York-New Jersey metropolitan area magnificent.[25] The Port of Oakland in California (a local government authority) runs 19 miles of real estate, an airport, and one of the world's largest shipping container ports on behalf of the economic development of Oakland. Incidentally, this airport is the one from which Amelia Earhart took off on her history-making attempt in 1937.[26]

Financing Authorities

Authorities are government-created nonprofits that operate very much as firms because they charge a price and obtain their long-term financing principally through the issuing of bonds (called variously revenue, industrial development, or tax-exempt bonds) that are sold in the bond market just as the bonds of any firm. The New York and New Jersey Port Authority, for example, cannot tax and receives no tax dollars. It is fully self-financing.

Authorities are financed primarily through fees and the debts that are serviced by these fees. The government that forms the authority may or may not choose to back its bonds, but usually they do not. The only claim investors are guaranteed are the earnings from the project that the bonds financed. Clearly, investors cannot walk away with a bridge or a tunnel. Therefore, the authority absorbs the financial and business risks of the project.

Authorities leverage much as firms do. They take any beginning investment from the governments that create them and then sell bonds to the public. These bonds may or may not be tax exempt. They are not tax exempt if 95 percent or more of their proceeds are for "private use." These are uses by commercial firms—largely those that the locality is trying to induce to stay or to re-locate in its area. The bondholders have no claims against the government—only against the income stream from the project financed.

Authorities as Instruments of Privatization

Authorities may be an interim step between transferring a function from the government bureaucracy to a firm or a nonprofit organization. The reverse, moving a function from the private to the public sector, is also applicable. Public transportation is an example. As recently as the 1950s much of public transportation was privately run. Today, public authorities finance and operate public transportation systems because private entrepreneurs were glad to unload.

The attempts to privatize airports (now run as authorities) have been heavily resisted by pilots. Baltimore port became more financially viable after it became an authority. The great Panama Canal is run essentially by an authority that contracts out work through a number of principal-agent agreements.

Agency and Faith-Based Organizations in Community and Housing Development

It is not possible to end this chapter without reference to the current debate about faith-based organizations and their effectiveness. Faith-based organizations have long been involved in housing and community development activities. Many have been involved in a very comprehensive way in various sectors including housing, jobs, business development and counseling, food and nurturing centers, schools, savings and investment, clubs, and clinics. Admitting the need to avoid the state intruding into a religious organization or proselytizing a religion, a principal-agent approach can be useful in evaluating certain potential benefits and pitfalls of government contracting with religious organizations for housing and community development.

Principal-agent theory implies that some communities and their institutions are likely to suffer from adverse selection; therefore, comparing secular and faith-based CDCs should control or at least account for the possibilities that even in the same community one suffers from more adverse selection than the other. Does one get more of the high at-risk cases that have a negative bias on the results? Are they harder and more costly cases to crack?

After accounting for adverse selection, is this difference in outcome or performance attributable to something other than doctrinal faith? If it is, then the successful treatment can be taught to secular organizations and the number of effective public policy agents would increase to the benefit of the society.

The danger here is obvious. If the doctrinal factors are determinative of success, then the efficient choice of CDC agents would require choosing and signaling which religious faith is most effective in community development. This is not a trivial constitutional and practical matter. Thus the court in *Freedom from Religion Foundation v. McCullum*[27] concluded that if it is the acceptance of a religious doctrine that makes a difference in the outcome of a program, such as a drug treatment program, then the government cannot fund it; if it is not religion as faith or doctrine that makes a difference, then there may be no characteristic distinction between a religious as compared to a secular treatment.

But the previous chapters point to the following forces. First, there is balanced theory that suggests that people of common interests tend to congregate and to have great influence on each other. Second, there is the theory of social capital that says that the repetitiveness of this interaction tends to cultivate trust, cohesion, cooperation, and motivation to a common good in which the sanctions that one member applies upon the other tend to be strong because each is affected by the other's behavior. Third, religious collection boxes provide for inexpensive financing and church members are a ready source of volunteers— the other resources of the organization may be brought to bear on the problem. Fourth, tax exemption and nonpayment of dividends add to the leverage effect. Fifth, such activities may not be inconsistent with the overall religious mission. As a result, the benefit/cost ratio is likely to be high. However, the political question, the question of intrusion, the question of constitutionality and efficiency, and the selection of cases are inescapable concerns.

Of course, I have not touched on the constitutional question, leaving that to the lawyers. The arguments range from the probability that even under the concept of separation of church and state there is no constitutional foundation for *not* funding faith-based organizations,[28] to the argument that even indirect payments may be a violation of the constitution,[29] to the argument that financing faith-based organizations does not necessarily imply support of them.[30]

Summary and Preview

This chapter demonstrated the logic and real-world application of the concepts in previous chapters by exploring various agency roles that nonprofits play in housing and in community development, and by focusing on programs involving tens of millions of dollars of investment by large, for-profit firms. The purpose is to demonstrate the reality of the concepts such as goodwill, leverage, agency, and principals, and also to demonstrate the benefits of nonexclusive contracts, adverse possession, the value of asymmetric information, and specificity of asset location.

This chapter also illustrated (a) why the government may contract with a nonprofit rather than a firm that is equally competent technically; (b) why the government would choose one nonprofit over another; and (d) why the application of the discussion to faith-based organizations is relevant to understanding the government's choice of contractors. The answer to these questions, as argued in the previous chapter, is traceable to a coherent mix of sociological and economic theories best understood within a principal-agent paradigm.

The next chapter continues to demonstrate the applicability of the concepts of the principal-agent paradigm to the performance of nonprofit hospitals. The emphases will be on provable performance relative to public expectations, and on the issues that are involved in balancing expert decision, community needs, and organizational survival. When may the agent justifiably dash the expectations of the principal? Can organizational or managerial self-interest benefit the public?

Chapter 7

The Performance of Agents

Acute Care Hospitals and Community Benefits

This chapter further explores perspectives gained when the nonprofit is seen as a social capital asset and agent of policy within a principal-agent paradigm. This chapter focuses on the nonprofit hospital as an agent of public policy—a valued part of the social capital of a community. It illustrates the public policy issues implicit in defining and in evaluating the performance of a nonprofit agent that is not a contractor to the government and yet has an immeasurable duty to advance community welfare. When the nonprofit is under contract to the government, the contract stipulates what is expected and the evaluation of performance is a matter of comparing the output agreed upon in the contract with what was actually done. Without a specific contract, there is no such easy guidance and the agent's performance may be open to dispute. Both situations are, however, open to dispute because both invite some degree of agent discretion.

When the organization is not under contract, the only guidance is its promise (its mission), and what it implies. But the mission is broad. It promises a class of performance, not specific details. The core problem for the government as the managing agent and for the public is establishing whether public expectations are being satisfactorily met and in a way that justifies compensation in the form of tax exemption.

But what is the basis of public expectations? Clearly, the agency of a nonprofit is based on the expectation that it will advance public welfare either directly or indirectly. The issue for the agent is uncovering these expectations prior to committing its resources in a manner that will not be construed as yielding insufficient public benefits to justify its exemption. But are the expectations realistic? Would meeting them risk the financial wellbeing of the organization? In making decisions, managers must balance public expectations, organizational survival, and their own self-interest. There are innumerable possibilities for conflict. What does moral hazard have to say about this?

Principal-agent theory implies that self-interest could lead to a moral hazard. This is especially so when there is an asymmetry in information. One interpretation is that this may enable the agent to take advantage of the principal. This chapter takes another view: Asymmetry in information leads the principal to judge the agent as working in its own self-interest, not being aware that only through the later course is the principal's interest best served. This is a variation of the "tragedy of common" discussed in chapter 2. In that tragedy, an individual pursuing his or her own self-interest eventually uses up all of the resources so that in the long run his or her self-interest or that of the community can no longer be served. Here, the pursuing of the organization's self-interest enables the long-run interest of the community to be served better.

The Public Mission of Hospitals

Nonprofit hospitals fit into the five-factor criteria of structured social capital delineated in chapter 3. Bazzoli, Chan, Shortell, and D'Aunno[1] report that some 71 percent of hospitals are in some form of a network. The most obvious of these is that both religious and sectarian hospitals are members of common owners. On the sectarian side, Hospital Corporation of America, Tenet, and Humana are examples. Examples on the religious side are Catholic hospitals, Seventh-Day Adventist Hospitals, and so on, and on the nonprofit side there are hospitals operated by fraternal groups, including the Shriners. Therefore, each individual hospital is not only a social asset but together they form a network of social assets. This network may be comprised of other hospitals and groups with which the hospital is affiliated. This chapter focuses on certain agency problems faced by individual nonprofit hospitals—since each is a separately chartered agent charged with advancing the health care of the public it serves.

Hospitals have always been categorized as one of the institutions that advance public welfare and therefore deserve tax exemption. A hospital is one of the most easily recognized and appreciated aspects of the social capital of any community. The pyramid for health and health-related services is as follows:

Advance Public Welfare

Health Services and Related Activities

Hospitals, hospital auxiliaries, nursing or convalescent homes, blood banks, mental health care, scientific research on diseases, group medical practice association, aid to the handicapped, nurses' register or bureau, hospital pharmacies, parking facilities, food services, health clinic, rescue and emergency services, care and housing for the aged, in-faculty group associations, health insurance (medical, dental, optical, etc.)

A hospital could provide any one or a combination of these tax-exempt services. Hospitals may also vary in specialization and emphasis, in reputation, in clientele, and in secular or religious affiliations. Furthermore, some are stand-alone and others are part of a chain or network.

Federal Public Policy and Expected Performance[2]

Hospitals, whether for-profit or nonprofit, have very much the same basic promise—healthcare of the community. Both try to use the latest and best diagnostic and therapeutic techniques and both charge for their services. Then, what allows one to be compensated by the public through tax exemption and the other not?

This question forced the Internal Revenue Service to come up with a set of criteria that it would use to distinguish between for-profit and nonprofit hospitals. The IRS started out with a definition that was adequate for decades. It said in Revenue Ruling 56–185 that to be tax exempt, a nonprofit hospital must be operated for the benefit of those who cannot pay.

But as a result of controversy, the IRS in 1969 issued Revenue Ruling 69–545, which applies today. It says that for a nonprofit hospital to qualify for federal tax exemption it must do the following:

1. The hospital should provide care to all insured patients, including those sponsored by government.
2. The hospital should provide full-time availability of emergency department services to anyone needing them.
3. The hospital should select its board of trustees from the community.
4. The hospital should provide medical staff privileges to all eligible physicians.
5. The operating surpluses of the hospital should be applied to capital replacement, expansion, debt amortization, improving inpatient care, medical training, education, and research.

Item five does not include the payments of dividends as a use of a nonprofit hospital's surplus. As a tax-exempt organization, nonprofit hospitals cannot pay dividends. For-profit hospitals can and often do. The surplus of the nonprofit hospitals must be used in one or more of the forms in item 5. All of these forms involve reinvesting the surplus in the hospital's mission.

In 1983, the IRS issued Revenue Ruling 83–157. It said that the nonprofit hospital does not have to have an emergency room if it fulfills the other conditions. In the case it considered, the state said that the emergency room would be duplicative and not satisfy any real need. Moreover, the ruling also said that there are certain specialty hospitals where emergency room service is out of the ordinary and therefore that criterion need not be satisfied.

Note the progression in definition by the IRS as to what may be deemed a nonprofit hospital worthy of tax exemption. Changes such as these arise from (a) challenges either by the affected class of agents or their competitors;

(b) new technologies including delivery systems, and therefore how the specific performance may be satisfied; (c) learning; and (d) unforeseen changes in public needs and how the public might prefer that these new needs be satisfied.

Public Policy of Individual States and Expected Performance

As a matter of public policy, states also have a strong interest in distinguishing between for-profit and nonprofit hospitals and justifying the latter's exemption from state and local taxes. Some state governments have established performance criteria for nonprofit hospitals to justify their tax exemption in the state and local jurisdictions.

These exemptions cover state and local income, property, and sales taxes and certain licensing fees. Thus, the nonprofit hospital operates under two defined relationships with governments and all they imply; one at the federal and the other at the state level. All states accept the supremacy of the federal law and then attach their own criteria. Among the states doing so are California, Connecticut, Massachusetts, Indiana, New Hampshire, Pennsylvania, Maryland, and Texas. Here are three examples.

In Pennsylvania,[3] all nonprofits (including hospitals) must do the following to obtain tax exemption or elect to pay a fee in lieu of taxes:

1. Advance a charitable purpose
2. Donate or render gratuitously a substantial part of its services
3. Benefit a substantial part of a class of people who qualify as subjects of charity
4. Relieve the government of a burden
5. Operate entirely free from a profit motive.

In Massachusetts,[4] the guidelines indicate:

1. The board and senior management of the nonprofit hospital should develop a plan stating how it will be implemented, including the allocation of resources and responsibilities.
2. There should be public disclosure of a formal community benefits plan to which the hospital is committed.
3. A specific target for community benefits should be identified. This target may be defined geographically, demographically, or according to health or charity-related status.
4. A comprehensive assessment of the health needs of the target population must be made and needs to be prioritized.
5. Implementation of the plan must be timely.

6. A report based on the above must be submitted to the Attorney General.

In Texas,[5] the most stringent state, a community benefit is defined as one or more of the following uses of the resources of the hospital:

1. A reasonableness standard: Charity care and government-sponsored indigent health care are provided at a level that is reasonable in relation to the community needs, as determined through a community needs analysis, the available resources of the hospital, and through the tax-exempt benefits received by the hospital.
2. Four percent of net patient revenue: Charity care and government-sponsored indigent health care equal to at least 4 percent of the hospital's net patient revenues.
3. One hundred percent of tax-exempt benefits: Charity care and government-sponsored indigent health care are provided in an amount at least equal to 100 percent of the hospital's tax-exempt benefits, excluding federal income tax.
4. Charity care and community benefits mix: Charity care, government-sponsored indigent health care, and other combined community benefits are provided in an amount equal to at least 5 percent of the hospital's net patient-revenue, of which charity care and government-sponsored indigent health care are provided in an amount equal to at least 3 percent of the hospital's net patient revenue.

These then are the public policy criteria that define the principal-agent relationship that distinguishes a for-profit from a nonprofit hospital. It is not in the concept of "charity" or "nonprofit." It is in specific classes of performance: How the agent is expected to perform for the principal, the public, in order to be compensated in the form of tax exemption.

Federal and State Policies within the Principal-Agency Framework

Principal-agent theory and the economic concept of externalities provide a framework for viewing the historical concern for charity care. Providers of medical care have more or better information about medical care and needs than individuals do, or can afford. Because society perceives itself as having an interest in keeping its individual members healthy, it is willing to make up the difference. It can do this through paying a subsidy to a for-profit hospital and/or paying a subsidy and tax exemption to a nonprofit hospital.

In the latter case, the tax exemption allows the hospital to attract outside resources in the form of donations and volunteer contributions that can only be spent on qualified health care (and cannot be paid as dividends to stockholders). This leverage significantly increases the resources and the corresponding benefits the community gets. Since the community through its taxpayers is paying for this benefit, it has a right to define what it expects from the nonprofit hospitals. Ergo: the list drawn up by the IRS and the states.

Public Needs, Public Expectations, and Hospital Performance

One of the central problems that leads to the formation of nonprofit organizations is the disincentive of consumers to reveal their preferences when they cannot be denied the benefits of a good or service. When a principal engages an agent to provide a service, the agent needs some way to determine the needs and expectations of the principal if these needs and expectations are not specifically stated in a contract or if the contract gives the agent wide discretion.

The lists of ways to satisfy community needs give hospitals complete discretion on the state level (perhaps less so in Texas), and it is on this level that questions mostly arise. Are the needs the hospital claims to be meeting in accord with public expectations? Can they do more? In a principal-agent framework, it is not just the output that counts, but that the output of the agent hospital satisfies public needs and expectations. This is particularly true if there is a pre-payment or reservation price paid. In the case of nonprofits, this payment is in the form of tax exemption.

In what follows, we pursue the problem from the political scientists' concerns with the distribution problem: What? How Much? For whom? When? As in the preceding section, much is drawn and recast from the experience and notes from the preparation of a previous paper.[6] Since writing that paper with many of these arguments, a Florida hospital filed suit, claiming that its bankruptcy is due to an attempt to enforce the community benefits law, citing some of the arguments given below.

What needs must hospitals satisfy at the state and local levels in order to merit tax exemption? There are several approaches to answering this question—all allowing discretion by the hospital.

1. It could be assumed that given the asymmetry of information, hospitals and health care professionals would know best and they should elect what is best for the community and do it; that is, depend on expert knowledge and give them discretion.
2. A list could be provided to the hospitals by the state with specific choices, and the hospital could elect from this list based on its superior information, capacity, and preferences; that is, depend on expert knowledge but constrain their discretion.

3. The hospitals could consult the public about its needs and, using some method such as a Likert scale, determine the intensity and implicitly the priority of these needs; that is, depend on consumer knowledge and their revealed preferences.

The last approach may give the best estimate of public expectations. It is also likely to be the least informed, since the public has no diagnostic capacity. It is also most likely to be impracticable, since the public has no information of the hospitals' capacity to meet certain needs. For these reasons, this option is likely to be the most disappointing. This option may not lead to the best choices either for the agent or the principal.

The first approach admits only to expert discretion. It may be the most informed, but it introduces the greatest opportunities for the agent to place its interests over those of the public. In these cases "trust," not as reliability but as faith and convergence of interest, is crucial. In the second case, expectations are bounded, but the hospitals have to have choices to reflect different organizational and community circumstances. This is the case in Texas. Each method contains the seeds for dispute. But the method that diminishes the use of the asymmetric expert information that the agent has but the public doesn't also diminishes the possible gains to the community. The risk of a moral hazard that this information will be used by the agent hospital for its selfish purposes may be worth taking.

What: The Hospital's Choice from the Government's Menu

All of the above procedures give the hospital a choice of how to meet its community benefits criteria. Choice is necessary when the agent is not a servant and when agents face different internal as well as external constraints. I have elsewhere distinguished two approaches.[7] One approach to this problem I labeled the demand approach. This approach assumes that external or environmental conditions drive the decision. Managers of hospitals are influenced primarily by the health conditions that surround them. They rank these needs according to severity and the risk to which they expose the community, and endeavor to treat these without regard to their self-interest—thus avoiding a moral hazard problem.

A second approach, called the supply approach, argues that managers place priority on retaining their tax-exempt status. They then select from the needs that public law specifically recognizes as advancing public welfare in a manner that qualifies for tax exemption. From this list, they focus on those that have the technical, physical, and financial capacity to satisfy with uncommitted or underutilized resources and that they may want to market to meet bona fide community needs. The hospital is motivated by self interests and its capacity to respond to specific kinds of medical needs.

The demand approach has the following shortcomings, although it is motivated by altruistic rather than selfish interests:

1. The need identified by the community may be inconsistent with the need specified in public law, and therefore its fulfillment does not allow the hospital to meet its requirements for tax exemption. This is especially true of the federal law that is need-specific, as described earlier in this chapter, and has supremacy over state law.
2. The need identified by the community may not be one that the hospital can economically and professionally respond to efficiently or with a high probability of success, and may be better met by another institution.

There are additional considerations. The hospital may choose to use its top surgical team principally for exceptional purposes. Why? Most surgeons and physicians are independent contractors and generally control the use of their time. The hospital could forego the room and equipment costs, but the utility of these depends upon having a willing surgeon. The hospital may choose not to offer its unusual machine (and its top staff) unless in an emergency. Round-the-clock nondiscriminatory services qualify. If the hospital has an unusual machine it may be a principal source of income for the hospital and its earnings may be necessary to pay the debt through which it was acquired. Moreover, its time may not be available—if it is so unusual in the community.

Research and education are qualified needs, but they, too, may blur altruistic with selfish interests. University hospitals can meet the tax-exempt requirement merely by doing research and education; but this is clearly within their self interests and not a major deviation from their overall mission and purpose. The charity patient in these hospitals gets outstanding care at the same time they serve the furtherance of a public good and the building of social capital in the development of knowledge and professional practice. Hence, the university, faculty, and students are more than secondary beneficiaries.

Many nonprofit hospitals meet a substantial part, if not all, of their community benefit requirements through free diagnosis for ailments such as cancer, high cholesterol, and high blood pressure. Others do so by free health education on drug use, stress management, diseases, pregnancy, parenting, and so on. Others do free transportation to and from the hospital. Others donate staff time, literature, and money to needy families.

Yet others choose to make charitable donations by encouraging and coordinating their employees in charitable activities after hours. These services do the following: (a) they are excellent marketing and recruiting strategies for potential patients; (b) they help the hospital to meet its tax-exempt requirements; (c) they help the community; and (d) they free the hospital to concentrate on delivering health care, utilizing all of its technical and scarce resources to make money. Point (c) may appear cynical; but a nonprofit hospital is required to plow back all of its profits into health care. It can, therefore, be argued that "in the long-run the community is better off" for these choices akin to point (c) even though they were driven by self-interest.

How Much: Public Expectations and the Hospital's Capacity to Perform

When the nonprofit enters into a contract, the amount it is expected to produce is usually specified. This is not the case in community benefits requirements, except in Texas, where the amount is based on the amount of tax exemption. This calculation is, however, based on the accounting data of the organization itself. This opens the door to asymmetric information, moral hazard, and dispute.

Calibrating benefits with the amount of exemption taken, as in Texas, is reasonable. Since exemption is a form of compensation, the hospitals are being asked to earn their pay. Even here where the amount can be calculated there is an invitation to dispute. As we have seen from recent corporate misdeeds, serious moral hazard can occur when the organization itself calculates these data or provides the data upon which others do their calculation. The profits of these corporations were vastly overstated. In chapter 9 we shall see that nonprofit organizations are also inclined to such fuzzy calculations when it suits them.

It is easy to overestimate the amount of community benefits the hospitals should provide based on the tax exemption they took. The income of a hospital, as with other nonprofits, is divided into two parts—the exempt and the taxable. In every state, and in the federal statues, the community benefits rule applies only to the exempt part: The provision of community service is to justify exemption. The dollar amount of exemption can only be determined after each hospital calculates its net exempt income and multiplies that by what would have been the tax rate on that income. There are two problems here.

One problem is a paradox created by the unintended consequences of moral hazard. To the extent that managers are persuaded by the moral hazard of trying to escape taxes by converting income to a nontaxable form (from unrelated to related business income), they risk increasing the community benefits requirements they impose upon themselves. Paradoxically, the net beneficiary is the local community.

Second, to the extent that the community requires the hospitals to provide benefits based on their overall net income rather than as a standard unrelated to that income or to exemption, it risks getting no benefits at all because many nonprofit hospitals report deficits at the end of some years. Therefore community benefits would be erratic, ranging from zero to some unknown amount, while the hospital gets tax exemption anyway.

The setting of expectations on the overall income of the hospital may also be managerially imprudent and therefore invite a moral hazard. A hospital has costs and other expenditure requirements that it cannot forego in order to meet free community benefits. Some of these are just the costs of routine operations; some are legal liabilities including pensions, debt service, and the maintenance of state-of-the-art equipment. These all reduce the amount the hospital may prudently make available. Fortunately for Texas hospitals, the law expressly recognizes these limitations.

This point deserves more explanation. State laws prohibit hospitals from making expenditures (or investments) that impair their future ability to function at high quality such as keeping up with technology and meeting quality standards and meeting the terms of other agreements. The amount that the hospital is free to dedicate to charitable expenditures where costs cannot be recovered is substantially less than its income. In the long run, self-interest and self-preservation (otherwise seen as moral hazards) serve the hospital and the community well if the hospital is in both good financial and technical standing.

For Whom: The Difference between Jurisdictional Demarcation and Service Markets

Who is the relevant community to receive benefits? As stated in chapter 3, the public that is the direct beneficiary is not necessarily the public that pays by means of tax exemption—the public with which the agent has a principal-agent agreement or the public (the state, city, or county) with which the hospital has a contract. Some years ago, several university hospitals undertook voluntary urban renewal programs in the neighborhoods in which they were located. To their credit, some of the hospitals were honest and did not call this charity. They recognized that the safety of patients and staff and the value of the hospitals' property were affected by the environment in which they were located. Many of these properties have escalated in value—a good predictable investment. Self-interest is served.

The "community" that is consistent with the hospital's self-interest will extend well beyond the "community" in which it is located. This target community, as in Texas and New Hampshire, is its market area. Thus, the hospital's self interest and the public's interest may go well beyond that immediate neighborhood. The hospital's market area is the area from which it draws its patients and from which a sizeable percentage of patients choose it over other hospitals—known as the Elzinga-Hogarty index. The hospital is concerned about this larger area that may cross jurisdiction, for those areas depend upon it, it depends upon them, and because it is the definition used to determine the competitiveness of the hospital for antitrust purposes.

For Whom: Asymmetric Information and Masking Self-Interest as Service

By hospital industry, federal, and state laws, a community benefit expenditure occurs if a hospital is not reimbursed for all or a portion of its costs for service to a patient. This may result from setting its normal price higher than Medicare or Medicaid would reimburse the hospital and accounting for the unpaid balance as a community benefit.

Herzlinger and Krasker[8] and Banks[9] have alerted that unreimbursed expenditures may also result from bad debt—the failure of the hospital to be able to collect from some of its patients. In either case, the hospital may (because of asymmetrical knowledge about the precise accounting for each patient) attribute all or a portion of these costs to community benefits. In this case, self-interest serves the hospital—not the community.

Adverse Selection and the Concentration of High-Risk Patients

The previous section dealt with issues of need, self-interest, moral hazard, and asymmetric information. This section deals with adverse selection and its consequence for the dispersal of community benefits through nonprofit hospitals as the agent for concentration and dispersal of high-risk patients. Sutton, Milet, and Blanchfield[10] found a concentration of charity or unreimbursed care in a few hospitals in California. Hattick and Ordos[11] find that one hospital in the state of Washington does 23 percent of the charity care in that state. Spencer,[12] in a study of the New York Prospective Hospital Reimbursement Methodology, showed that the program that was intended to spread charity care across hospitals by providing certain financial incentives ended up financing physician education, bad debt, overcapacity, and a concentration of unreimbursed care in teaching and public hospitals—often one and the same. Incidentally, this program was financed not through tax exemption but by a fund created by assessing third party (such as insurance company) payers.

A principal-agent framework would suggest that part of the concentration problem has to do with adverse selection. The location of a nonprofit hospital in a rural, poor community is likely to attract patients with a high risk of not being able to pay the full cost of care. Therefore, private for-profit hospitals are not likely to be attracted to those areas or to those patients. By staying away, they avoid the risk of adverse selection by patients. Consequently, nonprofit hospitals get a disproportionate share of the poor and are generally exempt from community benefits criteria.

Except for such clear-cut cases, using concepts such as "urban" and "rural" or "poor area" is likely to misinform expectations. The hospital's market area is likely to cut across or even hop and skip across these lines. Adverse selection suggests the following: The hospital in the lower income area would suffer adverse selection partly because most of its immediate residents are high charity risks. The residents in the area who can afford to pay or are insured may elect to go to the "better hospital in the better part of town" if not for the ambience, in the belief that it must be better quality. The rich residents of the "better" part of town are not likely to go to the poor area hospital; but the poor residents of the "better" area may if that is all they can afford. This results in adverse selection—a concentration of adverse cases in one area. To draw from the logic of regional economics, the distribution of charity care in this process would be determined by the distance and transport cost between the two hospitals.[13]

Thus, the amount of charity care a nonprofit hospital gives may be directly related to the distance and transactions costs of transporting a poor patient to the closest general, community, or public hospital. Little wonder that in most urban areas, the nonprofit hospital specializing in indigent cases—the general, community, and public hospitals—co-exists with the ones serving patients who can pay either themselves or through a third party. It is not coincidence that the ambulance races across town to deliver an indigent patient to the public or community hospital.

This does not mean, however, that the hospitals that minimize dealing with charity cases provide insufficient community benefits. They may choose to provide a different item in the menu of qualified benefits. The exercise of choice is one of the powers of being an agent. The community, general, or public hospitals are usually servants. They exercise no choice. Their "charity" care is involuntary and part of the expressed obligation in their principal-agent contract.

A Dispute between St. David and Government

Here is a specific example of a dispute over the exercise of discretion and choice of how to meet expectations. As described in the opening of this chapter, the IRS laid out a set of conditions that, if fulfilled, would indicate that the hospital was satisfying the community benefits criterion for tax exemption. This led to the case of *St. David's Health Care System Inc. v. United States of America,* the United States District Court, Western Division, Texas, Austin, Texas, decided on June 7, 2002.

St. David's Health Care System in Texas, a nonprofit tax-exempt acute care hospital system, entered into a joint venture with a for-profit hospital system, Hospital Corporation of America (HCA). To this venture, St. David contributed all of its hospital and medical assets, and HCA, which owns and operates over 180 hospitals nationwide, contributed the hospital and medical assets of its Austin, Texas, hospital. St. David's interest in the partnership as both limited and general partner was 45.9 percent and HCA's interest as both limited and general partner was 54.1 percent. The venture is managed by one of the HCA's local hospitals on behalf HCA as the managing partner. The governing board of the venture is constituted 50–50 between HCA and St. David. Chapter 7 describes the concerns of the IRS and courts about arrangements such as these.

In 2000, after reviewing the Form 990 of St. David, the IRS revoked its tax exemption, going back to the year 1996, when the partnership was formed. The IRS argued that such an arrangement indicated that St. David no longer existed for a charitable purpose but for the for-profit objectives of its partner. The central purpose of the venture, according to the IRS, was not to provide a community benefit. So it taxed St. David retroactively to 1996 (the year the partnership was formed) for approximately $900,000. St. David paid. But it took the IRS to court.

In 2002, the United States District Court cited above rendered its decision about the case. The hospital won (at least awaiting an IRS appeal). Here are the court's arguments as they relate to this chapter. Will they be sustained or applicable to other cases?

1. There is no indication in the regulations that all of the performances required by the IRS and listed in the opening of this chapter carry equal weight. This is especially so since the IRS indicated that it would look at the facts and circumstances of each case. Clearly, there is a suggestion that the hospital may exercise some discretion.
2. Noting that the key argument of the IRS had to do with control over the assets and therefore the commitment to charity and public purpose, the court made the following assertions:

   (a) It is clear that the presence of a community board is an argument in favor of tax exemption, but it is not clear that it is necessary if other criteria are met; and
   (b) It is also not clear that the persons who comprise this board must necessarily be from the community at large. The Court cites an earlier case where an HMO was granted exemption but all of its board members were from the HMO membership. They did not come from the community and were in de facto owners of the HMO; and
   (c) What anyway is a community board? The court asserted on page five of its decision that a community board does more than give "wealthy self-styled philanthropists something to do on the rare occasion that they are not playing golf. The purpose of a community board is to see that the public interest is given precedence over any private interests. Thus, if a board is structured to give such protection, it is clearly a community board." Therefore,
   (d) The fact that the votes were 50–50 is not relevant. What is relevant is that the partnership agreement stipulated that the chair of the board would always be an appointee of St. David. St. David would be able to unilaterally remove the CEO, an agreement that required that the community purpose always be met, and St. David reserved the unilateral right to dissolve the partnership if it failed to meet that purpose. Therefore, the provision of community benefits was protected.

The Court also had to address another claim. That is that the emergency service provided by the partnership did not meet what was intended by the listing of that service as a criterion. What was intended, it asserts, was free service to those who could not pay. The courts rejected that argument. Its rejection was based primarily on the following reasoning:

1. That it is clear from previous revenue decisions that there are some instances where fulfilling the emergency care criterion is not prudent and not necessary to meet the community benefits criteria (see the earlier discussion in this paper); and
2. That the fact that the hospital offers emergency care without first ascertaining the patient's ability to pay is sufficient because every hospital knows that by offering that service to every person who requests it, the hospital will end up with some patients who cannot pay; and
3. The court implies that making and living up to the offer is sufficient to meet a charitable obligation. Since there is certainty of some nonpayment when the offer was made and exercised, the fact that the hospital tries to collect later and fails is irrelevant.

Irrelevant? The IRS rebuts that it is not irrelevant because it implies that the hospital is treating as a charitable expense its collection failure. Bad debt now becomes charity. The court on page five of its decision responded to this by saying that the separation of bad debt from charity is not applicable to emergency care as it might be to other care, because the emergency care physician has no way of knowing a charity case from a bad debt case, someone who could pay but doesn't. Would the emergency physician be able to distinguish based on "skin color, the brand name of clothes worn by the patient upon entering the emergency room, or shaking a magic eight ball"?

And thus is illustrated the reality of some of the problems we discussed: (a) discretion; (b) what constitutes community and its benefits and how that can be satisfied for whom; (c) control over assets; (d) tax exemption as compensation; and (e) the mission as setting some boundary on expectations. But how far the boundary extends depends upon the source of the expectations as explained chapter 4 and who is expecting, among other things.

Expectations, Institutional and Managerial Survival

There are times when the management of the nonprofit must make decisions in the best interest of the survival of the organization, and, as public choice theory puts it, the interest of management itself. Brickley and Van Horn[14] find that both for-profit and nonprofit hospital managers focus on the financial performance of their hospitals as measured by rate of return on assets—not on altruism. Bryce[15] found that the rates of return on assets for nonprofit HMOs are equal to those of for-profits. Why would a nonprofit agent for the public and a for-profit agent for stockholders behave in the same way? What are the implications?

A hospital, for and not for profit, is an economic institution. As such it has to cover its costs and earn enough of a surplus to provide for a rainy day, to provide for growth as its market area grows in population size, and to provide for investments in repairs, additions, training, and new technologies. A hospital that continuously runs deficits caused by a negative cash flow cannot long survive.

Furthermore, most hospitals acquire properties, equipment, and supplies through debt. When a hospital issues a bond, that bond must be rated and competes with corporate bonds in the capital market. Its ability to attract investors depends upon the financial health of the hospital. Some hospitals can minimize this problem by borrowing through a hospital finance authority (discussed in the previous chapter) as set up by the state. That authority, however, must determine that the hospital has the ability to pay. The investors rely on the creditworthiness of the hospitals on whose behalf the debt is issued. This is their only source of interest payments. Further nonprofit and for profit hospitals and corporations compete in the same debt market where rates of return (adjusted for tax exemption) tend to converge among securities of equal quality. Market forces set these rates.

Thus, there is moral hazard. The managers are tempted to temper both bad debt and free care so as to enhance the hospital's credit worthiness and their own professional standing, wealth, and job security. Having a choice, they may elect some other form of community benefits. It would be the due diligence of the trustees that could persuade them otherwise, if that makes sense, because the trustees are, like the managers, entrusted with providing for the hospital's future. In the end, both for-profit and nonprofit hospitals are exposed to the same market discipline on which survival depends. In the end, personal and institutional survival may trump charity.

Leverage One More Time: The Faith-Based Hospitals

In chapter 4 the argument about leverage, social capital, mission, and goodwill as they contribute to the distinction between for-profit and nonprofit organizations was developed and illustrated in chapter 6 with housing. In a study[16] of 76 nonprofit hospitals in Texas, it was found that net patient revenues was a better predictor of community benefits expenditures for secular hospitals and that gross patient revenues was a better predictor for faith-based hospitals. In hospital accounting, net patient revenue means revenue gained directly from patient care. Gross patient revenues means net patient revenues plus revenues from other sources, including charitable contributions.

The implication of this is that faith-based organizations are better able to leverage—drawing additional dollars from charitable contributions, volunteer services, and from their religious affiliations in order to finance their community benefits. For-profit hospitals cannot do this. Further, Gloria J. Bazzoli, Benjamin Chan, Stephen M. Shortell, and Thomas D'Aunno[17] found that hospitals with centralized common owners generally have lower cost and superior infrastructure to hospitals that are only loosely aligned or affiliated. Hence, the lower cost of a religious hospital may have a lot to do with the common "ownership." This lower cost can be passed on in contracts, thus increasing the amount that every government contract yields.

Again, we return to the same theme: Social capital and the depth of the belief system that binds members, the commitment to the mission (this is especially noticeable with orders of Catholic nuns dedicated to charity care), the absence of leakage by the payment of dividends (and in the cases of nuns, competitive wages), the goodwill that religion has both to obtain donations in cash and in-kind (including volunteers) directly or through their affiliates, and the trust placed in them are possible operating and competitive advantages. The criterion need not be doctrinal faith.

Is Tax Exemption Worth It? Is the Compensation Enough?

Sutton, Milet, and Blanchfield[18] found a concentration of charity or unreimbursed care patients in just a few hospitals in California. They also found that for-profit and other nonprofit hospitals provide a similar level of charity care. The former does mostly patients on Medicare or Medicaid while the latter does mostly indigent patients. The difference is significant. With Medicare or Medicaid patients, at least some payment is guaranteed to cover part of the costs—and some hospitals make (or at least report) handsome earnings from serving and overcharging these patients (if recent settlements are any indication). In the case of nonprofits charity care is likely to be a total loss.

In comparing for-profit and nonprofit hospitals, Eggleston and Zeckhauser[19] concluded that nonprofit or public hospitals are best suited for situations that involve pure public goods or extensive externalities, where performance and qualify are not easily discerned by patients, who cannot make efficient choices. But Eggleston and Zeckhauser[20] also found no difference in the efficiency or offerings of for-profit and nonprofit hospitals and report that a study by Daniel Kessler and Mark McClellan found the same.

From a statutory point, however, the latter is required to meet community benefits requirements and the former is not a condition of exemption. When for-profit and nonprofit hospitals are compared in terms of community benefits requirements, Nicholson, Pauly, Burns, Bauermritter, and Asch[21] find that nonprofit hospitals spend less than we may expect on community benefits based on comparable expenditures of for-profit hospitals with the same rates of returns on assets and on equity. Rhinehart[22] finds that nonprofit hospitals spend less on community benefits than may be justified by their tax exemption. In standard economics, this implies, as some authors state, that the nonprofit hospitals are receiving some form of economic rent—payment for what they might have done anyway.

Agents have choices. One choice is whether to give up the tax-exempt status. Several hospitals have answered in the affirmative. One way is to convert from a nonprofit tax-exempt status to a for-profit status. The latter status allows them to sell stocks and therefore increase their capital. From the public's point of view, states have laws that require that the converting hospital pay a fair price for all of its assets both tangible and intangible, subject the conversion to public hearing, seek the approval of the attorney general, and assure that the community need will continue to be met.

But an implication from these conversions is that tax exemption may not be sufficient compensation to induce some hospitals to carry out a regime of community benefits. Thorpe, Florence, and Seiber[23] found that uncompensated care declined after conversion. Why might that be so? Tax exemption is applicable only to the income from activities related to the mission of the hospital. The list that qualifies is extensive. It includes income from an activity that is for the benefits of patients or employees such as the cafeteria, income from an activity conducted primarily by volunteers such as the gift shop, income from rental of space to an organization the hospital does not control, income from the sale of securities, interest income, royalties, income from donations, income from research, fees from leasing space to other hospitals, dividend income, purchase discounts and rebates, fees in joint ventures, and fees from contracting to other hospitals.

But income unrelated to the mission of the hospital (although a smaller part of the earnings of all hospitals) is taxed. The bottom-line question for the hospital, therefore, is whether the net savings from tax exemption cover the cost of providing the specific community benefits that are required (see the opening of this chapter), since this is a basic difference between a for-profit and a nonprofit hospital.

Why is the above an important consideration for the nonprofit tax-exempt hospital? Because if the economic rent argument is accurate, it implies that the hospital would have carried out community benefits even if it paid taxes, and voluntarily so, with full discretion as to how to do so, when, and how much to do—the very issues that are discussed earlier in the chapter.

The answer may lie partly in the fact that the tax benefit itself, while a compensation for performance, is not sufficient to explain the election of nonprofit hospital status. A for-profit hospital can substantially reduce its taxes (the price it is willing to pay to rid itself of specific community benefits performance) to zero from time to time and for an extremely long stretch at a time. It can do so by charging off bad debt, taking depreciation charges, deducting operating expenses, deducting operating losses up to several years back, deducting investment losses, taking tax credits, apportioning its revenues and expenses across the states in which it operates to favor low-tax states, and consolidating the earnings of all of its hospitals so that those with losses reduce the net gains. If it is part of a system it can reduce the gains of one unit by the losses in others. But it may not do so continuously and imprudently without threat to its stock price, its ability to issue bonds, and the job security of management.

None of these tax strategies is available to the tax-exempt hospital unless it has considerable income from activities that are not related to its mission. In short, the requirement to do community benefits may not be sufficient to induce hospitals to convert to a for-profit status. As empirical studies cited earlier show, they would do so anyway; and the tax exemption may not be sufficient to induce the nonprofit hospital to remain nonprofit—it could get some if not considerable more if it were for-profit.

Finally, note that the Emergency Medical Treatment and Active Labor Act of 1986 requires that any hospital (nonprofit or for-profit) that participates in the Medicare or Medicaid program has to at least stabilize patients before releasing them—without regard to their ability to pay. This means some amount of charity care is expected even for hospitals that do not do it for tax-exempt purposes.

The Origin of Nonprofit Hospitals and the Convergence of Values

A special edition of the *Journal of Health Politics, Policy and the Law* considered the questions of trust, asymmetric information, and the formation of nonprofit hospitals as stated by Arrow (chapter 2), who asserted that nonprofit hospitals exist because of the lack of information on the part of patients who must rely on the expert knowledge of the providers and that the trust that such decisions require is often best found in a nonprofit hospital where there may be a convergence of interest. The writings of two scholars in that edition are particularly relevant to this text. Needleman[24] argued that the evidence does not support the hypothesis that the public trusts nonprofit providers any more than they trust others but that the evidence supports the hypothesis that consumers choose nonprofit health care providers because of a combination of lower prices, higher quality, increased trustworthiness, and because of their provision of community services. Casalino[25] argued that asymmetric information is handled in part by intermediaries such as insurance companies that steer patients and influence their choices as they balance their own interests, those of the patients, and those of the providers. Here is another take on the issue.

If one categorizes all nonprofit hospitals, almost all will fall in one of three categories:

1. The first category are those that were originally formed by a state or local government and that are still operated by them, or that have been placed under nonprofit or for-profit management or have been converted to private nonprofit form or have been re-organized under a single authority such as described in the previous chapter. The point is that they are organized by government and usually receive some direct government appropriations.
2. The second category are those nonprofit tax-exempt hospitals formed by individuals who are risk-averse. They see the need for a community hospital. However, they do not see it as potentially profitable enough to risk their own investment capital or to attract other investors. But they do see or anticipate the leverage that the nonprofit form can offer through tax exemption, contributions, reinvestment of gains, volunteering—all as described earlier. Incidentally, these same individuals are willing to make current and long-term charitable commitments to the hospital because the "gains," tax deduction and honor, are immediate and not at risk.
3. The third are nonprofit hospitals organized and operated by fraternal or religious groups as part of their mission. Public hospitals tend to specialize in the lower income population with limited choice and are avoided by those who can choose otherwise—strong adverse selection and weak convergence of values.

The convergence of values is probably strongest in the third, where strongly shared values are easily signaled in names, where the origin of the hospital is based on a value system, and where the support of the organization may be based on an affiliation with a fraternal or religious group and monitored by its affiliates as described in social capital theory and theory of embeddedness, discussed previously.

But if the convergence of values is important, why do we find atheists in Seventh-Day Adventists hospitals, Jews in Catholic Hospitals, and anti-Semitics in Jewish hospitals? Why does the hospital population not reflect a one-to-one correspondence with values? The reason is that the convergence of values is not just the patients' but also the doctors'. Patients do not make unilateral decisions about where to go. Their choices are limited by the range of options the doctors have. And a good doctor's choices are limited by his or her affiliation and estimate of where the best care might be gotten for the particular malady of the patient. The patient remains dependent upon expert decision and, in an agency situation, with the physicians and the hospitals because the patient must rely on the judgment of both.

But the effect of asymmetric information may be reduced by the existence of vital information (through nonprofits and governments) about the mortality rates and reputations of hospitals. And what would they find? They might find what studies have found, that the mortality rates are lower in nonprofit hospitals than in for-profit ones. The mortality rates for for-profit

Table 7.1
Convergence of Values Based on the Origin of the Hospital

	Government private founders	*Risk-averse founders*	*Fraternal or religious founders*
Convergence of values	-	+	++

hospitals and public hospitals were about equal (120 per 1,000) patients, while for the nonprofits it was 114 per 1,000, and the differences were significant at 0.00001 level.[26] In a study of Canadian hospitals, Philip Devereaux and his colleagues found that the death rate in private for-profit hospitals was 2 percent higher than in nonprofit hospitals.[27] Thus, the convergence of expectations when there is mistrust of the profit motive, when the risks are high and asymmetric information persists, may lead to a reasoned (though not necessarily fully informed) choice of a nonprofit hospital. The evidence also indicates that there is some price stickiness in the demand for nonprofit hospital care. That is, that the demand for such care tends to vary very little with respect to changes in prices for their services. This is not the case with for-profit hospitals, where a price increase results in a decline in their use.[28] Rosenau notes that measures of performance, quality, and expectations among for-profit and nonprofit hospital and other healthcare providers are not consistent, although the weight of current empirical research may lean toward nonprofit providers as superior providers.[29]

Summary and Preview

This chapter demonstrates the application of the principal-agent paradigm to acute care hospitals with specific comparisons between the faith-based hospitals and the sectarians. Here the focus is on when performance is sufficient given the contractual understanding between the government and the actual facts and realities of nonprofit acute care hospitals. This is an actual, not a theoretical issue. All tax-exempt hospitals are required to demonstrate varying levels of community benefit expenditures (for which they do not receive full compensation) as a condition for maintaining their tax-exempt status. These expectations give a broad range of discretion. How do hospitals use their discretion in fulfilling this requirement? What are the measures for determining if the way this discretion is exercised is motivated by institutional or managerial self-interest or the interest of the community? Which is the relevant public that the hospital serves? How does selfishness masquerade as charity? How in these instances do community expectations conflict with reality? How do faith-based hospitals differ from sectarian hospitals? Does the concept of leverage as described in earlier chapters—more resources brought in from outside—seem to make a difference?

This chapter addresses these points and demonstrates, among other things, that institutional self-interest often serves both the community and the nonprofit agency well and may represent only a potential, not an actual, source of moral hazard. But the chapter goes further and continues the questions: (a) Why would the government contract with a nonprofit hospital when a similarly technically competent for-profit hospital is available? and (b) How do secular hospitals differ from religious hospitals in financing these community benefits requirements? The explanations go back to the discussions especially in chapters 2 through 5. The next chapter deals with nonprofits playing a role in shaping public policy. Nonprofits are not passive performers in the public policy process.

Chapter 8

Policy Formulation, Nonprofit Advocacy, and the Principal-Agent Framework

As social capital assets and agents of public policy, nonprofits are not passive purveyors of the public's will. Some seek to shape that will and to influence the policies that are promulgated in the name of the public. This chapter is about nonprofits as promoters of specific policy positions. Chapters 1–5 reminded us that a nonprofit association is a form of structural social capital formed by individuals with common interests and in which transactions among them are embedded with common understanding, objectives, trust, and a cooperative motivation to achieve a common goal and to take collective action to promote a common goal. Collective action need not be unanimous.

The common method used by associations to achieve these goals in public policy is lobbying and politicking of politicians, candidates, and executives responsible for writing and enforcing rules and regulations that activate a law once it is passed. This chapter will focus on the business association, mostly 501 (c) (6)s in U.S. law. But such associations exist throughout the world. Few countries are without a chamber of commerce or its equivalent and a common purpose of these and other associations to shape policy.

The Association as Social Capital: Sources of Coherence and Power

An association is the coming together of individuals or entities because of a common, identifiable interest. The congregation, the conglomerate, the political party are all associations. While loosely fitting associations may form social capital for other purposes, they are less appropriate within this context because the association must also be an agent and the agent must therefore be an identifiable person or entity capable of signing, discharging, or dispensing of a contract with the resulting exposure to reward or legal sanction. Therefore, this chapter focuses on the association as a formally organized nonprofit with a charter—a license of eligibility to work on behalf of a group with the ultimate beneficiary being the public. All associations, including the church, temple, mosque, or synagogue, which are tax exempt, fall into this category.

In the same way, business associations and professional associations are social capital assets. They meet all five distinguishing features laid out in chapter 3, except they do not get financed by tax-deductible contributions, but by dues and by tax exemption of a variety of revenues. Because dues are voluntary, they like donations, are indicators of the association's value to those who pay.

Various associations represent differing cognitive social capital, and these distinguish them. A business association is distinguished cognitively from others by its common interest in the affairs of business; and within these, business associations are further distinguished by particularistic interests. Accordingly, there are numerous U.S. and foreign associations within the liquor, restaurant, and grocery businesses, some representing a particular product or a particular stage in the supply chain from production to distribution to consumption. Together they form an ever-changing network (coalitions for and against) depending upon the public policy issue.

When Granovetter[1] and Uzzi[2] wrote their essays on business groups they were concerned with the interaction of productive units such as either vertical or horizontal integration. In this chapter we are concerned with associations in the way economists use clubs. Drawing from Buchanan[3] and Tiebout,[4] Cornes and Sandler[5] describe a club. A club is a group of individuals who voluntarily join together to share something in common:

1. Members of a club belong because the utility of membership exceeds the utility of nonmembership.
2. For a member, the net gain from membership must exceed the cost of membership.
3. Club goods usually involve congestion or crowding—the more people consuming it, the less available to others; there is potential rivalry over its consumption.
4. Clubs can limit their memberships to a subset of the population.
5. Clubs can institute mechanisms of exclusions such as a price for some products or a membership fee.

A club good is distinguishable from a public good in that a pure club good is made available only to members. But when an association lobbies for a highway, the public at large is affected. At the same time associations produce seminars, insurance programs, trips, and the like that may be completely closed to nonmembers. In short, a business association is of public policy importance not only because of what it does for its members but what the impact is on the public. Certifying physicians helps physicians and the public.

In the terms of chapter 3, business associations are structural social capital. They are permanent structures into which members have invested in anticipation of a flow of benefits the value of which may diminish or appreciate over time. Their members are bound by a shared value or vision and a shared set of norms that binds them—cognitive social capital. The stronger the latter and the more embedded, the greater the cohesive power of the association and in terms of chapter 5, the less its transactions cost. Also, in terms of chapter 5, the greater the number of business associations, the greater the diversity and competition they create within the policy arena. Associations are held together "club-like," but they are also agents. They exist to perform specific functions on behalf of their members.

An Association as a System of Networks

The association is a system of networks. We may identify these levels of networking in the business association world:

Intrafirm network (the firm member and its affiliates and subsidiaries and their affiliates and subsidiaries)

Interfirm network (the firm, its competitors, suppliers, and customers in any combination on a specific issue)

The firm and its business associations (firms belong to one or more business associations)

Interbusiness association (business associations form networks with other associations)

Internetworks (a network such as a federation connects with other networks).

This system of networking can be potentially formidable in making the business association an agent of public policy. Outside of the first level, however, the network is ad hoc, voluntary, and is rarely assured of a common position and assured just as many times of conflict and sometimes disinterest by some network members. The protection of steel came at the expense of other industries that purchase steel; the protection of the weak comes at the expense of restricting market share of the strong. The "network" is not an undifferentiated, unconflicted, static component of social capital no matter how strong the common bond. Networks are often unstable, ever-shifting coalitions formed to facilitate and effectuate a single collective action before disbursing only to be reconstituted (if ever) with different members and not infrequently to undo or to amend the former collective action.

Borrowing from the logic and language of Burt[6] we may argue that the entrepreneurial or brokerage role of the business association (that is, bringing parties to a transaction together), has value to the individual members, to the policy makers on whom they depend, and in connecting the various circles. They connect people, entities, agencies, networks, and systems. They broker between their members and others.

Examples of Associations: Their Policy, Positions, and Strategies

As Getz[7] in a comprehensive review of the literature notes, a central use of agency theory in political behavior of firms focuses on the reasons for corporate involvement in politics and public policy. This chapter is about the role of business associations as agents of public policy—representing the interest of their corporate members. What do they do? Why do they do it? How do they do it? What is the source of their power—other than money? Several specific topics will be discussed and the National Beer Wholesalers Association (NBWA) will be used as a specific example; but first, here are five examples of associations with different public policy agendas and their methods of influencing policy on behalf of their members.

The American Farm Bureau Federation

The American Farm Bureau's mission is to foster the implementation of policies recommended and developed by its members, representing over 5 million farming and ranching families throughout the United States. The federation is recognized as one of the strongest farm advocates, working largely through its "Public Policy Team," which is a network of lobbyists backed up by teams of specialists.

It lobbies in favor of the production of agricultural products enhanced by biotechnology. It opposes requiring that the inputs or technologies used in such processes be disclosed on labels. It favors the repeal of the death and capital gains taxes. It favors acceptance by all states of meat and poultry that first pass the inspection of any state with an inspection regime equivalent to the federal. It opposes increases or indexation of the minimum wage. It opposes monopoly practices by rail companies. It encourages its members to write the Environmental Protection Agency in favor of new rules reflecting the Supreme Court's decision that inland wetlands that are not navigable are not subject to federal control. The American Farm Bureau Federation is a 501 (c) (6) organization—meaning that contributions to it are not deductible and that it could exist exclusively for the lobbying purposes of its members.

Chesapeake Bay Foundation

Founded in 1967, The Chesapeake Bay Foundation is a 501(c)(3) organization, meaning that donations to it are tax deductible and that there are some dollar limits to its lobbying. It has some 80,000 members. It is dedicated to restoring and maintaining the quality and clarity of water, the diversity of life in the ecosystem, and the productivity of the 68,000 square miles of watershed in the Chesapeake Bay area covering (through a multistate agreement) the states of Virginia, Maryland, and Pennsylvania.

The foundation was the idea of business individuals alarmed by the deterioration of the bay area resulting from nitrogen runoffs from farmland and urban areas and from the exhausts from power plants and vehicles. It promulgates public policy and takes legal action when necessary to stem pollution. It undertakes programs to restore the bay's habitat and filtering mechanisms, such as forests, wetlands, underwater grasses, and oysters, through hands-on projects. It also conducts programs to educate citizens about their responsibilities for protecting the bay and its environment.

The Association of Community Organizations for Reform Now

The Association of Community Organizations for Reform Now (ACORN) is the nation's largest community organization of low- and moderate-income families, with over 150,000 member families organized into 700 neighborhood chapters in 51 cities across the country, according to its brochure. Among its national issues is opposition to lending where lenders charge extremely high interest rates to high-risk persons. It also advocates for more affordable housing, better schools, affordable utilities for lower-income individuals, and a living wage. Its principal tool is mass movement, such as public demonstrations and even sit-ins in local political offices.

National Association of Investment Companies

Founded in the 1970s, The National Association of Investment Companies (NAIC) member firms represent more than $4 billion in capital under management and include leading private equity firms, small-business investment companies backed by the U.S. Small Business Administration, and investment companies that are chartered by state and local governments. These experienced investors seek to fund companies that offer cutting-edge products and services within fast-growing markets.

In addition to facilitating the investment activities of its members, NAIC advocates, educates, and builds human capital. The NAIC advocates in favor of public policies that its members favor. It provides members with up-to-date information on industry developments, and it sponsors investment-related networking and professional development events.

The Business Roundtable

The Business Roundtable (BRT) is the association of chief executive officers of leading U.S. corporations with a combined workforce of more than 10 million employees in the United States. The Roundtable is committed to advocating public policies that foster vigorous economic growth, a dynamic global economy, and a well-trained and productive U.S. workforce essential for future competitiveness. The Business Roundtable studies issues, prepares position papers, makes recommendations, and lobbies the Congress and the president to support their views. A major aspect of its lobbying efforts is through personal contacts and publications. BRT is financed through dues calibrated to the company's sales and stockholders equity. The portion of dues used for lobbying purposes cannot be deducted either as a business or a charitable expense.[8]

The membership of the BRT is about 150 CEOs who jointly form the board of directors of the organization. The organization sets up task forces to study each issue chosen by the board. The head of the task force is an executive with corresponding subject responsibilities in the company whose CEO is the head of the task force, and all task force members are executives with expertise relevant to issues assigned the task force.

Agency Theory and the Business Association

As agents of public policy, there are some characteristics of business associations that make them operationally different from other nonprofits as social capital assets in the public policy process. The purpose of this section is to highlight these characteristics.

Members as Beneficiaries and Principals

Most nonprofits are not membership groups. The principals of an association, unlike other nonprofits, are its members—not the public at large. Membership is voluntary. Therefore, it can be presumed that the decision to join reflects the expectations that the benefits derived from membership in the association are equal to or exceed their costs. The renewal of membership is a renewal of expectations that benefits (even a different package) would exceed their costs. Therefore, the contract of the business association is with its members and to serve their common interest and expectations over time. The carrying out of the memberships' interest involves affecting the formulation, implementation, and evaluation of public policy. In this respect, the association, including the business association, is an agent of public policy.

Common Interest and Cognitive Social Capital

Zarhoodi[9] finds that exposure to the same regulations prompts similarity in political behavior of firms. Social capital theory claims that common interest, experience, and objectives that draw people into an association (such as the business association) binds their interaction among each other and strengthens the coherence of their political and policy views. Section 501 (c) (6) actually requires a demonstration of a common interest. Thus, the common interest is the cause for forming an association both in law and social capital theory. It is also part of the "trust" in which transactions among members may be embedded. Zukin and DiMaggio[10] note that even informal structural associations define a degree of embeddedness that characterizes transactions. Business associations are formed by firms that are competitors, and among them asymmetric if not incorrect information can be an advantage. Therefore, trust is likely to be less a motivating force than a common external interest and the informality of interaction less consequential in business associations due to the threat of anti-trust collusion.

The Cost of Membership and the Compensation of the Agent

As stated, business associations are tax-exempt organizations under Section 501 (c) (6) of the IRC. This means that dues paid to the associations that are used for lobbying and political purposes are not deductible as business or charitable expenses. Therefore, there is no tax incentive for member firms to support either type of advocacy. The fact that these advocacy activities are invariably well financed by member firms is evidence of the value members place on them and the use of the association as an advocacy agent.

In principal-agent theory, therefore, the principals (the members) comprise the primary source of compensation to the agent (the association). Donations are not tax deductible and neither are dues paid for lobbying or politicking. A rationale for this within the paradigm is as follows: The service rendered members is essentially a quid pro quo—they pay the association to protect and advance their interest and the association performs to the satisfaction of the members. It is the members' interest that leads the motivation, not the public's.

But to be tax exempt, the association must also serve a public purpose even as it attends to its members' interest; for example, a college accreditation board serves its members but it serves the larger public in signaling that the college has met certain qualifications. Therefore, some of the revenues of associations, including business associations, are tax exempt. The association does not pay taxes on dues it receives or on other business income.[11] This exemption is the public's payment for its share of the service performed.

The Contract and the Ultimate Power of the Principals to Enforce Compliance by the Agent

To be tax exempt, the association must exist by virtue of a written commitment (a statement of its mission) in its charter to exclusively advance a common business interest of its members. This common business interest may be industry related or related to the general economic environment in which the business operates, but it cannot relate to a specific corporation or franchise.[12] This means that the principal-agent relationship is organic because the association cannot exist in its exempt form short of this commitment—to expressly serve the interest of its members.

This commitment or contractual promise, the mission, is binding and appears both in the charter of the association and in its tax-exempt approval letter.[13] Moreover, in every state, association members have the right to (a) dissolve the association, (b) sue the management, and (c) vote for a change in management—assuming that managers are not able to hide all negative information forever. Unlike other nonprofits or firms, associations are subject to the monitoring and discipline of its members; that is, the power of the principals over the agents is direct.

Further, the mission cannot be changed or amended without the approval of the membership, the board, a filing with the state, and a filing with the IRS. Furthermore, the contractual relationship between the association and its members is basically unilateral in the sense that it binds the association, not the individual members. A member can walk away without recourse for the liability of the association. The association's liability does not extend to the individual members.[14]

The Effect of Exemption on the Ability to Finance Membership Interests: Leverage

The association cannot pay dividends—meaning that there is no leakage of this type as there is with a firm. Exemption makes certain association revenues, particularly dues related to the mission, rental income, interest, dividends, royalties, capital gains, sales of publications, and convention and educational fees, related to the mission tax free,[15] thus providing a financial basis for operating the association on behalf of its members. While unrelated business income may be taxed, it too must be used exclusively for the purpose of advancing the member's interest. Thus, the effect of tax exemption and nonpayment of taxes is to leverage the dues the members pay and to provide the association with more funds to impact public policy than it would otherwise have had.

Why Business Associations Choose This Form of Exemption

But this financial incentive does not explain by itself why business associations seek their tax exemption under Section 501 (c) (6) rather than the more common 501 (c) (3) that covers charities and educational institutions. The reasons are these: (1) associations do not need to demonstrate broad public financial support and therefore they can concentrate on membership interests; (2) the association is not limited in its lobbying as are other tax-exempt organizations, thereby allowing some associations to do unlimited legislative advocacy; and (3) while political advocacy is prohibited to other nonprofits, the association can conduct this type of advocacy directly and extensively although it must do so through a separately funded affiliate called a political action committee or PAC. With 501 (c) (3)s all forms of political advocacy are prohibited and legislative advocacy is limited to approximately 20 percent of expenditures.[16]

In order to accomplish both legislative and political advocacy as described earlier, associations have a broadly common organizational structure to separate the two. A PAC must be separate from the remainder of the association. The financing of the PAC and its operating activities must be segregated and distinguishable from the remainder of the association's activities, including legislative advocacy.

A PAC is an efficient way to raise an enormous amount of funds almost limitlessly. It allows the association to separate its politics from all of its other functions and therefore it allows members to do the same. The PAC is a single-product organization: support or oppose a candidate or a process. Association members with strong political views can "put their money where their mouths are" through their contributions to the PAC. The PAC is also an efficient operation, since it need not be more than a check-writing operation. Finally, the PAC is tax-efficient. If the association spends on politics, it risks a tax either on the expenditures or on its net investment income. But funds raised and spent on politics by its PAC are not taxed. As agents of public policy, the singular and common contribution of PACs is their input in choosing who will be the policymakers on all levels of government, who will not; who will be the policy implementers appointed by the successful political candidates, and the loyalty and attention they get from policymakers seeking to curry their financial support.

A PAC, described under Section 527 of the IRC, may be required to give notice to the IRS of its existence, and of its termination unless it is exclusively for candidates at the state or local levels, registered with the Federal Election Commission, or has assets less than $25,000. It may also be required to make disclosures to the federal government and to the public of persons who received more than $200 from it and persons who gave $500 or more to it.

Federal election laws, specifically 2 U.S.C. Section 441 b (b) (2)(c), prohibit corporations from making contributions to federal elections. But corporations may make contributions to cover the expenses of establishing, maintaining, and seeking solicitations to a PAC. Coors Brewery was advised by the Federal Election Commission (Federal Election Commission Advisory Opinion # 1994–6) that twice a year it could match its employees', directors', and officers' contributions to the Coors PAC by offering to make a charitable contribution to match each person's contribution to the PAC. Thus, while a member firm itself may not make a contribution to the PAC, it can induce, support, match, and pay expenses for its directors, officers, and employees to make such contributions. It simply cannot do so on its own behalf.

Legislative Action Committee

No separate organizational structure is required for lobbying. The association may lobby through a variety of channels. A common channel is through a department and a committee variously called government affairs, legislative affairs, or public policy. These departments may also contract with outside lobbying firms to assist them. There is no need to separate lobbying or legislative advocacy in a formal way as there is to do political advocacy. But, as in the case of political advocacy, registration and reporting are required. Those that do legislative advocacy (even through a hired outside firm) may have to disclose such activities under the Lobbying Disclosure Act of 1995 as amended in 1998, and annually report such activities, including expenditures, on their 990 POL forms to the IRS.

The Association as an Agent for Charitable and Educational Activities

Most large business associations have a foundation. This foundation also has to be separate from the remainder of the association by which it is administered. This foundation is used to make charitable contributions to activities not hostile to the interest of the members. The educational foundation serves to provide classes and courses for members, to print and distribute educational material to them, and to provide educational material to the public, such as the sponsorship of a concert or radio or television program that cannot be construed as propaganda or advertisement.

The Policy Process, Principal-Agent Relationship, and the Corporate Interest

We move from describing the structure of the association and the motive of the association in its principal-agent relationship with its members to the process through which the association discharges its agency function or promises to advance the interest of these members—its principals.

Two Routes to Impacting Policy Formulation and Revision

As Reilly, Hull, and Allen[17] explain, federal law with respect to business associations defines politicking as the advocacy of political philosophy or a candidate. It distinguishes this from legislative advocacy—and lobbying, or the attempt to affect the drafting of a bill, its passage, or implementation. Lobbying may aim to influence the general public; for example, to motivate them to write or express an opinion with respect to a proposed legislation. This is called grassroots lobbying. Lobbyists may influence a bill by being involved in drafting, supporting, or opposing it, supporting or opposing its signing, drafting the rules that will implement the bill after it is signed, or influencing the actual implementation.

A second type of advocacy is called politicking. This involves propagating a political philosophy and supporting or opposing a party or candidate. Under federal law, a business association (as a labor union) may do unlimited lobbying; but it cannot do substantial politicking unless it creates a segregated fund commonly known as a political action committee or PAC.

Both legislative and political advocacy yield a public good—one that has significant effects that go beyond those who consume that good. In addition, the consumption of that good does not deprive others from enjoying its benefits. There is no way to exclude others from benefiting from it even if they don't pay. While an association does political and legislative advocacy on behalf of its members, the benefits spillover to nonmembers of the industry and often to the general public (some of whom may not look too kindly on what others think is a benefit).

Policy Formulation: The Legislative Process

To influence policy formulation, the association must be familiar with and intervene into the policy process. Epstein and O'Halloran[18] argue that the way policy is made and the amount of discretion given to an agency to make the rules and to implement the policy all take place within a principal-agent context marked by asymmetric information. For example, a committee of the legislature drafts bills and in doing so often collects more information than the full legislature that votes. An influence of the association, therefore, is to provide this information as it advantages its members throughout this process, recognizing and exploiting the amount of information available or attainable at each point during the legislative process.

Once passed, the policy goes to the executive branch for implementation. Epstein and O'Halloran argue that the amount of discretion the legislature will give the executive branch to write the rules and to implement them will be greater (a) the more the legislature and the executive branch agree in philosophy and approaches to the policy, (b) the more legislators agree among themselves, and (c) the higher the uncertainty and the potential problems of implementing the policy. In (c) the legislature recognizes that its transaction costs for implementing a problematic policy may be higher than the executive branches', since the legislature does not have the same technical resources. Thus, the association must also target its energies; and sometimes it is best targeted outside of the legislative branch.

Policy Formulation: The Political Process

The effect of the association as an agent of its member firms may be to buttress the lobbying activities that each firm does on its own. This is especially true of large firms in the political process of affecting policy. Studies[19] (prior to the campaign reform act) have found that firm size and contracts with the government are consistent explanatory variables about the amount of political activities in which the firm invests. Studies have also found that this individual firm involvement is related to the degree to which the firm is in a concentrated industry. Zarhoodi[20] found that firms in concentrated industries are less likely to make contributions unless they are affected by government regulations.

More directly, Weidenbaum[21] a long-time observer, notes that firms have three ways of responding to the political or policy environment. They can choose (a) passive reaction to government policy initiatives, (b) positive anticipation of such initiatives, which could of course mean taking actions to avoid their impact, or (c) public policy shaping.

Yoffe[22] notes that some corporations may choose to be free riders because as Olson[23] noted, the product of lobbying and politicking is a collective good available to all members and even (at times such as the repeal of the death tax) to nonmembers. The corporation may choose to go it alone. Or, according to Yoffe, the firm may choose to be a "follower" and join forces with others. The business association is composed mostly of this latter group of businesses and business leaders that join together and follow a common strategy—at least within the association.

The business association may be viewed as a group strategy that responds to three agency problems identified by Lord.[24] These three agency problems are: (a) the difficulty that constituents have in monitoring their agent—the congressperson or elected official; (b) the difficult that constituents have, other than voting, to enforce their views; and (c) the difficulty the agent, congressional person, or elected official has in knowing the collective views of the principals. The association responds effectively to all three of these agency problems on the part of its members.

While the above deals with legislative issues, similar options are available to the firm on political issues. Alpin and Hegarty[25] and later Getz[26] identify various corporate strategies in the political arena. One of these is to finance PACs. Another is for the firm to provide information, and a third is to build constituents. This chapter will reflect all three of these strategies. Lord[27] finds that the effectiveness of corporate political activity is derived from the desire of legislators to serve the most politically active constituency.

Levitt finds that the PAC in turn has two ways of influencing a politician; that is, through his or her role-call votes on a bill and through affecting his or her winning an election. The latter has an effect as long as the politician is in office.[28] Alpine and Hegarty[29] concluded that the power of a group to manipulate a focal person is directly proportional to its power base and influence method. They also concluded that societal interest groups gain much of their power because of their fiduciary relationship with a broader cross-section of society. Translated, the broader the business association the greater its agency influence.

An Illustrative Case: The National Beer Wholesalers Association

Here is the case of the NBWA, founded in 1938, with the facts being drawn from its website as of late 2003 and early 2004. It is used to illustrate concepts of network, the range of policies that a business nonprofit may undertake even though they are not ones that the casual observer may think of as relevant, and the way at least one organization is organized to serve its members. One would think, for example, a beer association will be concerned only with spirits. But this is not the case. The principal-agent relationship of NBWA with its members is to provide leadership that enhances the independent beer wholesale industry; to advocate before government and the public; to encourage the responsible consumption of beer; and to provide and promote programs and services that will benefit its members.

The Organization's Political Base: The Number, Distribution of Principals, and Their Interests

The NBWA political base is made up of the 2,200 beer wholesalers who are members or principals located in virtually every congressional district. Its base extends beyond members, their families, and employees and their families, to the large number of retailers including grocery stores, bars, restaurants, and the consumers they serve and to the original producers of beer, since the wholesalers move the products from them (reducing their costs and increasing their immediate cash flow) to the various outlets.

The Core Messages: Shared Values as Cognitive Social Capital

All of NBWA's political and legislative advocacy activities are in conjunction with what NBWA refers to as "three core messages." One is the message that the beer industry promotes responsible consumption of its products and is making a difference by doing so. A second is that these family-owned businesses contribute more than beer to society. They also contribute jobs and taxes and make charitable contributions. The third core message is that moderate and responsible beer consumption could be healthy.

Members of NBWA are expected to comply with its association code. The first tenet in that code says that members will not market, promote, or condone activities or images that display irresponsible or illegal beer consumption. The second, that wholesalers should not market to or use in advocacy images, symbols, languages, locations, or music that would encourage beer drinking by the underaged. Third, members should not promote beer in a manner that advocates irresponsible behavior including ads that are sexual or anti-environmental, or display drunkenness or lack of awareness. Fourth, beer should not be promoted in a deceptive or misleading way, such as indicating that its consumption is needed for professional, social, sexual, or athletic success; and the qualities of the product or specific brands should not be exaggerated. Fifth, all advertisements should be in good taste—no lewd images and indecent language.

Political Advocacy

For accounting, reporting, as well as tax purposes, political advocacy by NBWA is conducted through a segregated fund that is separately financed by member firms, and their contributions to this fund are not tax deductible.

Tax laws require separate accounting and reporting and do not provide for tax deductibility of contributions. Accordingly, the political activities of NBWA conducted through its political action committee meet these conditions. Except for savings and investment, all PAC expenditures by law must be used for political purposes. The NBWA PAC (which is its name) receives contributions only from its member firms and it supports candidates and parties that favor member interests, and opposes those who threaten these interests.

Legislative Advocacy

The government or legislative affairs (or public policy) department may prepare Congressional testimony to be presented by a member or officer of the organization. It also responds to questions from various government agencies, Congress, and the White House. It tracks bills every step of the way, from their formation to their drafting, from their introduction to the debate and to their final markup in Congress, the vote in each house, the conference resolution of the two houses, and the signing by the president. It follows a similar route in state and local levels. It also responds to agency requests for comments on how the new laws will be implemented. It tracks and monitors feedback from members on problems in the implementation of old and new policies. Government affairs departments keep in close contact with federal, state, and local agencies.

The NBWA government affairs department uses two tools to assist the NBWA in legislative advocacy. It publishes a biweekly newsletter on legislative developments that informs members, solicits membership response, and invites their participation in lobbying activities. NBWA also participates in a legislative conference that brings members of the U.S. Congress, their staffs, and members of the beer industry to discuss legislative initiatives and issues of public policy of concern to the NBWA and its members. This three- to four-day conference, held annually in Washington, D.C., brings together members of the U.S. Congress and their staffs with member firms.

Example NBWA Legislative Issues

NBWA has favored capital gains and estate tax reduction or elimination (tax issues of broad economic interests) because its members are affected by these taxes in the transfer of ownership of their businesses at the time of death or through the sale of the business during their lifetime. Most beer distributors are small, family firms. Similarly, although federal long-haul driving regulations affect all drivers engaged in such activities, the specific interest of NBWA drivers is that they be exempt because most of them do not drive beyond 100 miles. But by being required to conform, member firms potentially suffer driver shortages and additional driver training costs.

The Five Core Competencies: The Source of Power of Business Associations

How are the five core competencies of a nonprofit as an agent of public policy manifested in the case of the nonprofit business association?

1. *Cognitive Social Capital:* A large group of individuals with a common purpose and motivated by common identifiable self-interest and their willingness to individually and collectively invest both money and energy in advancing that interest because they all are potentially equal beneficiaries either of each policy advocated or in the mix of policies. Thus, a member's harm by one policy supported by the organization may be more than compensated by the members' benefits from other policies for which the association lobbies.
2. *Goodwill:* An established and efficient channel of communication that allows members to reveal their preferences, to submit comments that help form a policy position, and that can be used to motivate members into action. Elected officials and policy administrators can also use this channel to communicate with members.
3. *Trust Derived from the Bounded Nature of the Mission:* The clarity and continuity of the association's mission and the organizational ability to (a) identify issues of broad or common interests, (b) support or oppose candidates sympathetic to those issues, (c) influence how or if legislation is written, (d) influence whether legislation is passed, (e) influence content and procedures of agency rules for policy implementation, (f) monitor implementation, (g) offer amendments to legislation and to agency rules and regulations after implementation, and (h) repeat this cycle over and over again.
4. *Leverage:* The ability to use tax-exempt dollars, and add their dues, fees, or special assessment to enhance any contract they may receive and perform within the organization's context.
5. *Trust Derived from the Contractual Nature of the Mission:* The confidence that those who contact or contract with the organization have that the association represents and speaks to the audience they wish to address or hear from; and that the association represents and is accountable to that audience in manners described in chapter 3.

Social Capital, Rent-Seeking Behavior, Competition, and the Number of Business Associations

In chapter 3 we argued that the greater the number of nonprofit agents of policy, the better. But that is not what the concurrence of the literature is with respect to business associations.

Bischoff[30] finds that public interest groups such as business associations grow with economic growth—at least in OECD countries. The question is whether the greater the number of public interest groups, such as business associations, the better off society. Social capital theory (described in chapter 3) implies that the greater the number of these associations the greater the social capital because the greater the "belonging," involvement in a common value, the ease of social control, communication, and cohesion. But Diamond[31] argues that the greater the number of competing associations, the greater the chances for legislative deadlock.

Public choice theory argues that lobbying, a primary activity of business associations, is often rent seeking at a social welfare cost because rent seeking is the attempt to seek private gains for one set of firms at the expense of others, or the remainder of society. An example is lobbying for tariffs that keep out lower-cost goods for the benefit of protecting the market share of domestic producers. Thus, all things considered, the greater the number of associations the greater the social cost of rent seeking.

To Becker,[32] pressure groups such as business associations are competitors among themselves for political benefits. Becker argues that a pressure group seeks to equalize its subsidies (benefits) with the cost of such subsidies (taxes). There are at least two limits to how far the group is willing to go. First, there is an internal limit because its members begin to have to pay more for the benefits. Second, the public reacts negatively as its costs in the form of taxes increase. If, however, the association of gainers could compensate the association of losers for their losses, then gainers would proceed until policies they favored were implemented. But the true cost of a policy is, as suggested by public choice theory (see chapter 2), not just the cost of the policy that is passed but the cost of those policies used in the bargain to "buy" passage.

But Ando[33] finds that while there is substantial competitiveness in the select category of interest groups she studied, there is no empirical evidence that increases in the expenditures by one side leads to increased expenditures by the other.

Summary and Preview

At the same time that a nonprofit is an agent of public policy it is also an agent to its members, responsible in part to promoting their interests in the public policy process. Further, while some nonprofits are implementers of public policy, as are housing and community development agencies and hospitals, other nonprofits help to formulate and evaluate policies. In this role, shared values and perspectives of members facilitate cohesion and collective action even when members are competitors. The strength of the association is based upon its composite of networks that are always shifting, emphasizing the importance of the sociology of network formation, especially in the mathematical sense that traces loci of concentration and activity.

The association has multiple roles in the policy process, but its nature in the formulation of policy and in its representation are the subjects of this chapter. The discussion is guided not only by the principal-agent paradigm but by empirical and game theoretical findings of scholars in political and lobbying behavior of organizations. Having recited the basic ingredients of the principal-agent paradigm as it might apply to these associations, some specific associations such as the National Beer Wholesalers Association were used to demonstrate the applicability of the principles. The chapter terminated with a discussion as to why and when member firms may choose a nonprofit association over a for-profit firm in some instances—paralleling the earlier question: Why would the government choose an equally competent nonprofit over a firm?

The next two chapters carry us along a different course. One of the problems inherent in any principal-agent paradigm is how the principal controls the agent so that the agent (in spite of the issue of moral hazard addressed in chapter 4) does what the agent wants. In chapter 2 we saw how the government does it when the nonprofit is under contract, and in chapter 4 we saw how it does it when the nonprofit is not under contract, and in chapter 5 we saw that it may reduce the risk by not hiring the nonprofit to do anything. Another way is to control the agent's ability to finance itself to do anything whether or not under contract. That is the subject of the next chapter.

Part IV

Problems of Regulating the Nonprofit Agent and the Foreseeable Challenges of Management

The relationship between a nonprofit and its public is governed not only by specific contracts, but by public regulations to keep the agent (in this case, the nonprofit) in check. As contracts are imperfect, so are regulations porous; but regulations circumscribe behavior beyond specific contracts. In many spheres, especially in markets where information depends upon constantly changing expert information, and where decisions must be timely, self-regulation is an alternative to government action. It is also potentially cheaper and more democratic. In capital markets, the public depends heavily on self-regulation by nonprofit organizations over firms and persons motivated by profits. The self-regulators help to keep the actuation of this motivation in bounds acceptable to public confidence and enable public participation. How does the government regulate the nonprofit on behalf of the public where the organization acts on a similar motive—raising money? Money drives firms as well as nonprofits; for without it, the latter is but a shell of promises made to the public that most certainly will not be fulfilled. But how does the regulator regulate without stifling the possibilities of fulfillment?

Chapter 9

Regulating the Finances of the Agent

In a principal-agent relationship the principal monitors and evaluates the agents. One of the ways in which the public exercises these oversight functions over the nonprofit as an agent of public policy is to control critical aspects of its financing. This is done partly by requiring that the nonprofit demonstrate a high level of public financial support. The theory here is that the lack of public financial support may be an indicator of lack of public interest or perceived value of what the organization is doing.

In one test of public support for 501 (c) (3) organizations, the organization must demonstrate that at least one third of its total financial support comes to it from the public—meaning donations from corporations, individuals, foundations, and the government. In another test this amount can be lowered to 10 percent if the organization can show that it has public involvement in its activities and governing body or in the use of its facilities.[1]

In addition to these requirements, the federal and state governments and watchdog agencies commonly use a metric known as the fundraising expense ratio to determine if the 501 (c) (3) organization is abusing its tax-exempt privileges or deceiving the public in solicitation campaigns. What is the public interest in this ratio? Is there a moral hazard associated with this ratio and its use? What are some of the dilemmas resulting from the application of these ratios to control agent behavior? These are the issues this chapter faces.

The Fundraising Ratio and Its Various Uses

Krishman, Yetman, and Yetman[2] studied 100,000 organizations nationally and 719 in the state of California and found that these organizations tend to overstate their yield ratio and understate their expense ratio. Why? As Tinkelman[3] argues, donors are impressed with high-yield ratios and the higher the yield ratio the more they give. This suggests a moral hazard: Nonprofits using their control of contractual and accounting information to give them ratios that are viewed favorably by the public or to resist divulging the very low yield of their fundraising campaigns. One reason this occurs that is particularly of public interest is because of the large amounts of what is collected that is paid by the organization to the fundraisers themselves (particularly private firms) and also that may be used for other "administrative" expenses.

The fundraising ratio is not only a signal to the public and government agencies as described above; the ratio is also the principal indicator of fundraising efficiency (Kotler and Andreasen,[4] Bryce,[5] Dove,[6] Greenfield[7]). Tuckman and Chang[8] (1998) find that the ratio varies by mission across the nonprofit sector. Moreover, Barber, Roberts, and Visvanathan[9] find that the ratio varies with the type of donor the organization is targeting. It is higher when the organization targets donors who need a lot of information.

Using data from Form 990, the organization's annual report to the IRS, the fundraising ratio is calculated by dividing an organization's current year's fundraising expense by its current year's revenue from fundraising. Froelich, Knoeple, and Pollak[10] find that the fundraising ratios otherwise reported by organizations are reliable when compared with IRS data. The fundraising expense ratio is used as an ethical standard and these standards may vary among the different groups[11] that set them. The reciprocal of the expense ratio is the rate of return on an organization's investment in fundraising. The higher the ratio of fundraising revenues to expenses, the higher the yield. What is the basis of the public policy interest in the fundraising expense ratio?

Bases for Public Policy Interest in Fundraising Ratios

Organizations receiving federal income tax exemption are also exempt from income, sales, and property taxes and some fees at the state and local levels in accordance with their laws. Furthermore, under Section 170 of the IRC and corresponding state and local codes, donations to these organizations are deductible. Thus, from a public finance perspective, a public interest arises because of the tax expenditures (tax revenues foregone at all levels) due to tax deductions and exemptions. Tax exemption is costly to the public treasury.

Public interest also arises because the primary reason for giving an exemption and a deduction is because the purposes of these organizations are the advancement of public welfare and the relieving of the burden of government to solely provide or finance certain services or products, the absence of which increases social problems and costs to society.[12] Hence, there is a public interest in the percentage of tax-subsidized fundraising that is not used by tax-exempt organizations to directly carry out their agency functions but, instead, are diverted to fundraisers or management in the form of compensation.

Another basis for public policy interest in fundraising expense ratios is private gains. All of the assets of tax-exempt organizations under Section 501 (c) (3) of the IRC are to be used to advance public welfare—not private gains (or personal benefits). Therefore, a use of these assets that produces disproportionate shares of fundraising revenues for for-profit fundraisers implies a use for private gains, as the IRS implied in a recent case in which the IRS revoked the tax exemption retroactively 15 years on charges of inurement (benefit) because the organization got only one-fourth of what the fundraiser collected.[13] Moreover, it may also imply that the principal motive or consequence of the fundraising was this private gain.

A 2003 Supreme Court case illustrates the concern in an elongated way. In Federal *Election Commission v. Beaumont, et al.*[14] North Carolina Right to Life, a nonprofit advocacy group, sued the Federal Election Commission, arguing that the ban on corporate political contribution is an infringement on its free speech. The law, they argued, should not apply to nonprofits operating as public agents—not for private benefits. This is especially so, they argue, because nonprofits with limited resources do not have enough money to make a difference in a campaign. Moreover, they argued, they were not making a contribution to the campaign, they were merely spending money to express their freedom of speech, protected by the First Amendment.

The court rejected that argument and said the history of court cases and the history of Congressional actions on the law do not support this argument in favor of an exemption for nonprofits. The law, according to the court, was intended to prohibit corporations (nonprofits are corporations) from developing slush funds to corrupt the political process, to undermine campaign reform, to give corporations undue political influence, and to prohibit the use of funds raised in ways and for purposes not intended by donors or shareholders, who may even be in disagreement with the purpose or cause for which the funds are used by the corporation. Accordingly, the prohibition against the use of donated funds for political purposes by nonprofit organizations stands.

Public interest is also aimed at reducing fraud and misrepresentation, in encouraging giving and participation in the voluntary sector, and in the exercise of First Amendment rights of freedom of expression and association. To achieve this balance, states have charitable solicitation laws that cover registration, licensing, disclosure, acknowledgement, receipts, recordkeeping, and accounting. At the same time, the single most used reason for court decisions on the fundraising ratio relates to this public policy interest; namely, the preservation of the right of free speech and association, the financing by nonprofit organizations in this connection, and the avoidance of fraud perpetrated on donors. In particular, donors should not be led to believe that their funds would be used to finance the production of the organization when they are being disproportionately used to cover the administrative costs of the organization or contractual costs of fundraisers. But how is disproportion measured?

A recent U.S. Supreme Court case, *Illinois Ex Rel. Madigan, Attorney General of Illinois v. Telemarketing Associates, Inc. et al.,*[15] illustrates the point. VietNow, a Vietnam veterans nonprofit group, hired Telemarketing Associates to solicit on its behalf. They signed a contract giving 85 percent of the fees to the telemarketers and 15 percent to the Vietnam veterans group. In soliciting, Telemarketing represented that a significant part of the funds raised would be going to the organization for specifically identified purposes. The Attorney General of Illinois filed suit indicating that that advertising was knowingly deceptive and false. The U.S. Supreme Court noted that previous decisions stated that barring fees above a prescribed level was a restraint on free speech, but that this case did not involve such a "prophylactic proscription of high-fee charitable solicitation." The issue in this case, the court concluded, was fraud, and decided that states (19 had joined Illinois) do have the right to take action when fundraisers seek to mislead donors.

Steinberg[16] has developed an argument as to the limits of this concern for high fundraising ratios. He begins by quoting Chief Justice Rehnquist in Schaumberg that there is no necessary connection between the percentage of fundraising revenues retained by fundraisers and a fraudulent solicitation (a low fundraising ratio is not a deterrent to fraud) and that some causes may have high fundraising costs and yet be preferred by some donors just as high-priced goods are.

Steinberg adds that donor interests such as the social benefits from a ball may exceed the charitable purpose, therefore, paying more than the charity retains for charitable purposes is not fraudulent. The donor knowingly obtains benefits in excess of the percentage of the donation used purely for charity. A high fundraising ratio may result from fixed fundraising costs (such as space and equipment); consequently, he argues, what should matter to the donor is the additional value that his or her contribution brings.

Rose-Ackerman[17] argues that this ratio could serve as a barrier to entry to certain industries in the nonprofit sector—securing those that can meet the target and barring those that cannot. As a consequence the ratio contributes to less competitive markets.

The Supreme Court of the United States has consistently ruled against state laws that place numerical limits on fundraising ratios.[18] Specifically, in Munson and in Schaumburg,[19] the Court, while acknowledging the merits of its intent, declared a 25 percent expense ratio as too broad a restriction on speech and association because it did not distinguish between organizations with truly high fundraising costs from others. But in the specific case of *United Cancer Council v. Commissioner,* 1999, the IRS declared the fundraiser's expense ratio excessive.[20]

Some state attorneys general (e.g., from California, New York, Connecticut, and Washington, among others) annually publish the expense ratios of telemarketing fundraisers based on the past year's operation of those firms in the specific state, and almost all states offer guidance in charitable giving and refer potential donors to ethical guides by the Council of Better Business Bureau (CBB) of a 35 percent limit on fundraising expense ratios.[21]

Aside from these legal purposes, sometimes the fundraising ratio is used as a means of accountability. Ebrahim[22] correctly notes that accountability is complicated by the fact that the nonprofit is both a principal and an agent—indeed at any one time it may be conducting multi-agency functions resulting in conflict or compromise—and that these vary from nonprofit to nonprofit organizations and Chisolm[23] and Lowery[24] are correct also in noting that nonprofits are not subject to the type of market forces that may impose discipline or accountability on firms and they also are not subject to the electoral pressures that may cause accountability in government. Consequently, most of the accountability of nonprofits results from the imposition of state and federal laws, but the imposition of these laws may be counterproductive. Bogart[25] finds that major theories give conflicting views on accountability. In this vein, is the fundraising ratio set as a standard of accountability unambiguous in its consequences?

With this background, this chapter extends the line of inquiry by looking at fundraising as practiced by nonprofit organizations. They set fundraising targets such as in capital or annual campaigns and then try to meet those targets at the lowest fundraising ratio (least cost) possible. Why is this analysis important? First, because fundraising is an essential part of demonstrating public support consistent with the underlying theory that the nonprofit is an agent of the public. At the same time, a ratio set as a standard may limit the amount of fundraising an organization can do to meet its true needs to finance its mission objectives as an agent of public policy when such objectives are not completely or even partially supported by contracts. The following section looks at one aspect of this inherent conflict and its consequences.

Unintended Consequences of Ratios as Standards

This section will demonstrate how a ratio set as a standard, even if only a voluntary ethical standard as opposed to a mandatory legal one, could lead to unintended consequences that go beyond the organization's ability to satisfy its financial needs from fundraising. One consequence is the possibility of "excessive" fundraising while in compliance with the standard. This is the kind of ethical lapse with which the American Red Cross was charged due to its fundraising in response to the September 11, 2001, tragedy.

Depicting a Fundraising Expense Cycle

To understand the impact of the fundraising ratio norms set by state and private agencies on managerial decisions, we must understand the fundraising expense cycle of these organizations. Every organization has a different profile and every one at a given time may be at a different point. Let us focus on the shape of the fundraising ratio curve in figure 9.1. This curve is intended to depict one frame in a fundraising expense cycle. We shall shortly explain why the curve rises, reaches a peak, and falls to a minimum and why this process repeats itself over and over again although the peaks and the valleys of this cycle will differ as the organization benefits from the experiences and expenditures from the previous cycle. This cycle is like a wave, so we can relegate our analysis to one portion because after it starts to rise again we would merely be repeating the results demonstrated. Why may a fundraising expense curve take this form?

Every fundraising campaign has an initial gearing-up period, starting at zero in the extreme case. During this stage I period, the fundraising expense ratio in figure 9.1 is likely to rise faster than revenues as the focus is on designing, planning, staffing, creating, and evaluating lists—all activities preparatory to the actual campaign. This gearing-up stage has costs that may include acquisition of space and equipment, the costs of mailing, advertising, entertaining, travel, mailing-list creation, and donor assessment, and other costs aimed at increasing contact and cultivation of donors. This rising cost peaks where the unit cost of funds raised is highest, and the yield (being its reciprocal) is lowest.

But if the initial costs are so high, why would the yield be so high, that is, 0.75 in figure 9.1? Because often campaigns are launched only after larger donors are committed and approximately a third of the campaign goal is reasonably assured and booked. For some organizations, especially the young and less well-known and connected ones, the expense ratio could be extremely high at the outset. Indeed, they could begin well above one, indicating initial losses.

The organization may spend on fundraising as long as that expenditure yields a net gain. To spend \$100,000 to get \$110,000 is a 10 percent rate of return. To spend \$100,000 to get \$1,000 is a 1 percent rate of return—just about what the organization gains in 2004 in a savings account. Therefore, the investment in fundraising makes sense as long as the expense ratio is less than one, indicating that the revenue from fundraising exceeds the cost of raising it. When the expense ratio is equal to one the organization is breaking even and is unlikely to go beyond that point since it would be receiving less than it spent unless it is capable of making the sizeable investment or have sizeable gains in revenues that would bring it back down the curve.

The reader might at this point consider the following—all of which will come into play:

1. Fundraising is properly classified as an investment because expenditures on it are undertaken to produce returns in contributions and donations at a future date. Those revenues from fundraising are not guaranteed; fundraising has often failed to meet its target.
2. Nonprofit organizations work with limited budgets, and the investment in fundraising must be compared with the benefits that would come from other expenditures—such as the requirement that the organization expend on its mission promises or invest the same sum in a risk-free and effortless investment such as short-term U.S. obligations.
3. To carry on fundraising until the yield is so low is analogous to trying to maximize revenues. This is good in theory, but Oken and Weisbrod[26] find no evidence that nonprofits are revenue maximizes from

fundraising. The reader is alerted to a discussion below about the cost of excess fundraising. In short, unlike a firm, the organization is not motivated by maximizing revenues; rather it is motivated by getting what it needs to meet its target and its commitment as an agent to the public. Put another way, the demand for the service of a nonprofit is not limitless. Therefore the nonprofit's need for capital during any period has a calculable limit.

4. A high expense ratio is analogous to high price/earnings ratio (P/E) on a stock. It implies high risk-taking and is likely to detract the more conservative or skeptical investors—donors. High expense ratios are not attractive to many potential donors just as high P/E ratios are not because investors see the firms with such ratios as speculative, overvalued.
5. The managers of the organization must contend with the fact that if the ratio well exceeds what is considered reasonable by the local attorney general or the public (as described in a Canadian case at the end of this chapter) this could cause negative public reaction and a decline in donations.

Given these, there is a strong built-in bias against operating at high expense ratios even absent an ethical standard. There is a strong incentive to reduce the fundraising expense ratio and hasten on to stage II—bringing the ratio down.

In stage II increases in revenues from the campaign begin to exceed increases in these costs so that the fundraising ratio begins to decline. On the revenue side, the speed and continuation of decline in the fundraising ratio will depend in part on the number of donors contributing large sums at a given time, but it will also depend on a continuity of contributions or else the decline would occur only in periods when the large contributions are received. Thus, a continuing decline requires a continuous fundraising effort—mostly of variable costs in the form of keeping contact, generating more contact, and the costs of receiving, recording, and responding to donors. This is consistent with the year-round fundraising done by organizations. But stage II and thereafter may also necessitate larger and larger expenditures by the nonprofit to reach a larger and perhaps less responsive or less accessible audience.

Stage III represents a flattening or bottoming out of the curve where the fundraising ratio is again low and the fundraising yield is correspondingly high. Fixed costs would have been spread, marginal costs can be stabilized, and donor response may be high. This is where every organization would ultimately want to be—making lots of money from fundraising at the lowest expense ratio possible below or no greater than the ethical standard. But organizations do not simply begin there; they must operate even at less advantageous points. They cannot simply close down because they do not have the optimal financing—neither can firms. However, if the organization

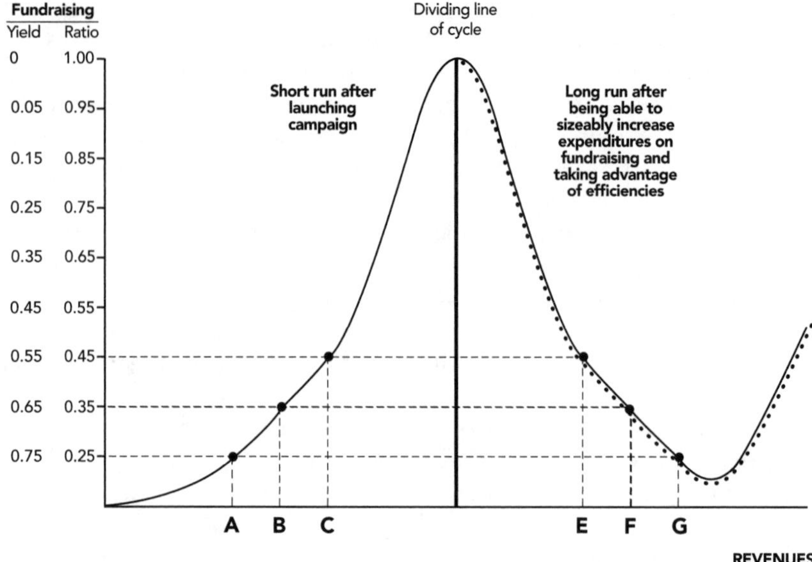

Figure 9.1 Fundraising cycle

increases its efforts to harvest an even less responsive or inaccessible new donor pool and goes beyond this minimum point, the additional cost of fundraising could rise faster, causing the fundraising ratio to again begin to slope upward.

Setting the Fundraising Target

Every organization with a fundraising operation sets a specific numerical target or range of how much it aims to raise at the end of a year, a campaign, or some other period. This goal-setting is part of stage I. Through very disciplined planning this specific amount or range is based on the organization's estimate of its total financial needs to meet its mission objectives for that period (build a building, give so many scholarships, feed so many people).

But every nonprofit organization has only three specific sources from which it may obtain capital to meet these needs. By standard accounting, operating, and tax procedures, these sources are earnings from (a) business activities, which are divided into earnings from related business, such as fees it may charge for its services to its clients, and earnings from unrelated business activities, which include profits from activities unrelated to the fulfillment of its mission; (b) earnings from investment activities such as dividends and capital gains; and (c) gifts and donations it receives.

Knowing the amount it must fundraise to meet these needs is simple arithmetic. It is the amount needed to meet the targeted need minus the amounts expected from related and unrelated business plus the amount expected from earnings from its investments portfolio including dividends and capital gains. The difference between the target and this sum of (a) and (b) above is the amount the organization must receive in the form of donations and contributions if it is to meet its target. This procedure is common real-world practice.

For convenience, we have chosen to call this calculated need the organization's "true fundraising need." This is the specific goal based on overall financial need and objective that an organization (National Public Radio, United Way, universities and colleges) announces at the beginning of fundraising campaigns or cycles as its fundraising goal or target. It is a specific number, calculated based on needs, which organizations, especially large ones with budgetary processes, do as a matter of common practice.

Independent Determination of Target, Standard, Costs, and Fundraising Cycle

An organization's fundraising expense ratio lines are really the least cost of fundraising by the organization over a range of possible targets and times. Therefore, for any target, there is a minimum cost to meet it. This cost is determined by such factors as the nature of the mission and the efficiency of the fundraising operation. On the other hand, the fundraising target or true need is determined by how much the organization needs to raise from fundraising (as explained above) to finance its mission objective for that period. External forces set the standard without taking into account either the fundraising efficiency of the organization or its specific needs. In what follows, we shall see the static and dynamic consequences of the collision of these three forces.

Social Capital, Goodwill, and Fundraising Efficiency

The fundraising efficiency of a nonprofit is more than its technical skills. It is part of those elements that make up its goodwill (name recognition, public responsiveness to its mission, its mailing list and reach to the wealthy and generous, its communication channels, the trust it has earned). It is also related to its social capital (its attachment to affiliates, the closeness of bonds, and the commitment of its members plus their own personal wealth or capital, the size of its network, and the density of its relationship). These factors have been discussed in all of the previous chapters.

The Three Key Concepts

The three key concepts in the following demonstrations are these: (1) Fundraising expenditures are investment expenditures—the organization undertakes them in anticipation of donations and contributions that exceed the expenditures, therefore it will proceed with such an investment as long as the returns exceed the cost as indicated by an expense ratio less than one. (2) The organization calculates its needs from fundraising based upon the money it needs to meet its mission objectives minus the amount it will get from all other sources in order to meet that financial need. It does not backward plan. It does not say: This is the amount we raised; therefore, this is what we need. We shall see by reference to the American Red Cross the consequence of backward planning when it becomes visible and public. (3) The ethical standard ratio is set as an independent standard that covers all organizations and is a best average judgment. All of these assumptions represent what happens in the real world everyday.

Dilemmas of Controlling Fundraising through a Fundraising Ratio

Let us try to simulate a real problem of an organization operating in the long run when it has the most favorable opportunity to adjust to any ratio set as a standard—specifically, it can start on one side of the curve and move to the other. It is flexible, it can learn, it can grow.

Case I

If the organization has an operating fundraising ratio 0.25 it can easily meet a fundraising target of A without violating the standard. But, why wouldn't it not move up to the standard of 0.35 where the amount it could raise would be B, which is greater than A? Indeed, if the organization's production function for fundraising is one that economists refer to as linear homogeneous—meaning that its collection of funds is proportionate to its fundraising expenses so that, for example, doubling fundraising expenditures means doubling the amount received—then, the fundraising ratio will remain constant—in this case at 0.25 and this organization could raise as much as G, which is even greater than A or B without violating the standard. What inhibits the organization from going that far if its target is only A?

First, fundraising is an investment. Thus, there is a cost for going after more funds and an uncertainty about the outcome. The fact that a nonprofit knows that it has a ratio of 0.25 does not mean certainty that once it starts its fundraising the public will respond as quickly or as positively as it expects, which would in the interim cause its ratio to rise even, probably, above the standard. Second, there is public scrutiny (including scrutiny from the IRS) on excess accumulation of funds and public scrutiny on the opulent use of funds, including excess compensation. Whether either of these things matters depends upon the organization and the facts and circumstances. Clearly, universities are allowed to accumulate large endowments (although some endowments, such as those at Harvard and Princeton, have caused some concern and have led the schools to voluntarily be more charitable to less wealthy students). Social and health service organizations are not looked at so kindly. Their accumulation is looked at as a failure to do their duty.

Case II

In Case II the organization has a fundraising ratio of 0.45, which is higher than the standard. Even if the standard were an average or the median or the mode, by definition some organizations would exceed it as long as there is some variation in the population of organizations, as in reality there are. Therefore every standard that is set by definition imposes a disadvantage on some organizations—those that fall above it. Let us investigate such a case.

At 0.45 the organization cannot meet any budgetary needs it has from fundraising unless the need is B or below. But at 0.45 the organization still finds such an investment worthy because for every $100 the organization spends to raise funds, it receives $54—a gain. Since the organization is already violating the rule, if its production function is also one of constant returns, it is tempted to raise as much as E. While it faces the same constraints as in Case I, the moral suasion of the standard is diminished, since no matter what the organization does it will violate it.

In Case II, the organization has the following options: (a) abide by the standard and not meet its needs from fundraising, (b) violate the standard and meet just its needs, or (c) violate the standard and exceed its needs since it is in violation anyway.

Case III

In Case III, the organization is just at the standard 0.35. This is okay as long as B is equal to the amount it targets to raise from fundraising. If it is, the organization may well operate at that level even though its production function for fundraising is marked by constant returns to scale, which means that it could probably go to F and raise substantially more funds. Why would the organization not want to do this?

Excess Fundraising: Public Reactions and Organizational Strategies

In the cases above, there is the possibility of the organization collecting more than its target need. Presumably, most organizations try to raise as much as they can from fundraising and any unexpected excess can be incorporated into the mission without a problem. This is not always so true or so simple. To begin with, this assumes that organizations seek to maximize their revenues from fundraising. But Oken and Weisbrod found no evidence of this. Rather in every day practice, organizations in their fiscal and strategic planning set targets (as described earlier) and try to meet them. Those targets are invariably announced publicly and results are also announced or at least available in the organization's annual filing. Therefore, there are at least five reasons why organizations that are visible are careful of excess fundraising.

1. There might be public rebuke. That is what the American Red Cross experienced after September 11, 2001,and after the 1989 earthquake in San Francisco. This chapter closes with a similar public outcry about a group in Canada.
2. There is the social cost of diverging funds from other organizations, some responding to the same social needs. Among those who sounded the early warning against the American Red Cross were other organizations reacting to the calamity that felt that the American Red Cross was unethical or diverting funds from other organizations.
3. There is the promotion of secondary spending within the organization. The American Red Cross's choice of using the excess to update its computer system, and its ability to respond, was unacceptable to donors even though the changes were needed and not illegal. The chief executive officer was let go for having made that decision.
4. Excess fundraising increases the risk level of fraudulent behavior.[27] Auditors are taught to see excess cash as a red flag, and its continuity without justification or offsetting expenditures will prompt local investigations. Some believe that this is the result of recent federal legislation; to some extent it is, but this power has long resided with local attorneys general—and some of them have used it.
5. While one may argue that excess cash allows the organization to expand the range or depth of its permissible activities, this is not the case if funds were given for specific and restricted purposes. This was the basis of the claim against the American Red Cross, and previously against an order of priests in Maryland, and led to the case *Secretary of State of Maryland v. Joseph H. Munson Co. Inc.*

While the examples drawn are identifiable with the events of September 11, one should note that this was not the first or second time that the American Red Cross ran into this problem. The case is just convenient for illustration.

A Variety of Managerial Responses

A standard is useful only if managers care. The evidence is that managers are sensitive to how the ethical ratio may affect their fundraising. An organization can qualify for The Better Business Bureau's Alliance for Wise Giving seal of approval (for which it pays a fee of $1,000 to $15,000) if no more than 35 percent of all its expenses go to fundraising. This label helps in fundraising. Okten and Weisbrod found no evidence that nonprofits seek to maximize revenues from fundraising.[28] Presumably, this is so even among those who could.

Hall,[29] Hall,[30] Greenfield,[31] and Levi[32] give anecdotal evidence that fundraising is influenced by public perception of fundraising costs, and Weisbrod and Dominguez[33] provide empirical evidence that fundraising expense as a proxy for information dissemination has a positive correlation with donations and therefore on managerial decisions. Okten and Weisbrod[34] find that fundraising expenditure increases donation probably because it implies more information and advertising to potential donors (the information effect). At the same time they find that high expense ratios correlate with low donations because a high expense ratio is interpreted by a potential donor as a high price for the output of the nonprofit organization (the price effect). These imply that managers care about the way standards affect public perception.

Finally, one managerial option is outsourcing of fundraising. Contracting out allows the organization to minimize its direct investment in fundraising (office space, personnel, equipment)—much of which would be borne by the contractor. Thus, the risk that the flow of donations would be insufficient to cover investment costs is substantially shifted to the contractor, who is paid on a performance basis (for example, 80 percent of the amount the contractor collected). The effect is to increase the need for vigilance over contractor abuse, and malfeasance between management and contractor—collusion between two agents of the public at the latter's expense.

The Sensitivity of Organizations to a Standard

How do managers adjust when initially operating at a higher ratio than the standard? Without empirical evidence, we can describe several possibilities that are consistent with the reaction of managers to the imposition of a standard.

To do this, let us borrow from Okten and Weisbrod's finding that donations respond to two effects. One is the price effect and the other is the information effect. The price effect discourages donations by suggesting to donors that too large a percentage of their contributions is being diverted to managers and fundraisers and away from programs. Thus, other things equal, the higher the expense ratio the less incentive people have to give. The second, the information effect, encourages people to give by reaching more people with the kind of information that induces them to give. Thus, when an organization tries to reduce its expense ratio by reducing its expenses, it is likely to reduce the number of people adequately informed about the organization's needs. The final results on the organization's fund raising will depend upon which effect is stronger—the price or the information effect.

Let us compare these three scenarios.

1. Where the two effects are equal.
2. Where the information effect is greater than the price effect.
3. Where the price effect is greater than the information effect.

These scenarios were developed graphically by the author in an unpublished paper[35] using the Cobweb Theorem with the information effect having an upward slope and the price effect a downward one.

Scenario 1. Where the Effects Are Equal

Suppose the decline in fundraising expenditures reduces the information benefits at the same rate as it increases the price (cost) reduction benefits. This means that the amount of donations lost because of the lack of information will be offset by the amount of donations gained because donors are impressed by the lower ratio. But the results are not that simple in a real-world fundraising cycle.

The fundraising ratio to which people are reacting in this year's solicitation is the fundraising ratio that is published and based on the past. So, a reduction of fundraising expenses will bring about an immediate reduction in the benefits from information. There is no immediate price benefit because this year's actual ratio that is targeted to be smaller to meet the norm will not be known to donors until next year. In fact last year's high ratio will at least continue to discourage the same number or amounts of donations as it did before.

Suppose the organization was meeting its needs at any higher ratio. This combined effect, last year's expense ratio, and this year's reduction in information, will cause an immediate drop in donations below the level where the organization met its needs.

Seeing this drop below needs, a manager must choose whether to conform or meet the organization's need even at a higher ratio as it did before trying to adjust downward. But if the information effect is equal to the price effect every additional expenditure would lead to no net gain in donations because one effect offsets the other. A manager suspecting this outcome may have no incentive to try to meet the standard.

The organizations that best fit Scenario 1 are those with established and narrow missions and narrow solicitation markets. Information in such a market tends to be redundant to the same pool of people—an equal number of whom or amount may be added as turned off. In this category are also organizations that feel that they are doing as well as they can—satisfying their needs and getting a fair return on their investments in fundraising.[36]

For these Scenario 1 organizations there may be no strong incentive to take the risk of voluntarily reducing their fundraising expense ratio. Why, they may ask, experiment if the outcome is not likely to be materially better?

Scenario 2: Where the Benefits of Information Are Greater Than from Cost Reduction

Let us now suppose that the benefits from information are substantially greater than the benefits from reducing the price. There are a number of organizations, such as health-related organizations, that can disseminate information that have greater value to the receiver than the donations the receiver will make.

When the organization cuts expenses, the benefits from the spread of information will be cut substantially more than the benefits from price reduction. The initial impact is a decline in donations due to the reduced information, but also because consumers will be using the higher expense ratio of the past and they will be no less discouraged than they were before. Consequently, there is no immediate encouragement of net new donations based on the lower cost.

Hence, as before, the manager may try to increase expenditures on fundraising so as to at least meet the organization's needs. But this time the information effect is substantially greater so that the additional expenditure on fundraising produces more donations due to the information than reduces them due to the higher cost effect.

A manager recognizing this is likely to conclude that as long as the expenditures on fundraising do not exceed the cost of raising these funds, spending more will increase funds raised even to excesses. But, this temptation is limited by the costs of excesses discussed earlier.

Scenario 3: Where the Benefits from Cost Reduction Exceed the Benefits from Information

For some nonprofits, those dealing with the poor, donors may be more repulsed by the high price (cost) of fundraising than they are attracted by more information. Local organizations have a limited pool of potential donors; therefore, the benefits from more information contacts is likely to be less than from the benefit due to reduction in price or cost of solicitation.

Hence, when the organization reduces fundraising expenses the initial response is very much as before. The information effect produces a drop in donations, but because donors are responding to last year's numbers the drop is not immediately offset by the improved expense. The organization is now below the amount it needs. When it tries to adjust back it may do extremely well. This is so because its benefits on the upswing come from both the additional information, but more so, because donors are attracted to the improvement in expense ratio and may give more.

But this result comes in the future, not necessarily in the current year when expenses are lowered. Whether this organization will be able to hold at the standard is another matter. But, for the reasons given, it has the least risk from trying because any corrective increase in expenditures would probably generate a better response than it would in either of the preceding two scenarios.

Toward a Typology: Balancing Information and Cost and Ranking by Probable Levels of Noncompliance to Fundraising Ratios Set as Standards

The preceding discussions lead to the following typology:

1. Organizations where the information effect exceeds the price effect are the least likely to voluntarily follow a standard. This is so because the more they increase their expenditures, the more donations they receive because potential donors are less influenced by the expense, price, or cost factor than by the benefits of information—its content, quality, and frequency. These organizations can be successful even with high fundraising ratios.
2. Organizations where the price effect exceeds the information effect are the most likely to be influenced by the standard because potential donors to these organizations are more influenced by the expense than by the information so that the decline in donations due to the latter is more than compensated for by the rise due to the former.
3. Organizations where the information and the price effects are equal would be neutral at best because increases in donations due to the price effect are offset by decreases due to the information effect.
4. In organizations where the cohesion described in social capital theory is strong, trust is strong, and cooperation toward a collective action is strong, the fact that there is a public standard that is voluntary may have little influence on that organization's willingness or ability to raise funds among its own members (churches, lodge, and alumni associations) or among members of the public depending upon the strength of the organization's goodwill.

Admittedly, research and theory can go beyond this simplified approach of action-reaction. Some consideration of the time lag between the two and the path that different organizations may choose once confronted with the realization that their fundraising ratio does not conform to the standard may be of some future research interest.

Toward Improvements in Measurement and Accountability

No standard is perfect and watchdog agencies have explored various ways of making the standard better. Perhaps more procedural methods such as greater disclosure,[37] better internal oversight,[38] and improved reporting,[39] including the movement toward social accounting by nonprofits may be effective[40] with less distortion even as watchdog agencies continue as they now do to recognize the need to go beyond numbers. Both public choice theory and the theories of first, second, and third best choices discussed in chapter 4 remind us that public policy may introduce its own distortion. It is therefore necessary to continually discuss probable improvement in these ratios.

Because the fundraising ratio varies by mission-type as observed by Tuckman and Chang in the opening of this chapter, some distortions in the fundraising ratio could be removed by calculating a benchmark fundraising ratio for each mission type. But I believe a significant improvement could occur by calculating the ratio for each organization as a four-year moving average. This would help to smooth some of the distortions due to learning and startup as described in this chapter. It would also smooth the effects of unusual events affecting either costs or revenues from fundraising and the mismatch that occurs when expense is incurred and the recognition of revenues it generates.

Under current accounting practices[41] there could be a considerable lag between expense occurrence and when the revenues they generate can be recognized. Under required practices, revenues cannot be recognized until all material uncertainty of their being received and controlled by the nonprofit organization are removed. Thus, an expenditure to get a donor to pledge a million dollars two years from now is recorded as an expenditure but the revenues are recorded when it (not just a promise) is unconditionally received. There is a natural lag in the fundraising process since it takes time to cultivate donors and, in particular, most large donors. The use of a four-year period makes sense since it correlates with the four-year period the IRS uses for the public support test for 501 (c)(3)s, the very organizations to which standards apply.

Greater Disclosure and a Narrowing of Asymmetric Information

Greater disclosure has several advantages: First, it narrows the range of asymmetric information. Second, it gives donors discretion and choices where in some cases, either for the reasons given earlier in this chapter or for reasons of costs impediments, the fundraising ratio is high. Third, as the book has argued earlier, the existence of asymmetric information has given rise to countervailing organizations such as Guidestar and the National Charities Information Board and the Better Business Bureau that provide donors with information about the organizations to which they wish to give. Fourth, both in the United States (as described in *Illinois vs. Telemarketing Associates*) and in Canada (as described below), failure to disclose accurately places the organization and the contractor at risk.

A decision (2001) of the Ontario Superior Court of Justice in the *AIDS Society for Children (Ontario),* 105 A.C.W.S. (3rd) 1044, reflects a public interest when the arrangement is likely to be contrary to public policy. The case concerns the group hiring a fundraising firm to raise funds to build a hospice for children suffering form HIV/AIDS. The arrangement ended up with an 80/20 split between the fundraiser and the nonprofit organization, with the latter getting the smaller portion. As a result, there was a public appeal to the government that went to court on behalf of the public.

The court decided that the AIDS Society for Children, a nonprofit, has a fiduciary responsibility to the public from which it raised money. The society and its trustees also have the responsibility to be sure that those funds are used for the charitable purposes for which they were intended and to disclose how the funds were used, including fundraising costs. The fundraising company, according to the court, using language of the principal-agent paradigm discussed in this book, was an agent of the AIDS Society for Children and the latter was the principal in this principal-agent relationship.

Since the company is an agent of the nonprofit, the latter cannot relinquish the obligation to inform the public about the use of its donations and to make sure that the money is used for the charitable purposes for which it was intended. Therefore, while the court concluded that it could not rule on the prudence of the 80/20 split, it could rule that the failure to disclose the split was a misrepresentation and contrary to public policy, as in *Illinois vs. Telemarketing,* referred to earlier.

Before closing this discussion and moving on to a discussion of self-regulation in the next chapter, we should note that there is a persuasive argument about the need for third-party regulation in the non-profit sector. Fleishman[42] argues that public trust is the single most important asset that nonprofits have. Therefore, having a strong independent third party, such as an independent federal agency, to monitor, impose regulations, and disseminate information about individual nonprofits would build and sustain public trust and confidence in them; and, by implication, donations and participation in the sector would grow. Put within the context of the principal-agent paradigm, there would be more confidence in the agency functions of the nonprofit.

Summary and Preview

In this chapter recognition was given to the fact that principals monitor their agents and that a principal may limit the powers of its agent to act on its behalf. One way to monitor and limit the agent is by monitoring and limiting its financing or its compensation. This chapter reviewed the judicial history of government concerns over fundraising by nonprofits and the attempts to limit fundraising practices to be consistent with public policy interests by setting a minimum standard by which fundraising revenues should exceed fundraising costs. The chapter culminates in a discussion of the utility of these standards in restraining abusive solicitations of organizations of various types and the potential utility of greater public disclosure in restraining this abuse.

With this chapter, the reader of this book will have gone from (a) discussing the various forms of public policy functions nonprofits perform, to (b) placing this performance within a principal-agent paradigm, to (c) using that paradigm to uncover and to expand on critical insights based on concepts of other disciplines in addition to economics, to (d) illustrating these applications in real-world practices in areas such as health care and housing and community development, to (e) seeing how the nonprofit influences the formulation of policy in the business sector, and, finally, to (f) seeing how the public sector tries to control the financing of the nonprofit as its agent. The next chapter shifts the discussion from the nonprofit being the regulated to being the regulator—not of large markets as in chapter 2, but of its members, be they individuals or other nonprofits, such as in a federation. The United Way is an example of a federation. The chapter begins where the book started—with markets—and then raises the questions, can this model be extended and what would it take?

Chapter 10

The Nonprofit as a Self-Regulator

In previous chapters, particularly in the second, we discussed the nonprofit as a regulator over market transactions and gave some examples. The purpose of this chapter is to demonstrate in some detail what a nonprofit self-regulator does. Self-regulation is not a matter of writing and posting ethical codes. It is a matter of exercising the legislative powers of writing rules, the policing powers of law enforcement, and the judicial powers of making judgments that are terminally costly to others and the custodial powers of influence and public confidence. Nowhere are these simultaneous powers more invested in nonprofits than in the capital markets such as the New York Stock Exchange and the Chicago Board of Trades.

But as the OECD study referred to in chapter 2 notes, the trend to what it calls distributive governance—where governance extends to quasi-governmental bodies—is growing and therefore it is of interest to this theme: the nonprofit as social capital and an agent of public policy. In this role, the nonprofit is being used instead of government to keep check over its members, who supposedly play an important role in the welfare of the public. As chapter 2 indicates, self-regulatory bodies vary in their power and method of influence. In education there are nonprofits that do accreditation and certification—methods of screening and signaling in an asymmetric model. But there are also professional baseball, football, and basketball leagues associations—all nonprofit associations. They, too, are self-regulators with the power to set rules, to judge when those rules are broken, to penalize, to enforce penalties, and to arbitrate. The Ganeen Bank experience described in chapter 4 is also based on a self-regulatory format.

The self-regulating organization has a multiple agency. It is an agent for its members, but it is also an agent for the public. Clearly, this can result in conflict. A self-regulatory body, however, needs public confidence and the confidence of the government that it will do what is right for the public even if that conflicts with some other membership interests. Thus, when it was demonstrated that the National Association of Securities Dealers (NASD) had a serious conflict in its ownership of the Nasdaq that might have contributed to the public being duped by some of its members, it sold it to concentrate on its regulatory powers even though there was no evidence that the organization itself was culpable.

From a principal-agent perspective, the principal focus is whether the agent has the capacity and the incentive to carry out the public's good even when the self-interest of its members or itself may be threatened. What does it take for an organization to be the ultimate self-regulator? This chapter goes through a description of the NASD and then it itemizes ten cognitive social capital characteristics that the author hypothesizes enable a nonprofit organization to be a successful self-regulator—to govern its members on behalf of the public.

The Public Policy Purpose of Self-Regulation

This regulatory function is performed on behalf of the public because misbehavior reverberates with deep consequences and costs to the public and from which the public cannot protect itself partly because of asymmetric information. The information the public has is less than adequate or timely and as in Coase's Theorem, referred to in chapter 2, the negative effects and costs are more than the individual parties can settle among themselves. Furthermore, in these situations, individual members acting voluntarily among themselves would not necessarily produce the best solutions for themselves or for the public.

Students of public policy would recognize the Prisoner's Dilemma as such a situation. Here confronted with a problem and unaware of what the counterparties will do, one selects a strategy that leads to less than the best results for the two or the public. Diekmann and Lindenberg[1] also discuss other such dilemmas including their own, a volunteer dilemma, one in which faced with a common problem, one person acts while the others stand by only to benefit freely of that action. Voluntary action even among individuals who share a common interest may not lead to the best results for the group.

The essential point of all of this is to say that there are large-scale transactions where there is asymmetric information (in substance and timeliness) not only on the part of the public but on the part of the government, where the moral hazard of persons acting in their own self-interest can produce high and widespread social costs. In the securities market, where timeliness is of essence, the slow pace of government will not do. Recognizing this, countries throughout the world have created self-regulatory systems often outside of the government bureaucracy. Accordingly, this chapter is about the National Association of Securities Dealers (NASD), a self-regulatory organization with significant control over the format of securities transactions in the United States. But the chapter also features principles that have application to (a) a broader array of nonprofit organizations, and (b) a single nonprofit with a larger membership base.

Self-Regulatory Organizations (SROs) and the Market as a Common Pool Resource

The self-regulatory organizations to be described below can be seen as agents of control over a common-pool resource of general public interest.

Recall from chapter 2 that a common-pool resource is one in which there is (a) limited or imperfect excludability, and (b) there is "subtractability"—meaning that the more the resource is consumed the less it may be available to others over time due to the diminishing of the resource or at any specific time due to congestion. The common resource to be described in this chapter is the public market for transactions in securities—stocks, bonds, and their derivatives. This market is capable of being congested, and the market and its agents can be overloaded. One of the roles of the agent is to manage this congestion and queuing process in general given that each stock exchange is its own self-regulatory organization by law.

Unlike the typical common-pool resource, the public market for transactions in securities is replete with assets that are privately owned—the stocks and bonds issued and traded. As Ostrom[2] has argued, common pool resource management is consistent with collective ownership of the common-pool property or with individual ownership. Ownership comes with rights (a) to access, (b) to transfer (called the rights of alienation), (c) to withdraw, (d) to manage, and (e) to exclude, as per Ostrom and Schagler described by Ostrom.[3] Individuals have these rights with respect to the securities, but not with respect to the market or transactions. Further, as Ostrom[4] argues, some common-pool resources are owned by no one—thus providing for relatively easy access. The public market for transactions in securities is of this type. No one owns the market (a network of transactions) although individual securities and institutions engaged in various aspects of the market may be individually owned. But access to the market is generally open to all who wish to buy and sell.

In terms of the earlier chapters, what makes a market work is trust based upon (a) a convergence of complementary interests—a transaction to buy must be complemented by a transaction to sell; (b) a known set of performance expectations of and by each party in the paradigm—boundaries of expectations in the mission of each; (c) a dependency as in the network theory of exchange—the function of the network is not only to make others know what each has to offer but to make buyers and sellers meet each other and provide both with an organized format in which to conduct their transactions; (d) a recognition that the scope of the network allows for greater efficiency—each part is interested in improving its position by increasing the network form which it buys and sells; (e) a recognition of the utility of having transactions that are subject to asymmetric information managed by a third party—in this case the self regulator of licensing, advertising, and sanctioning or screening and signaling the public and other players about who is authorized to be in the game; (f) the expected reciprocity of treatment as sides change in the transaction process (today's buyer is tomorrow's seller); and (g) conformance to the same set of rules about how transactions within the principal-agent paradigm or the organized market format will be conducted and the known risk of not being allowed to play if one does not comply. The market self-regulator is a structural social capital asset and agent performing a public policy function central to the operation of any capital market and therefore of any market economy.

Three Examples of Self-Regulatory Organizations (SROs)

By virtue of federal law[5] all firms and their associated persons doing securities business with the public in the United States are members of the National Association of Securities Dealers. The NASD registers member firms, writes rules to govern their behavior, examines them for compliance, and disciplines those that fail to comply. It also provides education to industry professionals and investors and operates the world's largest securities arbitration and mediation programs. There are over 5,200 broker firms, and over 650,000 individual securities representatives who are members of NASD. As of 2004, the NASD had over 2,000 employees.

But, as stated earlier, the NASD is not the world's only self-regulatory body of its type—although it is notable in its scope and size. The Swedish Security Dealers Association was founded in 1908. It is a membership organization of all banks and institutions practicing on the Swedish Stock Exchange. Its express purpose is to further the common interest of these institutions in the trading of equities, bonds, futures options, and derivatives. It develops and enforces rules concerning the exchange of securities, but it has less than 50 members.

The Trinidad and Tobago Securities Exchange Commission (Act 32, 1995, Part 3) sets up rules by which the commission may certify self-regulating organizations. This act bars any person from running a business as a security exchange or clearing agency or as an association of securities companies unless that person (or organization) is registered as a self-regulatory organization under the act. It further holds that to be a self-regulatory organization, that person or entity must engage in the securities business, be an independent corporation with its own charter and seal and must have the power to sue and be sued, be incorporated in any "state" but registered in Trinidad and Tobago, and have a body of rules for the admission and governance of its members.

Hence, while this book focuses on the NASD, SROs are not unique to developed countries or Western countries, or countries with a long market-driven tradition. SROs are also found in former nonmarket countries.

The International Network of Self-Regulatory Organizations in Financial Markets

The International Organization of Securities Commissions is an organization totaling 172 members (including affiliates and associates) of securities commissions and security-related nongovernmental organizations, such as the World Bank, throughout the world, including developed and developing nations such as the United States and Barbados and market-driven as well as formerly nonmarket countries such as Albania and Belgium.

The International Organization of Securities Commission describes the self-regulated organization as a voluntary organization authorized by law to regulate securities markets.[6] These SROs, as they are called, do not write legislation; instead, they write rules through which they enforce and re-enforce the regulations of government agencies. They have monopoly powers in the sense that people or entities wishing to carry out specific securities business must be members of that organization by the laws of each country. This means that such persons are subject not only to the government agency's (usually called a securities and/or exchange commission) regulation but the rules of the SROs, which are "voluntary," nongovernmental organizations comprised solely of the people and entities doing securities business in that country. The International Organization of Securities Commissions is a bridge across countries both for the government agencies that are members and the SROs that are also members; and it provides a forum for multilateral exchange of information and learning. The network is global.

The Advantages of Self-Regulatory Organizations

Empirically, Milhaupt [7] and Kim and Kim[8] have shown the effectiveness of these nonprofit organizations in Korea, Taiwan, and Japan. The International Organization of Securities Committees studied self-regulatory organizations throughout the world and concluded that they are advantageous because[9]:

1. The financial industry is complex and the SROs have an in-depth knowledge of the markets, the players, and the regulations and reduce the need for replication of this expertise in government.
2. The motivation of members to make self-regulation work is strong because it improves the environment in which they operate and make profits.
3. The contractual relationship between the SRO and the people it regulates gives it a global network.
4. Transparency and accountability are no less in an SRO than in a government entity, which may be subject to the same types of pressures. Moreover, it is to the self-interest of the members of the SRO to be known as regulated.
5. SROs are more flexible in their rulemaking than governmental agencies and legislative bodies.

6. With the globalization of markets, communication, and information sharing, standardization is enabled by SROs.

In short, the existence of these organizations and their networks facilitate global financial transactions.

Kumar[10] while generally in agreement with these, points to the possibilities of conflict of interest in self-regulatory organizations, particularly deriving from what we may describe as the buddy system and from the temptation to put what is best for business above what is best for consumers—including the protection of some members. In short, he notes the moral hazard in chapter 4.

Noting that the SROs are associations with the first responsibilities to their members, DeMarzo, Fishman, and Hagerty[11] model this moral hazard of an SRO choosing an enforcement contract that may be more favorable to its members than to the customer. The incentive is to choose a common policy to which all of the members are subject but that is lax compared to a contract designed by the customer. In this case, an alternative group of suppliers may be formed that is more consumer friendly. This alternative, however, is nullified by the rules that require membership in one common organization. What this implies is that where this moral hazard problem exists, the free market solution of growing competitive regulators is unavailable. If that is the case, what are protective remedies? We shall make some suggestions after the following example.

The National Association of Securities Dealers as an Example of the Extensive Regulatory Reach of an SRO

The Securities and Exchange Acts of 1933 and 1934 (especially Section 15A) recognize and provide the legislative foundations for the operations of self-regulatory organizations in the United States. These are all national securities exchanges, registered security clearing agencies, and registered securities associations.

This paper focuses on one, a registered securities association called the National Association of Securities Dealers, or NASD, notable in its size and the scope of its regulatory reach. All securities brokerage, clearance agencies, and their representatives and their associated persons must belong to NASD in order to be in the securities business in the United States. The following is derived from an interpretation of the organization's manual.[12]

The Basic Laws

As other SROs, the NASD is certified, registered, and regulated by the Securities Exchange Commission (SEC) as a self-regulatory body. Its mission is to carry out the following basic laws, for which the SEC is the overseeing government agency:

1. The Securities Exchange Act of 1933, which governs rules of communication, information dissemination, and content of securities.
2. The Securities Exchange Act of 1934, which governs a wide range of marketing, registering, and behavioral activities, including the role of self-regulatory organizations
3. The Investment Company Act of 1940, which governs investment advisors, such as mutual funds.
4. Regulation T, which governs the credit that brokerage houses extend to their credits—margin accounts. Unlike the previous three, Regulation T is a Federal Reserve Bank regulation—not an SEC regulation.

When the NASD is enforcing these laws, it is not deemed to be a legal agent of the SEC or to have governmental powers, but rather as a private entity under the imprimatur and oversight of the SEC. In 1975 Congress passed a law indicating that SROs have no governmentally derived powers, but act under the imprimatur of the SEC.[13]

NASD as a Regulatory Organization

The NASD is a Delaware membership-based, nonstock, nonprofit corporation incorporated in 1936 by industry leaders influenced by the market collapse during the Depression. It has the following missions:

1. To promote through cooperative effort the investment banking and securities business, to standardize its principles and practices, to promote therein high standards of commercial honor, and to encourage and promote the observance of federal and state securities laws by and among association members;
2. To provide a medium through which its membership may be enabled to confer, consult, and cooperate with governmental and other agencies in the solution of problems affecting investors, the public, and the investment banking and securities business;
3. To adopt, administer, and enforce rules of fair practice and rules to prevent fraudulent and manipulative acts and practices, and in general to promote just and equitable principles of trade for the protection of investors;
4. To promote self-discipline among members and to investigate and adjust grievances between the public and members and between members;
5. To register with the Securities and Exchange Commission as a national securities association pursuant to Section 15A of the Securities Exchange Act of 1934, as amended, and to establish and provide a medium for effectuating the purposes of said Section; and

6. To transact business and to purchase, hold, own, lease, mortgage, sell, and convey any and all property, real and personal, necessary, convenient, or useful for the purposes of the NASD.

The members of the NASD have no voting rights except those normally accorded nonprofit corporations in the state of Delaware, and these include the right to vote on by-law changes and for the board of directors. Voting for directors is determined on a plurality of members present at the annual meeting or represented through proxy. The governors serve up to three years and two consecutive terms. Members comment but do not vote on rules.

The NASD is a parent company of three separate but wholly owned subsidiaries. One deals with regulations, one with markets, and one with arbitration. These are the three major functions of the association. The association names the directors of the subsidiaries, initiates and coordinates action by the subsidiaries, administers certain shared functions such as technology, and ensures that the subsidiaries act in furtherance of the association's purposes.

To appreciate the regulatory reach of the NASD and the internal structure required to exercise these functions is the purpose of the next sections.

The Regulatory Subsidiary and Its Functions

The regulatory subsidiary develops and administers its own budget and procedures and has its own management staff (including directors). It has the following functions:

1. To establish and interpret rules and regulations and to determine to whom and how they will be applied,
2. To establish rules concerning the public or private sale of securities, financial responsibility, membership requirements, the settlement of securities transactions—such as an order to buy or to sell—and advertising practices,
3. To do all investigative and surveillance work to ensure compliance with NASD rules, to determine if such rules are disobeyed and to determine and apply appropriate penalties, and to determine through education and examinations whether a person meets the qualification of membership without which the person cannot engage in the public sale of securities, and to investigate complaints against members and take appropriate actions, and
4. To interface with Congress and others with respect to the above functions.

The Marketplace Subsidiary

In 2000, the NASD sold the Nasdaq but it continues its regulatory market functions. The market subsidiary has the following functions:

1. To operate an automatic system for the support of the Nasdaq and other stock markets,
2. To provide a telecommunications system that links buyers' and sellers' orders, provides quotations, transaction reports, and comparisons,
3. To develop, adopt, and disseminate rules governing over-the-counter and other market trading procedures and listing requirements and delisting procedures, to set requirements for participation in these markets, and to set market procedures for the efficiency of securities transactions on these markets,
4. To represent the NASD before the Congress and others with respect to these functions.

The Dispute Resolution Subsidiary

The Dispute Resolution Subsidiary has the following functions:

1. To provide rules and regulations concerning disputes involving members,
2. To advise as to the necessity of rule changes concerning resolution of disputes between members, among members, customers, and associated persons members,
3. To conduct arbitration, mediation, and other dispute resolution programs,
4. To assess fees,
5. To represent the NASD before the Congress and public on the above matters.

NASD Rules

To carry out its regulatory function under the basic four laws alluded to above and through the structure just described, the NASD has its own rules. These rules, however, are generally subject to review and approval or rejection by the SEC, but are not subject to voting by NASD members.

The NASD has rules of conduct, rules of markets, and rules of procedures. The rules of conduct refer to rules concerning (a) the filing of misleading information as to membership or registration, (b) failure to register personnel, (c) restrictions on the purchase and sale of initial equity public offerings, (d) the trading ahead of customer limit order, (e) market confirmations, (f) fair dealing with customers, (g) mark-up policy, (h) "breakpoint" sale—the lower commission paid as the customer buys a larger volume, (i) manipulative and deceptive quotations, (j) firmness of quotations, (k) failure to act under provisions of code of arbitration procedure, (l) refusal to abide by rulings of the committee.

Under the market rules (a) issuers of securities are required to inform NASD prior to issuing certain information to the public so that NASD may determine if trading in the security should be halted, (b) issuers must disclose to the public information contained in NASD staff determination about the issuer or its trading practices, (c) NASD reserves the right to close its markets when there are unusual price movements—especially if other markets are closing, (d) the independence of directors is verified by assuring that over the past three years they or a close relative or associate had no relationship with the business that would compromise their independence as directors, (e) the eligibility for being listed or de-listed on the Nasdaq is established, (f) terms of settlement and reporting of confirmations and transactions, including how to calculate price and quantity, are established, and (h) the procedures for making buy or sell orders of prohibited communications are established.

The procedural rules include: (a) making the NASD manual available to consumers, (b) providing information to the NASD as requested and required, (c) keeping records of trades in a prescribed way (such as dates of trade, office and agent carrying out the transaction, price, and security symbols) and (d) establishing procedures for investigations, hearings and selection of hearing officers, rules of evidence, rights of parties, decisions, settlements and review procedures, penalties including suspension, reinstatement, and cancellation of membership and public disclosure of disciplinary decisions.

Extending the SRO Model to Public-Private Partnership in Nonstatutory Regulatory Spheres

Shifting some of the burden of regulating certain market functions from the government to the nonprofit organization that is an association of the participants in that market has several advantages. First, it shifts some portion of the cost of disseminating, explaining, and enforcing regulations to the beneficiaries themselves, who pay the dues that support the organization's regulatory function.

Second, the gain is not only financial, it is also, in terms of management, of a less sizeable bureaucracy for such purposes within the government. In 2004, the NASD employed approximately 2,000 persons.

Third, there is the potential for greater efficiency since the regulated and the regulators are much the same in familiarity with the nature of the transactions and those nuances not easily observable by outsiders or for which the outsider may not carry the same level of credibility or interest. For example, disputes among members may hardly concern the public, yet they may eventually create precedents that affect the public by affecting all members. Thus, a dispute of this type may be more urgent to members and the association than it would be to a government agent or public interest group.

Fourth, in a broader civil society and sociopolitical sense, these organizations represent a "privatization" of government functions with the associative benefits of "self-governance" and a reduction of the intrusion of government in private transactions—an elaboration of democracy.

When an association is given a statutory status as a self-regulatory body and when it has monopoly power in the sense that one has to be a member to carry out a line of business, the key source of its power to regulate the behavior of its members is obvious—the power of law. The questions arise: What are the conditions that may enable an association to have its members voluntarily submit to its regulatory dictates absent such statutory blessings? How does an association earn such status without the benefit of legal compulsion?

In the financial industry, for example, states recognize financial advisors such as certified financial advisors (CFA), certified life underwriter (CLU), chartered financial consultant (ChFC), and chartered financial planner (CFP), and may require them to register as financial advisors, pay certain fees, and be recertified periodically. But these organizations do not have the self-regulatory statutory powers of the NASD. The same thing is true in law and real estate and other professions; although less true of some state medical boards.

Yet, it is to the advantage of these associations and their members to induce legislators to "trust" their ability to police their members in lieu of the heavy weight of the government's hands. We specify association rather than any other type of NGO. As Bryce[14] writes, associations are distinctly different. Not only do they have members, but their responsibility is to advance public interest through the advancement of membership common interests. What are the factors that may empower such associations (short of the statutory imprimatur) to exercise such powers over their members? The focus here is not on listing all internal and external capacities, not on finance, but on certain organizational capacities as they may relate specifically to the function of self-regulation—the regulation of their members. A theoretical framework for the list will then follow.

This author posits the following for consideration:

1. A contractual relationship between the members as principals and the association as their agent is needed. This contractual relationship expresses the specific types of functions the association promises to carry out on behalf of its members, in return for which they provide financial support to the association; for example, in the form of dues. This "contract" need be more than an understanding of the purpose of the association, its bylaws, and the conditions of membership. Clearly, an ethical code is not good enough, for it is merely an unenforceable promise to perform in a specific, unenforceable way. What is required is a formal acknowledgement by each member that he or she will abide by the rules and decisions of the organization. See the discussions of expectations in chapters 4–7. This is important because in these organizations rules and regulations facilitate the implementation and effectiveness of public law.

2. The members of the association must make up a significant part of the market for the products or services they represent. "Significant" may be in the form of market share, or total number of participants—sufficiently so that their behavior in the marketplace is determinative of outcomes, public expectations, and the behavior of others in the business. Here, the trick is to avoid inferences of collusive behavior. Does the association really act as a cartel? One of the reasons for seeking legal protection is that a self-regulating organization can easily run afoul of antitrust laws.
3. The activity must encompass transactions that are important to the function of members. It must matter to them and to the industry as well as to the public at large. The force of the association and its regulations are diminished to the extent that they can be avoided.
4. The association must have the ability to assign penalties and to exclude nonmembers from some rights that would enable them to operate as well as members can. Thus, the organization's membership adds value. Also, by attracting new members the scope and effectiveness of the network provided by the organization is expanded—adding to the incentive for members to comply rather than be expelled from the organization, thereby losing all of these advantages and values.[15]
5. The association must be publicly recognized as authoritative, as representative of its membership and as having some power over its members. This public recognition can come from history, confidence from evidence of performance and of the consequences of its sanctions, governmental endorsements (e.g., the American Red Cross)—that is, from measures other than by legislation. This is important because to the extent that customers or potential customers know these facts about the association, the fear that it will act upon a member may moderate that member's performance with the public. This is the principle of the Better Business Bureau or of being disbarred or defrocked.
6. The association must have some facility to communicate among its members—partly to serve them notice, to give them guidance, to make them aware of trends, to seek their input, and to communicate their decisions, including punitive ones. This is tricky business because unless properly structured, the organization could be sued for injury. This is not unusual, except that the organization would not have the umbrella of immunity that a government agency might.
7. The association must have some assurance of perpetuity. The members, the public, and those with whom the members interact must have some "assurance" that the association will be around, enabling it to enforce its sanctions and increasing the potential to eventually uncover future and past wrongdoing.
8. There must be a commonality of interest best served through an association of common-kind members. The members of a cattle

association have a common interest best served by a cattle association. Accordingly, special needs are attended, as they would not be in a broader association of farmers. Moreover, the organization must be open to accepting newly qualified members.

9. The members must find that the association is trustworthy. This means that it is fair with them, it is reliable, it is accountable, it is receptive to their views and concerns within itself and with the broader public, and it is predictable in the sense that it has an unwavering mission and a clear strategy to meet that mission effectively.
10. The organization must have the ability to scan the environment, evaluate and assess threats and opportunities to the members, provide authoritative interpretation and categorization of government regulations, practices, and procedures, and derive rules by which both the association and its members must behave to be in compliance with government regulations. This is so because the organization and its members must operate within the ever-changing boundaries of statutory and administrative policies set by government.

The above are not devoid of theoretical backdrop about social capital, as alluded to in earlier chapters. Yamagishi[16] found support for his hypothesis, called a structural/goal expectation hypothesis, and it applies here. It states that people tend to cooperate if they expect others to cooperate and if they are aware that in the absence of cooperation the collective objective would fail. Yamagishi argues that to ensure the cooperation of members in large groups, sanctions are employed. Thus, self-regulatory organizations need sanctions since, as in the case of the NASD, what is being controlled is not merely an individual's action, but the integrity and ability of the network to function. This is what constitutes a market.

The hypotheses above also relate to social capital in its cognitive form, as an element that binds and leads to a complementary (not necessarily equivalent) form of behavior due to complementary objectives—a buy order is matched by a sell order. Therefore, there is the need for a common understanding about behavior expectations among members and between the members and the agent.

Beyond the statutory power to force participants to be members is the theoretical concern about how to induce membership and reduce freeridership. Olson[17] hypothesized about inducing membership by making the benefits that the members receive greater than the cost of membership and by inducing membership through the provision of certain private goods (travel tours, life and health insurance, investment vehicles, and so on) that will not only attract members, but for which a fee can be charged to help defray costs and therefore reduce the effect of freeriding. Existing research reveals two problems. Individuals may miscalculate (perhaps purposefully) either their costs or their benefits,[18] or they may find that the private goods are not sufficient inducements since they could, if they chose, obtain those goods elsewhere.[19] For these reasons, the scope of the self-regulatory organization has to be sufficiently wide or encompass elements that are essential to the success of anyone engaged in the activity over which self-regulation applies.

Not only is the scope of the self-regulator important, but so also is the size (number of members, persons, or transactions covered), at least from the perspective of monitoring the behavior of members. Agrawal and Goyal[20] find that too small a group means that the cost of full-time monitoring across the board—covering all relevant activities—may be too expensive and impracticable for each person to do or for the group to afford a third-party monitor; and for a very large group, the average cost may exceed the benefit for each member. In the above hypotheses, when the self-regulator monitors essential activities, the relevant cost to the nonmembers is not the marginal cost of membership but the opportunity cost (total loss) for not being able to play or to play at a severe disadvantage.

With respect to permanence, the above hypotheses agree with Weesie, Buskens, and Raub[21] that the power of some relationships depends upon their being embedded in permanence over time so that one would expect not to escape. This permanence may be embedded in a relationship, an institution, or a network. The self-regulator has permanence through its corporate form (an institution) that allows it to survive beyond the persons writing the laws and enforcing them, and also allows it to be an agent of the public. It can encompass the complete network of players: in the case of the NASD, those who issue and sell securities to the public and their affiliated parties in these transactions. Again, scope in the above discussion refers not only to essential activity, but also to the scope of players.

How does a self-regulatory organization get started if not by statutory declaration? Organizations such as the American Bar Association and the American Medical Association wield self-regulatory powers without statutory assignment of such powers. The organization may in due course evolve to be recognized, or it may be initiated by prominent members and then recognized by the public and eventually become statutory (roughly the case of the NASD). One study[22] of the self-regulation of the train, water, and electricity industries in Great Britain charted a hoc period, followed by a formal assignment and development of regulatory powers, which was followed by the eventual strategic regulatory management of firms in the industries.

Or, the self-regulator could get started through the DiMaggio and Powell[23] framework of organizational adaptation through mimicking best practices; as organizations mimic successful behavior among each other, they professionalize it through in-house training and institutionalize it through the self- regulatory agency that can enforce these practices by means similar to factors (a) through (g) listed earlier in this chapter.

Or the formation could follow the logic of Coleman, Parsons, and Heckathorn and the order of Oliver, Maxwell, Teixeira as follows. Commenting on Talcott Parsons's theory of the Prologomena, Coleman[24] interprets him to be saying that common values lead to common goals. Institutional (in the case of this chapter, organizational) control is often needed to bring compliance to meeting common goals. Control and conformity are achieved partly through a common commitment to the goals and through positive and negative sanctions on individuals or entities that stray. Four types of relationships of individuals or entities to the group are possible. The individual may be a developer of sanctions, one who follows the sanctions, one who disobeys them because of his or her own personal interests, or one who enforces them.

But Coleman goes on to add that sanctions imposed on an individual have spillover effects on others and on the group as a whole. Therefore, the group has an interest in each person, and each person has an interest in compliance by every other. Heckathorn[25] has shown that the effectiveness of this group-mediating control depends upon the heterogeneity of the group, the capability of the outside source to monitor a sanction, the strength of the sanction, and the cost and efficacy of various enforcement measures the group can take against the individual members.

Oliver, Maxwell, Teixeira[26] find that there is a critical mass that is important in collective action, and that the order of recruiting members is important to achieving that mass. If the production function of the benefits the members receive from the organization is one of diminishing marginal returns, it temporarily favors free riders since a surplus of contributions is likely to occur. In other words, as members are added and charged the same dues as those before, these new members are cognizant that their dues add less to the output of the organization than the members who preceded them. Presumably, then, at some point the contribution of a person adds nothing to the output of the group and the person may just choose not to contribute and to take a free ride.

Therefore, the collectivity is better off if the least willing contributor contributes first, since his or her marginal contribution would yield impressive results in their eyes. The collectivity could also maximize its contribution by starting with the least willing, since the most willing (or committed) is less likely to be detracted by the diminishing marginal contribution of his or her contributions.

When the production function is characterized by increasing marginal returns, one dilemma is that expecting that the contribution of others may more than compensate for his or her refusal to contribute, no one contributes waiting for the others to do so first, thus making his or her contribution unnecessary. On the other hand, an "irrational" person may contribute just to stimulate others to contribute, with each successive person being impressed by the increasing marginal benefits of his or her contribution. The question: Who is on first?

Summary and Preview

Scott[27] writes that as self-regulatory organizations rise in importance, they call forth for a different type and consistency of public scrutiny. Ultimately, as Rao[28] argues, self-regulators that have statutory or public approval are the most effective. This chapter recognized that there are many certifying and regulatory nonprofits that do have public acceptance, but not necessary statutory approval. One of the most fascinating in-between organizations is the Governmental Accounting Standard Board (GASB), which, like the Financial Accounting Standard Board (FASB) discussed in chapter 2, is operated by the Financial Accounting Foundation, a 501 (c) (3). It sets rules by which government accounting is done, but it is not created by law. The legitimatizing role is reversed: GASB determines the clarity, consistence, comparability, and legitimacy of how governments account for the public's treasury. Thus, we close this chapter having discussed the principles that may increase the effectiveness of nonprofits as self-regulatory bodies—as social capital agents of public policy with the general mission of control, certification, and public confidence, especially where markets are asymmetric.

This chapter considered the regulatory role of nonprofit organizations over large financial market functions. In particular, it considered and explained the role of the National Association of Corporate Dealers (NASD) as a statutory regulator of the behavior of brokers and dealers and their associated parties in the securities market. The chapter not only discussed the sources of such power, but the realm over which that power is exercised and the manner in which it is exercised. Finally, the chapter considered the question: What factors may enable other associations to be self-regulatory when a statutory imprimatur is absent? The question and the chapter go to the heart of the challenge of public-private sharing of governance, which the OECD refers to as distributive governance. The next chapter considers the implications that the central theme of this book may have for the management of nonprofits viewed as social capital assets and agents of public policy.

Chapter 11

The Implications for Strategic Planning and Positioning

This book is about perspective: The nonprofit as a social asset and agent of policy within a principal-agent paradigm. This paradigm informs and reflects operational realities and strategies. This chapter is about some implications of the theme for managerial perspectives in daily operations but mostly for strategic planning and positioning of the organization. The chapter is divided into two parts: first are the implications from the perspective that the nonprofit is a social capital asset, and second are the implications from setting this asset in a principal-agent paradigm.

Nonprofits as Social Capital Assets and Some Implications for Management

A basic theme of this book is the nonprofit as a social capital asset. Chapters 3 and 4 argue that the nonprofit can be described as a structural social capital asset in a principal-agent framework because:

1. It is a composite of assets and is itself a long-lived asset—a capital asset that is a legal person capable of entering into a contract. It can function as an agent and is licensed to function as an agent of the public by both the state in which it is incorporated and the federal government. This is witnessed in its charter and in its receiving tax exemption.
2. All property rights over the organization and its assets, except in the case of creditors, are owned by a collectivity, a group, a community, or a society, to which all properties must be distributed if the organization terminates. In this sense, exclusive ownership of the assets by the society or community, the nonprofit is social.
3. It is a long-lived asset with an expected flow of benefits. Since the community owns the asset, it also owns the benefits that are expected to flow from it. Over its life, the asset and its benefits might grow, become obsolete, or diminish in quantity and in value.
4. The acquisition of the assets, and their maintenance, results from the investment by the community or group in the form of donations, tax deductions, and tax exemption. All of these represent costs, called tax

expenditures, to the public. Therefore, they are indirect payments by the public.

5. Because of the above, the nonprofit is obliged to be accountable to the public in the same manner that a public firm is obliged to be accountable to its shareholders. Accordingly, both are obligated by law to report to the public annually. Agents are accountable to their principals.

For management this implies that accountability and transparency are not merely ethical imperatives. Accountability and transparency may be equally categorized as duties of management to the owners of these assets for whom a long-term flow of benefits is expected. It also implies that management's role over these assets is first and foremost as trustees or custodians—the persons to whom those social assets are entrusted.

Given that role, the three concepts that should guide management's decisions over these assets may be described as PAD:

1. Preservation: The management's first responsibility is the preservation of these assets.
2. Accretion: The management's second responsibility is to grow these assets to meet future needs.
3. Distribution: The management's third responsibility is the distribution or disposition of these assets only in accordance with the purposes for which they were intended and also on a schedule that would allow them to last as intended.

Chapters 3 and 4 also imply that the cognitive concepts of social capital are best used to distinguish among nonprofits. That is to say, concepts such as norms, networks, or shared beliefs or values that enable the organization to take collective action are best used to distinguish nonprofit organizations. The organizations may be distinguished not only because they may have different values or shared visions, but by the degree to which these are embodied in the organization. For example, two different museums are two different structural social capital assets because of the five factors above. However, they are distinguishable not merely by the artifacts they carry, but by the values (art principles, philosophies, specialties, missions) they follow.

The managerial implications of the cognitive concept of social capital as it relates to nonprofit organizations are that it enhances management's ability to behaviorally and sociologically differentiate the organization in the marketplace. It also enables greater internal cohesion and external support, including financial support from those who share a common view. Marketing based on this shared value also enhances the ability of the organization to take collective action as it rallies members or communities around a passion they already share and have already invested. All these managerial implications of social capital apply whether the organization is an association or a nonmembership organization, faith-based or not. The properties of cognitive social capital as developed and used in this book are:

1. They are intangibles embodied in the product, process, or service of the organization.
2. They are sociological—the interaction among human actors or entities and those sociological factors such as norms, culture, regulations, and trust that govern these interactions.
3. They are accessible to all members of the collectivity or group to which they pertain and not subject to individual property rights. The group owns them.
4. They add economic and/or social value and can reduce contract costs—production or transaction.
5. They are identifiable and therefore can be taken into specific consideration by those who wish to engage, join, or hire the group.

Implications from Concept of Agent of Public Policy

The second set of implications is derived from combining the idea of the nonprofit as a social capital asset and the use of those assets by the management in forwarding public policy within the principal-agent paradigm.

The Rise of Competitors and the Need for Reassessment of the Operation

The nonprofit being a social capital asset implies its ownership by the community. It also implies that the organization's value to the community is based on its potential use in advancing the community purposes over a considerable period of time. Once the investment has been made in the nonprofit, a return in terms of a long-term flow of benefits is expected without regard to government or market failure.

In today's world, this view is significant because entrepreneurial imagination has turned many "market failures" into market successes; and the concept of market failure often means nothing more than the failure of an entrepreneur to figure a way to make a profit out of the enterprise. The success of Fed Ex and UPS by unbundling "mail service" and taking the profitable part and leaving the unprofitable part to the U.S. Post Office is not unlike private companies unbundling information, collection services, accounting services, from social services delivery, leaving the more costly population to serve to the nonprofits. While the literature focuses on the intrusion of nonprofits into "unfair" competition with small firms, the real problem for the nonprofit manager may be just the reverse—an increase in the concentration of adverse selection without the potentially profitable segments that can allow the program to internally finance itself.

Hence, the imagination of nonprofit managers must always point to the fact that there may be formidable competition from other sectors. FAIR requires this competition and so may its progenies over time on all levels of government. As discussed in chapters 3–5, activities that are not profitable and may be consequences of adverse selection may be best suited for nonprofits rather than firms, but they increase the need for outside subsidy, internally earned income, and fundraising. The success of the latter depends upon the public's valuation of the expected flow of benefits from the nonprofit. Assessing and communicating its ability to meet expectations and needs will become a major challenge of the nonprofit manager. One cannot market what one cannot do; and if what one can do is not wanted one cannot sell it or give it away. The principal-agent paradigm is a reminder that the nonprofit is under contract for specific performance of a need consistent with public policy. How is the public policy purpose being served by the organization valued relative to its competitors?

Marketing and Branding the Organization through the Concepts of Social Capital

In a competitive market, the ability to differentiate an organization is what defines its niche. The concept of social capital in its structural, but especially in its cognitive form, offer differentiating, marketing, binding, branding, and contract-bidding themes to nonprofit organizations in the public policy process. The norms and values that differentiate one organization from another are also the norms and values that attract like-thinking clients and supporters and bind them into the potential for greater collective action called for in the public policy process and described in this book. The networks may offer distinctive efficiencies in cooperation, operation, and communication. These have economic value and can be embodied in the production process, final product, or service. The skillful cultivation and strategic use of cognitive social capital is a responsibility of management in positioning an organization.

Customer First as a Contractual Obligation

One of the great dangers of entrenched bureaucracies is that they become their own principal. The principal-agent paradigm is an effective retraining tool because it focuses the attention and energies of the staff on the true client—the public. In associations, such as business associations discussed in this book, the members are the direct clients, with spillovers to the public. The essence of the paradigm is that the nonprofit exists in service of the public. This coincides with the concept of the mission as a contractual promise to serve the public in specified ways. For the nonprofit, "customer first" (to serve the public) is not a slogan but the reason for being.

The Market for the Nonprofit as the Public

For the nonprofit the number of individual customers might be small but the consequences, because of external effects, may go beyond the individual served and spillover to the public. Thus, the concept of "public" in public policy is central and requires management to ascertain the public it serves with each good or service it produces. The "public" is often substantially larger than the direct beneficiaries of these goods or services. This is partly because of externalities or spillover effects; it is also partly because of the distinction between principal and beneficiary. In public policy the former is larger than the latter, with different metrics of performance.

Tax Exemption as a Reservation Price

The nonprofit needs to ascertain that the public values the purposes it claims to serve and that it serves those purposes in ways that justify tax and other fee exemptions. In a principal-agent paradigm an exemption is partly a pre-payment for a public service. It's a lay-away price—a price to reserve the capacity of the organization and to have it available to serve the public need. It is not an entitlement due to "charitable" intent. It is the "price" the public is willing to pay for a service and to reserve the capacity of the organization to provide that service over a long period.

Tax Deductibility of Donations as Prices and Metrics of Value

In the principal-agent paradigm donations, tax exemption and contract payments are compensations for the specific performance of the nonprofit. The first two, donations and exemptions, are based more on the history of past performance and the expectations that the past is prolog. The other, contracts, is based on the expectations and promise of future specific performance. Having offered and accepted the donations, exemptions, or payment, the organization is legally obligated to perform. Performance is not an option for nonprofits and it is not merely an ethical issue. It is a contractual obligation.

The Potential for Conflict, the Promise to Perform, and Corporate Communication and Intelligence

When the nonprofit is viewed within a principal-agent paradigm, public needs and expectations become driving forces. While public ignorance does contribute to erroneous expectations, expectations are initially set in the voluntary commitment to a mission by the organization and its founders. Mission statements are cognitively bounded. They are statements of promise that generate public expectations. This confidence or trust is based on the knowledge that the mission is a permanent contractual promise that the sole purpose of the nonprofit is to discharge that mission, and that the mission is clearly understood by all parties to the contract—the nonprofit and the public, and the government as the representative of the latter.

Placing the nonprofit in a principal-agent paradigm means that the nonprofit manager must give attention to (a) the relationship between the organization and the community and the government as the community's agent; (b) the relationship between the organization and the government, the public's representative; (c) the expectations that derive from that relationship—recognizing the various sources of such expectations; (d) the current and future capacity of the organization to meet those expectations; (e) the risks and discretion associated with the choices the organization must make connected to those expectations; and (f) the maintenance of external communication flowing in and out of the organization to its principal—the public.

Note that in the principal-agent paradigm choice is not only the result of resource limitation. It is also the result of the expectation that given the resources available, choice must also be made because an agent is hired precisely because the principal is hiring the presumed ability or intelligence of the agent to make discretionary decisions or choices on the principal's (the public's) behalf.

The Role of Organizational Selfishness

The nonprofit is a social capital asset from which a long-term flow of benefits is expected. A fundamental conflict is between public expectations or demands and organizational capacity and responsibility to survive for future service. Short-run sacrifices are often the foundation for long-run capacity building for the future. The nonprofit manager has to weigh short-run and long-run optimality decisions. Is the capacity to deliver in the future impaired by today's decisions?

The wisdom and consequences of this choice depend in part upon whether the nonprofit is under contract or not. Specifically, government contracts as discussed in this book contain a number of remedies that the government may impose. When not under contract, the government still holds the ultimate power of dissolution for failure to be a functioning organization. The power to involuntarily dissolve a nonprofit is vested in every state government.

The Custodial and Trustee Duties of Management

When the nonprofit is viewed as a collection of assets and an asset itself belonging to and for the purpose of the community or group, accountability is a duty. The nonprofit is a custodian of other people's (the community's or group) assets and the custodial responsibilities can be seen as neither secondary nor as a nuisance.

The custodial duties imply more than ethics, the preservation of assets, and the making of conservative and prudent judgments. They also imply the duty of care. A hallmark of this duty is due diligence. Due diligence is the exercise of curiosity and courage. It is the asking for explanations and the tenacity to keep asking until an intelligible answer is given.

The principal-agent paradigm implies that questions of due diligence may be divided into two parts. One part deals with issues of preservation, accumulation, and distribution of the assets of the organization (PAD). The emphasis in this first part is on the capacity of the organization to deliver. Does it have that capacity? Does it continue to build for the long-term and how much? Is the future jeopardized?

The second part of due diligence relates to the agency function of the organization. Having preserved and grown the asset and its capability, is the organization performing consistently with the public policy intent? The fact that an organization may be performing consistently with its mission is not enough. Can't more be done, or is it impossible?

Principal-Agent Theory and Performance as Both an Efficiency and an Ethical Issue: Integrating Efficiency and Ethics

In the principal-agent paradigm the need for oversight is inherent in the relationship between the principal and the agent, and a code of ethics serves to reinforce that relationship. Accordingly, some ethical codes should emanate from expectations of performance given the public purpose of the organization. A review of many ethical codes of nonprofits reveals a conscious and good-faith effort to assure the public as donors or supporters, but with little connection to the contractual promise of the organization to perform in a particular way. The failure to continuously perform reasonably within the promise of a mission should be interpreted both as a performance (contractual) as well as an ethical breach. In the extreme, it is both. Thus, an organization that raises funds to build 20 homes for the poor but uses the funds inefficiently (not necessarily unethically) to build only one, has performed both inefficiently and unethically. Unlike a firm, a nonprofit charged with a public purpose performs unethically when it continuously performs inefficiently. It misuses public resources and leaves public purposes unattended for reasons other than those that may be normally and occasionally expected.

A good beginning model for tying performance and ethics is offered by the National Society of Fund Raising Executives (now the Association of Fundraising Professionals). They charge their members with the ethical responsibility to ensure that the institutions for which they raise funds use those funds for the purposes for which they were intended.[1] Furthermore, policing an organization's performance is not as difficult an oversight problem for directors as it may appear at first blush. Every year, every nonprofit organization with an asset size of $25,000 or more is required to file with the IRS a truthful statement containing what it did. Associations are also required to report this to their members. Those reports are good initial sources of performance measures.

Self-Regulation, the Self-Regulator, the Public, and the Government

In a principal-agent paradigm where nonprofits are agents and governments are the managing agents, the latter has a duty to oversee the former. Therefore, self-regulation by the nonprofit sector (or by a nonprofit of itself) is not a sufficient substitute for the regulatory responsibilities of the government over the sector. Indeed, in its inherently governmental duties, the government's responsibility is to oversee both the agent and any organization acting as a self-regulator over the sector or itself.

The self-regulator is not without its inherent conflicts and contradictions as a triple agent, that is, to the public, to the sector, and to the government to the extent that it is an agent of the latter by assuming some of its regulatory responsibilities. Therefore, self-regulation, as important as it undoubtedly is, can neither be a panacea nor an escape from this book's central theme. The self-regulator is a social capital asset and agent of the public's policies to which all of the discussions in the previous chapters apply and upon the self-regulator lies a uniquely different and larger burden to serve the public's interest, to make sure that others so serve, and to reduce the asymmetry of information that leaves the public vulnerable.

A hopeful contribution of this book applies to those who regulate nonprofits through the setting of fundraising ratios. The issue is not whether or not there is an ethical purpose behind such a ratio; there is a useful one. Rather, it is to factor in that many nonprofits have a strong, very rational incentive to forego such ratios as constraints on their duty to serve the public interest. Therefore, this book created a typology and reasons why there are variations in the incentive to comply and an implicit challenge for the oversight organizations to find another way. Good rulemaking is also about understanding the incentive for rule-avoidance.

Along the same theme is the ability of the organization to regulate its members; that is, self-regulation. While this book focuses on the financial markets, many nonprofits are members of federations and some of the same thinking would apply. The ultimate form of self-regulation is the ability of the organization to serve (a) as a legislative body (writing its own rules); (b) an enforcement body (enforcing its rule and specific government regulations); and (c) a judiciary (meting out penalties and enforcing them). Can the nonprofit sector control itself?

The Five Factors of Competence as Strengths

This book described five core competencies of nonprofit organizations. They are: (a) trust as derived from the convergence of interests and purpose; (b) trust as a contractual promise derived from the character of a mission; (c) leverage; (d) goodwill; and (e) social capital in its cognitive form. What is important about these competencies is that they are all within the capacity of the management to cultivate and thereby make the organization competitive and relevant in the public policy process.

The argument for leverage implies a need for nonprofit managers to be concerned about the pricing of contracts. The bringing of other resources to enhance the outcome of the government contract (leverage) is tantamount to subsidizing that contract. A fixed-price contract (one in which the agent agrees to perform a function at a pre-fixed price (regardless of additional or final costs) could induce cost cutting among nonprofit providers just as among for-profit providers. In both cases, the underlying motive is the same. The contract requires a performance that is more expensive than that for which it pays. The difference between the firm and the nonprofit is that the nonprofit may have access to lower cost sources of the additional capital required (donations, contributions, grants from foundations, volunteering), which it can freely allocate to any program within its mission. In essence the nonprofit subsidizes the specific government contract, and not the reverse.

The nonprofit manager has certain strategies to reduce unreimbursed subsidies to the government. These include renegotiating contracts terms. They also include alternative methods of pricing, such as performance-based pricing, which allows milestones to be set and compensation to vary by attainment of milestones. Many government contracts allow for certain cost adjustments.[2] These strategies also include negotiating (when applicable) for cost reimbursement contracts. In cost reimbursement contracts, the government may set a stop-loss limit beyond which it would not go, but the contractor may charge the government and be paid within this limit based upon the actual project costs. The acceptable costs are set in the contract. One specific contract term that may merit scrutiny is the overhead rate. This is the organization's cost to which the project contributes and, therefore, is not solely responsible. Overhead costs that are unreimbursed strain the organization's resources.

While these strategies will help to recover costs, they will not diminish the importance of leverage in competitive bidding. The ability to bring more resources to the project than the contract has paid for, even when it pays full costs, plus a fee, is always a positive for the public (the principal) and for the nonprofit in fulfilling its purpose. A responsibility of management is to build on all those factors that lead to leverage as described in chapter 5, and achieve a competitive advantage for the organization.

Zero-sum Games, Faith-Based Organizations, Pareto Optimality, and Public Policy

The studies in chapter 3 found that faith-based organizations not only receive more donations and volunteers than secular organizations, but that religious participants are also the major donors and volunteers to secular and to religious organizations. In a world in which the pool of funds available for donations or volunteers is not increasing faster than needs, this makes every dollar or hour given to a religious nonprofit one less given to a secular one. This is a zero-sum game and the faith-based organizations may be said to crowd out the secular ones—assuming that they are equally efficient. Why? Because the donors and volunteers have fixed budgets and available hours so that what is given to one type of organization comes from the potential that could be given to another.

Roughly speaking, a Pareto Optimality position is reached if the percentage going to the faith-based organizations and secular organizations are proportionate in dollar terms to the public problems each tackles. In this case, a Pareto Optimality means that society's overall welfare could not be improved by transferring more dollars or volunteer hours from the secular to the faith-based or reverse. Public welfare is being taken care of best we can, given the resources we have.

We shall never know if we have arrived at a Pareto Optimality position. But we have arrived where it causes us to conjure up some final thoughts. The debate over the constitutionality of government contracting to faith-based organizations must be matched by the debate over the most efficient use of government contracts. This book shows that five factors of confidence—particularly the potential for leverage—would frequently favor faith-based organizations because of volunteering and donations that increase the potential resources brought by these organizations to the problem; and the social capital that could decrease the internal transaction cost, thereby reducing the overall contract cost to the government. The critical assumption is that faith-based organizations use their own resources (directly or indirectly) to augment the public policy outcomes financed by government contracts.

The Pareto Optimality and zero-sum theory imply that if nonprofit organizations are to continue being the prominent players in the public process this book describes, the long-run objective may be served by a debate about how to increase the size of the pool of supporters and those five factors delineated in this book that increase the competitive position of a nonprofit.

Twenty Specific Implications from the Perspective of Nonprofits as Social Capital Assets and Agents of Public Policy

Looking at nonprofits within this general context—nonprofits as social capital and agents of public policy—leads to the following specific implications that are discussed in this book.

1. The nonprofit is a prominent player in the public policy process. A significant role of many nonprofits in this process is managing social

and economic risks. But others regulate markets or provide for greater efficiency of firms and governments.

2. The participation of nonprofits in this process is properly depicted within the principal-agent paradigm. Within this paradigm the nonprofit is a public agent to conduct a number of functions on the public's behalf. These functions run the gamut of market regulation to social service provision.
3. The nonprofit organization meets five criteria that allows it to be classified as a social capital asset.
4. For an asset to be an agent of the public, it has to have the legal capacity to make promises to perform on behalf of the public, to be compensated and to be penalized; therefore, cognitive social capital cannot be an agent. Structured social capital can.
5. But cognitive social capital can facilitate the agency function and differentiate among organizations in a competitive environment. Cognitive social capital, as developed in this book, has economic and branding values that can be priced and traded and are ultimately embodied in the process, product, or services the organization produces.
6. Networks of nonprofits lower transaction and production costs but also provide signals to the public about performance expectations.
7. In today's competitive environment where federal and state contracting laws require competition among firms, governments, and nonprofits, large firms operating across states have an advantage. The power of the nonprofit to survive this competition is based upon its unique core endowments described in this text as five factors of confidence. These five go beyond the concepts of market and contract or government failures. They help to explain why a nonprofit may win a bid over an equally qualified firm for a contract. Importantly, they are within the power of nonprofit managers to cultivate so as to increase the organization's competitive position in all contract bidding.
8. Within the paradigm, contract payments are for specific performance and to some extent may represent a reservation price or even economic rent. Indeed, to the extent that a nonprofit raises additional funds or incurs unreimbursed costs associated with the performance of the government contract, the subsidy is from the nonprofit to the public and not the reverse. It may be this possibility and power of leveraging that is determinative during periods of government budget constraints and lower political preference for social programs.
9. Within the principal-agent paradigm, the deductibility of donations and tax exemption of nonprofits are public payments in expectation of performance; in a sense, they are prices the public pays in anticipation of performances by the organization on the public's behalf.
10. Advantages such as greater trust, lower transaction cost, and unspecified contracts beg questions such as on what basis does the government trust a nonprofit more than an equally qualified firm? A review of the actual government contracting procedures further begs the

question. Trust is argued to be based on two factors: (a) trust based on the contractual and bounded nature of the mission; and (b) trust based on the mutuality of shared objectives between the government and the nonprofit.

11. The principal-agent paradigm, when coupled with public choice theory, focuses on issues of performance, expectations, trust and self-interest of nonprofit managers and government officials. Is the policy in which the nonprofit participates in the best interest of the very public both it and the government are obliged to serve? This question is in two forms: (a) the policy may introduce its own distortions and harm; and (b) there is some amount of self-serving interest that motivates government officials as well as nonprofit managers.
12. The principal-agent paradigm points to the moral hazard of self-serving at the expense of the public. But this is not just a moral question. When are managers justified in placing the interest of the organization above the public?
13. The nonprofit as a social capital asset and agent is not passive. It attempts to shape public policy and how policy is implemented. Understanding a network as cognitive social capital and how networks are articulated help in appreciating the power of business associations in influencing public policy. It is more than money that counts. We must turn to the theories of network formation, interaction, and stability, the theory of collective action and to principal-agent concepts to fully understand this role.
14. Nonprofits in the policy process are not sacrosanct. They too are involved in some degree of rent-seeking, defined as the transfer of resources toward one group's interest at the expense of others or the community.
15. In any principal-agent paradigm regulating the behavior of the agent is a challenge, but the agent can also be used as an instrument of self-control—regulating itself and its members on behalf of the public. Sports associations, educational certifying associations, medical associations, securities boards such as the New York Stock Exchange and other stock exchanges—all play both backward and forward roles as agents. What makes these work? Are these models extendable to reduce the burden of government and the efficiency of regulating not only nonprofits themselves but society by using nonprofits as an agent of regulation and enforcement? This is not a quixotic question. Most housing associations, certifying boards, and even nonprofit prisons work this way.
16. Faith-based organizations are no different to other nonprofit organizations in fitting into the principal-agent paradigm as agents of public policy. But faith-based organizations differ along the five-factor scale introduced in this book. The argument in this book, and upon which the five factors are founded, is not moral or constitutional, but economic. Moreover, they justify the choice of nonprofits as a busi-

ness decision governed by considerations of rate of return and net present value. Notwithstanding, faith-based organizations do pose a Pareto optimality problem since the evidence is that donors and volunteers make zero-sum choices.

17. All of the above have implications for managerial vision and the competitive positioning of the organization. For example, when goodwill is treated as a business concept (not in a big lump called social capital) and when cognitive social capital is distinguished from goodwill as a business concept, the contracting opportunities for the nonprofit are affected. Goodwill can be leased, bought, and sold without the involvement of the organization. It is alienable. The only way to get the cognitive social capital of the organization is to hire it.
18. Accordingly, the reader will find that definitions matter. For example, for something to be defined as a social structural capital asset, it must meet an operational and verifiable definition of a capital asset as well as a social asset. It must have a recognizable and stable (not necessarily permanent) structure, and there must be some enforceable community property rights over the assets. Similar criteria are designed in this book for each key concept and each is related to identifiable stages in the public policy process.
19. Each stage of the public policy process involves a collective action on the part of the nonprofit. A principal contribution of cognitive social capital in the public policy process is the cost and efficiency with which it allows the nonprofit to carry out the required collective action. Indeed, that collective action may be the nonprofit's only raison d'être.
20. The principal-agent paradigm, the mission of the nonprofit, and the role of the nonprofit in public policy as a social capital asset are not always aimed at promoting conformity, cohesion, and social continuity. Often the objective is the encouragement or accommodation of the reverse—dissent, discontinuity of norms and beliefs that delay or discourage socioeconomic development or exploration and innovation. The principal agent paradigm is applicable without moral judgment or normative implications. It does, however, provide a positive framework in which every nonprofit may be assessed as a social capital asset and agent of the public's interest.

This book argued that nonprofits are significant players in all phases of the public policy process—from design and formulation, to implementation and evaluation. While the processes of formulating and getting a policy adopted through the political process are fundamentally standardized, implementation varies because of policy content and purpose. Therefore, in closing, is there a typology that suggests itself with respect to the generalized roles that nonprofits play as implementers of public policy—at least as suggested by the content of this book—and, specifically, where distinctly different nonprofits are seen as having a common public policy purpose?

Implications for a Functional Classification of Nonprofits

Given the argument that from a public policy perspective what a nonprofit does may be more functionally descriptive than its origin, is it possible to come up with a typology of generalized public policy purposes played by distinctly different nonprofits as they implement distinctly different public policies?

A hospital is intended to attend to the health needs of a population. A social service center may be involved in reducing juvenile delinquency. They are very different, except that they both are specializing in managing significant social risks. Therefore, they are both classified in Table 11.1 below as principally managers of social risks. Similarly, the school and the museum are different, but they both are incubators and stores of the public's long-term and valued assets. A certifying agency and a consumer information service organization are different, but they are both principally concerned with asymmetric information—signaling the public about the value and quality of a good or service after testing. They both facilitate transactions where asymmetric information is a problem. A water authority and a community development corporation are distinctly different, but they both facilitate transactions (reduce transaction and production costs) of governments, firms, and households.

Table 11.1 is this author's suggestion of the rudiments of such a functional typology as is evidenced, demonstrated, or referred to by specific examples throughout this book. Obviously, some organizations may fit more than one role. But, owing to mission commitment and resource constraints, most organizations can appropriately be characterized by one role—that role being its principal purpose.

The Chicago Board of Trade (CBOT) is a self-governing, self-regulated, membership nonprofit corporation. It operates a leading market for trading futures contracts and options in Treasury securities as well as a variety of agricultural and other products. It has rules and regulations concerning these transactions that its members must follow. The objective is to make transactions equitable, efficient, and reciprocal, and to cause each transaction to move with some certainty of expectations by buyer and seller.

On the other hand, the National Association of Insurance Commissioners (NAIC) is deeply involved in the nature of the insurance contract and the nature of the transaction between the insurance seller and the buyer. Insurance contracts are what lawyers refer to as contracts of adhesion. This means that there is a recognized asymmetry of information about the contract. The insurance company is more knowledgeable about the contract than the potential buyer, who has no opportunity to amend the details of the contract. The buyer takes it or leaves it. In the case of CBOT and its members, facilitating the transaction is an identifiable principal objective. In

Table 11.1

Selective Types of Public Services Performed by Nonprofits in the Public Policy Process

Service	*Description*
Regulation	Regulating members, markets, and transactions; e.g., in financial markets
Risk-taking / management	Assuming and attending to society's risks; e.g., hospitals, social services
Intermediation	Standing between government and the public, business and the public, and between various segments of the public, markets, or government; e.g., business, professional, labor, and other associations, and advocacy groups
Innovation	Advancing community welfare through innovation and discretion; a bearer of investment (as opposed to social) risks; i.e., experimental laboratories
Market facilitation	Facilitating market decisions through reduction of transaction and production costs of persons, firms, and governments; e.g., infrastructure and environmental improvement where asymmetric information is not the issue
Facilitation (asymmetric markets)	Reducing the impact of asymmetric information with or without being an alternative provider; e.g., consumer information services
Custody / management of community property rights	Incorporating, representing, protecting, and managing the property rights of a group or collectivity in the absence of assignable private property rights; e.g., a housing association
Channeling of diffusion and centering of collective action	Diffusing information and taking collective action; e.g., a political action committee, religious and fraternal organizations
Generation / preservation of community social capital	Incubating or storing of society's tangible and intangible assets; e.g., schools, museums, and religious organizations

the case of the NAIC, dealing with the problem of asymmetric information is. Therefore the NAIC preoccupies itself with the nature of the contract and the preparation of the agent to fairly explain it to the public. Thus, we distinguish in Table 11.1 between just facilitating a transaction where asymmetric information is not the key issue and one in which it is. Nonprofits serve the public in both situations but with different objectives.

As an aside, let us note that CBOT collaborates with and competes with the Chicago Mercantile Exchange. In an interesting twist, the latter demutualized (went from a nonprofit mutual corporation to a for-profit holding company) in 2002, two years after the former reorganized as a Delaware nonprofit corporation. Even in high finance, the world may not be easily divided into activities that are naturally nonprofit because of market failure and those that are not. Making the understanding of what makes a nonprofit competitive, rather than what makes it exclusive, is a driving consideration of this book.

Furthermore, there is no assumption that these roles listed in Table 11.1 are exclusively or inherently nonprofit (i.e., because the market or government fails). Within the hospital and social services sectors are firms making a handsome profit, nonprofits making little or none, and governments running deficits. A basic contention of this book is that in each of these roles, the nonprofit has competitors among firms and governments as required by federal (and many state and local government) procurement laws. Accordingly, the five factors of comparative advantage of nonprofits over firms are crucial to understanding why, when, and under what competitive criteria nonprofits may be chosen for government contracts; that is, win the competition fairly and squarely.

A Foreseeable Danger: Breaking the Link Between the Nonprofit and the Public

We cannot end this book without first asking the question: Given the argument of this book, is there a foreseeable danger of public policy concern connected to the theme of nonprofits as social capital and agents of the public's policies? The answer is yes. The source of the foreseeable danger is the trend toward contracting out of public services to firms. The logic goes as follows:

While firms are certainly attracted by the profit motive, the increasing involvement of firms in government contracting in the social services is associated with several factors. First, there is a deliberate public policy to privatize and to encourage competition among firms, nonprofits, and governments, with the hope of increasing efficiency in the delivery of public programs. Second, many of these programs have been unbundled so that some parts are more clearly profitable and more attractive to firms, for example, the separation of technology and management from actual service delivery. In the first two parts of this triad, firms generally have the advantage; and in the second, depending upon the service, they can be competitive if they are willing to live with a low profit margin, as is common in many social services.

Third, even when a contract yields a low profit margin, it may be attractive to firms (according to Kennedy and Cannon[3]) because it is a reliable source of revenues, it helps to cover the firm's overhead, and it gives the firm market credibility that it can use to its advantage. Furthermore, a point that is often misunderstood, working within a low profit margin is not inconsistent with maximization of profits and does not require the organization or firm to cheat. Grocery stores operate with extremely low profit margins. Low profit margins encourage a firm to increase administrative efficiency and to duplicate itself across many government purchasers of the same service. Grocery stores live with lower margins, partly by keeping selling and managerial costs down and by creating standardized chains.

What the above scenario foretells is a probable environment of increased competition in the social service sector from firms operating simultaneously in several states and local governments across the country and the need for nonprofits to prepare to be competitive within such an environment by doing the same, or to be the subcontractors to firms for the service delivery tasks where the task-performance portions of the contract are not unbundled in the original government's purchase order.

The danger of subcontracting arrangements is that the nonprofit would be one step removed from its principal—the public—unless provisions are made under these subcontracting or partnering arrangements for direct reporting of the nonprofit to the government. In a subcontracting relationship of a nonprofit to a firm, the firm is the proximate principal. Such subcontracting arrangements are fraught with all the principal-agent problems discussed in this book—only the nonprofit now answers to the firm and its cost objectives. We end up with the nonprofit being a facilitator of the firm's profit motive by assuming its performance risks. In this kind of world, partnering with the partnership responsibilities specified in the original bid submitted to the government will often be a superior arrangement to subcontracting.

Notes

Chapter 1

1. The Internal Revenue Service, *Annual Report of Commissioner and Chief Consul* (Washington, D.C.: U.S. Government Printing Office, various years up to 1989) and the United States Revenue Service, *Databook,* 1997) p. 23.
2. Joel Sobel, "Can We Trust Social Capital," *Journal of Economic Literature,* Vol. 41, 2002, pp. 139–145.
3. Charles E. Lindblom, "The Science of Muddling Through," *Public Administration Review,* Vol. 19, No. 2, spring 1959, pp. 77–88.
4. Robert A. Dahl and Charles E. Lindblom, *Politics, Economics and Welfare* (Chicago: University of Chicago Press, 1953).
5. Amittai Etzioni, " Mixed Scanning: A Third Approach in Decision-Making," *Public Administration Review,* Vol. 27, 1967, pp. 385–392.
6. James Wilson, *Bureaucracy: What Government Agencies Do and Why They Do It* (New York: Basic Books, 1989).
7. John Forester, "Bounded Rationality and the Politics of Muddling Through," *Public Administration Review,* Vol. 44, 1984, pp. 23–30.
8. Kenneth Arrow, "Observations on Social Capital," in Partha Dasgupta and Ismail Serageldi, eds., *Social Capital: A Multifaceted Perspective* (Washington, D.C: World Bank, 2000), pp. 3–5.
9. Ibid.
10. Robert Solow, "Notes on Social Capital and Economic Performance," in Partha Dasgupta and Ismail Serageldi, eds., *Social Capital: A Multifaceted Perspective* (Washington, D.C: World Bank, 2000), pp. 6–9.

Chapter 2

1. Mark Golstein and Moshe Justman, "Education, Social Cohesion and Economic Growth," *The American Economic Review,* Vol. 92, No. 4, 2002, pp. 1192–1204.
2. Avern Ben-Ner and Benedetto Gui, "Introduction," *The Nonprofit Sector in the Mixed Economy* (Ann Arbor: The University of Michigan Press, 1993), p.6.
3. Mancur Olson, *The Logic of Collective Action* (Cambridge, MA: Harvard University Press, 1965).

4. Burton A. Weisbrod, *The Nonprofit Economy* (Cambridge, MA: Harvard University Press, 1988).
5. Ibid., esp. p. 25.
6. Myron J. Roomkin and Burton A. Weisbrod, "Managerial Compensation and Incentives in For-Profit and Nonprofit Hospitals," *Journal of Law and Economic Organization,* Vol. 15, No.3, Fall 1999, pp. 740–787.
7. Cagla Okten and Burton A. Weisbrod, "Determinants of Donations in Private Nonprofit Markets," Vol. 75, 2000, *Journal of Public Economics,* pp. 255–277, and Burton Weisbrod and Nestor Dominguez, "Demand for Collective Goods in Private Nonprofit Markets: Can Fundraising Expenditures Help Overcome Free-Rider Behavior?" *Journal of Public Economics,* Vol. 30, 1986, pp. 83–95.
8. Nancy Wolff, Burton A. Weisbrod and Edward Bird, "The Supply of Volunteer Labor: The Case of Hospitals," *Nonprofit Management Leadership,* Vol. 4, 1993, pp. 23–45.
9. Ben-Ner and Gui, "Introduction," esp. p. 8.
10. Dennis Young, *If Not for Profit, for What?* (Lexington, MA: Heath, 1983), esp. pp. 55–74.
11. Estelle James, "The Nonprofit Sector in Comparative Perspective," in W. W. Powell, ed., *The Nonprofit Sector: A Research Handbook* (New Haven: Yale: University Press, 1987), pp. 397–415.
12. Ben-Ner and Theresa Van Hoomissen, "Nonprofit Organizations in the Mixed Economy: A Demand and Supply Analysis," in Ben-Ner and Gui, "Introduction," pp. 28–58.
13. Ben-Ner and Gui, "Introduction," p. 8, footnote 6.
14. Henry B. Hansmann, "The Role of Nonprofit Enterprise," *The Yale Law Journal,* Vol. 89, April 1980, pp. 835–898.
15. David Easley and Maureen O'Hara, "Optimal Nonprofit Firms," in Susan Rose-Ackerman, ed., *The Economics of Nonprofit Institutions* (New York: Oxford University Press, 1986), pp. 84–93.
16. Eugene F. Fama and Michael C. Jansen, "Agency Problems and Residual Claims," *Journal of Law and Economics,* Vol. 26, 1986, pp. 327–349. Quote is from 342.
17. Oliver E. Williamson, "Public and Private Bureaucracies: A Transaction Economic Cost Perspective" *Journal of Law and Economic Organization,* Vol. 15, No.1, 1999, pp. 306–341.
18. Ben-Ner and Gui, "Introduction," p. 44.
19. Herrington J. Bryce, *Financial and Strategic Management for Nonprofit Organizations,* 3rd ed. (San Diego: Jossey Bass, 2000), pp. 42–48 and 618–649.
20. Kenneth Arrow, "Uncertainty and the Welfare Economics of Medical Care," *American Economic Review,* Vol. 53, 1963, pp. 941–973.
21. Michael A. Spence, "Job Signaling," *The Quarterly Journal of Economics,* Vol. 87, No. 3, 1973, pp. 355–374, and Spence, Michael,

"Informational Aspects of Market Structure: An Introduction," *The Quarterly Journal of Economics,* Vol. 90, No.4, 1976, pp. 591–597.

22. George Akerlof, "The Market for Lemons: Qualitative Uncertainty and the Market Mechanism," *Quarterly Journal of Economics,* Vol. 84, 1970, pp. 488–500.
23. Sanford J. Grossman and Joseph Stiglitz, "On the Impossibility of Informational Efficient Markets," *The American Economic Review,* Vol. 70, June 1980, pp. 266–293. Joseph Stiglitz and Andrew Weiss, "Credit Rationing in Markets with Imperfect Information," *The American Economic Review,* Vol. 71, No.3, 1981, pp. 393–410. Michael Rothschild and Joseph Stiglitz, "Equilibrium in Competitive Insurance Markets: The Economics of Markets with Imperfect Information," *Quarterly Journal of Economics,* Vol. 90, No.4, 1976, pp. 629–649. Joseph Stiglitz, "The Theory of Screening, Education and the Distribution of Income," *The American Economic Review,* Vol. 65, No. 3, June 1975, pp. 283–300. Douglas R. Arnott and J. Stiglitz: "Moral Hazard and Nonmarket Institutions: Dysfunctional Crowding Out or Peer Monitoring," *American Economic Review,* Vol. 81, 1991, pp. 179–190.
24. Ronald H. Coase, "The Nature of the Firm," *Journal of Law, Eonomics and Organization,* Vol. 3, No. 47, 1988, and *The Firm, The Market, and the Law* (Chicago, IL: University of Chicago Press, 1988).
25. Roger A. Lohmann, "And Lettuce is Nonanimal: Toward a Positive Economics of Voluntary Action," *Nonprofit & Voluntary Sector Quarterly,* Vol. 18, No. 4, Winter 1989, pp. 367–383.
26. Lester M. Salamon, *Partners in Public Service: Government-Nonprofit Relations in the Modern Welfare State* (Baltimore: MD, 1995), esp. pp. 32–52.
27. Burton A. Weisbrod, "Toward a Theory of the Voluntary Nonprofit Sector in a Three-Sector Economy," in Susan Rose-Ackerman, ed., *The Economics of Nonprofit Institutions* (New York: Oxford University Press, 1986), pp. 21–44.
28. James Douglas, "Political Theories of Nonprofit Organizations," in Walter W. Powell, ed., *The Nonprofit Sector: A Research Handbook* (New Haven, CT: Yale University Press, 1987), pp. 43–54.
29. Joseph Nye, Philip D. Zelikow and David C. King, eds., *Why People Don't Trust Governments* (Cambridge, MA: Harvard University Press, 1997). David G. Carnevale, *Trustworthy Government : Leadership and Management Strategies for Building Trust and High Performance,* (San Francisco: CA: Jossey-Bass, 1995). Peter D. Behn, "Government Performance and the Conundrum of Public Trust," in John D. Donahue and Joseph S. Nye, Jr, eds., *Market-Based Governance* (Washington, DC: Brookings Institution Press), pp. 325–348.
30. Russell Hardin, *Trust and Trustworthiness* (New York: Russell Sage Foundation, 2003), and Russell Hardin, "Trust in Government," in

Valerie Braithwaite and Margaret Levi, *Trust & Governance* (New York: Russell Sage Foundation, 1998), pp. 10–11.

31. John Boli and George M. Thomas, " World Culture in the World Polity: A Century of Nongovernmental Organizations," *American Sociological Review,* Vol. 62, No.2, 1997, pp. 171–190.
32. John Walton and Charles Ragin, "Global and Sources of Political Protests: Third World Responses to Debt Crisis," *American Sociological Review,* Vol. 55, No.6, 1990, pp. 876–890.
33. Alan Kuperman, "Tragic Consequences: How and Why Communal Groups Provide Genocidal Retaliation," paper presented at the American Political Science Association, San Francisco, August 30–September 2, 2001.
34. Carlo Borzaga and Alceste Santuari, "New Trends in the Non-profit Sector in Europe: The Emergence of Social Entrepreneurship," OECD, *The Non-Profit Sector in a Changing Economy* (Paris, France: OECD, 2003), pp. 32–59, esp. p. 32.
35. Marco A. Mena, "The Non-Profit Sector in Mexico: From Informal to Formal Recognition," OECD, *The Non-Profit Sector in a Changing Economy* (Paris, France: OECD, 2003), pp. 96–105.
36. Herrington J. Bryce, "Preface," *Management in the Non-profit Sector* (Lefkosa, North Cyprus: The Management Centre, 2000), p. 9, and Guilden P. Kucuk, Emete Imge, Kani Kanol and Meral Akinci, "Successes and Failures of the Non-Governmental Organizations in North Cyprus in the Way of Democratic Participation," (Lefkosa, North Cyprus: The Management Centre, 2000), pp. 140–153.
37. Peter Berger and Richard Neuhaus, *To Empower People: The Role of Mediating Structures in Public Policy* (Washington, D.C: American Enterprise Institute for Public Policy Research, 1977). Peter Berger, Richard Neuhaus, and Robert Novak, eds., *To Empower People: From State to Civil Society* (Washington, D.C: The American Enterprise Institute, 1996).
38. Steven Kelman, *Making Public Policy* (New York: Basic Books, 1987), esp .pp. 271–296.
39. Richard O. Zerbe, Jr., and Howard E. McCurdy, " The Failure of Market Failure," *Journal of Policy Analysis and Management,* Vol. 18, No. 4, Fall 1999, pp. 558–578.

Chapter 3

1. Alejandro Portes, "Social Capital: Its Origins and Applications in Modern Sociology," *Annual Review of Sociology,* Vol. 24, No.1, 1998, pp. 12–37.
2. Tom Schuller, Stephen Baron, and John Field, "A Review and Critique," in Stephen Baron, John Field, and Tom Schuller, eds., *Social Capital: Critical Perspective* (New York: Oxford University Press, 2000), pp. 1–38.

3. Kenneth Arrow, "Observations on Social Capital," in P. Dasgupta and I. Seraglio, eds., *Social Capital: A Multifaceted Perspective* (Washington, D.C: World Bank, 2000), pp. 3–5.
4. Robert Solow, "Notes on Social Capital and Economic Performance," in P. Dasgupta and I. Seraglio, eds., *Social Capital: A Multifaceted Perspective* (Washington, D.C: World Bank, 2000), pp. 6–10.
5. Marc Hooghe and Dietlind Stolle, "Introduction: Generating Social Capital," in Marc Hooghe and Dietlind Stolle, eds., *Generating Social Capital: Civil Society and the Institutions in Comparative Perspective* (New York: Palgrave MacMillian, 2003), pp. 1–18. Schuller, Baron, and Field, "A Review and Critique."
6. Edward J. Glaser, David Laibson, and Bruce Sacerdote, "An Economic Approach to Social Capital," *The Economic Journal,* Vol. 112, No. 783, Nov. 2002, pp. 437–459.
7. Robert Putnam, *Bowling Alone: The Collapse and Revival of American Community* (New York: Simon Schuster, 2000).
8. Glaser, Laibson, and Sacerdote, "An Economic Approach to Social Capital."
9. Herrington J. Bryce, *Financial and Strategic Management for Nonrprofit Organizations* , 3rd ed. (San Diego: Jossey Bass, 2000).
10. Vincent Buskens, "The Social Structure of Trust," *Social Networks,* Vol. 20, No. 3, July 1998, pp. 265–289.
11. Oliver E. Williamson, *Markets and Hierarchies: Analysis and Antitrust Implications, A Study of the Economics of Internal Organization* (New York: Free Press, 1975). Oliver E. Williamson, *The Economic Institutions of Capitalism: Firms, Markets, Relational Contracting* (New York: Free Press, 1985); Oliver E. Williamson,. "Comparative Economic Organization: The Analysis of Discrete Structural Alternatives," *Administrative Science Quarterly,* Vol. 36, 1991, pp. 269–296.
12. Rachel E. Kranton and Deborah F. Minehart, "A Theory of Buyer-Seller Networks," *The American Economic Review,* Vol. 91, No. 3, June 2001, pp. 485–509.
13. Matthew O. Jackson and Asher Wolinsky, "A Strategic Model of Social and Economic Networks," *Journal of Economic Theory,* Vol. 71, No. 1, October 1996, pp. 44–74.
14. Paul DiMaggio and Hugh Louch, "Socially Embedded Consumer Transaction," *American Sociological Review,* Vol. 63, 1998, pp. 619–637.
15. Joel Polodny, "Networks as Pipes and Prisms of the Market," *The American Journal of Sociology,* Vol. 107, No. 1, July 2001, pp. 33–60. Joel M. Polodny, "A Picture Is Worth a Thousand Symbols: A Sociologist's View of the Economic Pursuit of Truth," *The American Economic Review,* Vol. 93, No. 2, May 2003, pp. 169–174.
16. Nancy Katz, David Lazer, Holly Arrow, Noshir Contractor, "Network Theory and Small Groups," *Small Group Research,* June 2004, pp. 307–332.

17. Ibid.
18. Karen S. Cook and Joseph.M. Whitmeyer, "Two Approaches to Social Structure: Network Theory and Exchange Analysis," *Annual Review of Sociology,* Vol. 18, 1992, 109–127.
19. Putnam, *Bowling Alone,* esp. p. 19. Lewis M. Feldstein with Don Cohen, *Better Together: Restoring the American Community* (New York. Simon and Schuster, 2003).
20. James Coleman, *Foundations of Social Theory* (Cambridge, MA: Belknap Press, 1994).
21. Frances Fukiyama, "Social Capital and Development, the Coming Agenda," *SAIS REVIEW,* Vol 22, No. 1, winter-spring 2002, pp. 23–28.
22. Clarence N. Stone, "Civic Capacity and Urban Education," *Urban Affairs*, Vol. 36, No. 5, May 2001, pp. 595–619, and Clarence Stone, Jeffrey R. Henig, Bryan D. Jones, and Carol Pierannunzi, *Building Civic Capacity: The Politics of Reforming Urban Schools* (Lawrence, KS: University Press of Kansas, 2001).
23. William Raspberry, "Watching for a Groundswell," *Washington Post,* November 1, 2004, p. A21.
24. D. Byrne and D. Nelson, "Attraction as a Linear Function of Proportion of Positive Reinforcements," *Journal of Personality and Social Psychology Bulletin,* Vol. 4, 1965, pp. 240–243.
25. Elinor Ostrom, *Governing the Commons: The Evolution of Institutions for Collective Action* (Cambridge, UK: Cambridge University Press, 1990).
26. Marc Granovetter, "The Strength of Weak Ties," *American Journal of Sociology,* Vol. 78, 1973, pp. 1360–1380.
27. Walter Powell and Laurel Smith-Doerr, "Networks and Economic Life," in Neil Smelser and Richard Swedberg, eds., *The Handbook of Economic Sociology* (Princeton, N.J:. Princeton University Press and Russell Sage Foundation, 1994), pp. 369–402.
28. Samuel Bowles and Herbert Gintis, "Social Capital and Community Governance," *The Economic Journal,* Vol. 112, No. 483, November 21, 2002, pp. 419–436.
29. Herrington J. Bryce, *Financial and Strategic Management of Nonprofit Organizations,* 2d ed. (Upper Saddle, NJ: Prentice Hall, 1992), p. 127–128.
30. Putnam, *Bowling Alone.*
31. Ibid.
32. Anidrudh Krishna, *Active Social Capital: Tracing the Roots of Development and Democracy* (New York: Columbia University Press 2002), pp. 55–84.
33. Richard A. Couto, and Catherine Guthrie, *Making Democracy Work Better: Mediating Structures, Social Capital and the Democratic Process* (Chapel Hill, N.C.: University of North Carolina Press, 1999).

34. Elenaor Brown and James Ferris, *Social Capital in Los Angeles: Findings from the Social Capital Community Benchmark Survey* (Los Angeles, CA: The Center on Philanthropy and Public Policy, 2001).
35. Christiaan Grootaert and Thierry van Bastelaer, eds., *Understanding and Measuring Social Capital: A Multidisciiplinary Tool for Practitioners* (Washington, D.C.: The World Bank, 2002).
36. Ibid., esp. pp. 152–236.
37. Coleman, *Foundations of Social Theory.*
38. Rory McVeigh and Chistian Smith, "Who Protests in America: An Analysis of Three Political Alternatives-Inaction, Institutionalized Politics, or Protest," *Sociological Forum,* Vol. 14, No. 4, December 1999, pp. 685–702.
39. J. E. Williams, "Linking Beliefs to Collective Action: Politicized Religious Beliefs and the Civil Rights Movement," *Sociological Form,* Vol. 17, No. 2, July 2002, pp. 203–222.
40. Sheila Suess Kennedy and Wolfgang Bielefeld, *Charitable Choice Results from Three States* (Indianapolis, IN: Center for Urban Policy and Environment, Indiana University-Purdue University, 2003).
41. Colin J. Baier and Bradley R. E. Wright, "If You Love Me, Keep My Commandments: A Meta-Analysis of the Effect of Religion on Crime," *Journal of Research in Crime and Delinquency,* Vol. 38, No. 1, February 2001, pp. 3–21.
42. Mathew R. Lee and John P. Bartkowski, "Civic Participation, Regional Subcultures, and Violence: The Differential Effects of Secular and Religious Participation on Adult and Juvenile Homicide," *Homicide Studies,* Vol. 8, No. 1, February 2004, pp. 5–39.
43. Norma D. Turner, Kristi H. O'Dell, and Gayle. W. Weaver, " Religion and the Recovery of Addicted Women," *Journal of Religion and Health,* Vol. 38, No. 2, 1999, pp. 132–147.
44. P. M. Flynn, E. W. Joe, K. M. Broome, D. D., Simpson and B. S. Brown, *Journal of Substance Abuse Treatment,* Vol. 25, No. 3, October 2003, pp. 177–186.
45. Christian Research Association, *Social Capital and Religion in Contemporary Australia* (Melbourne, Australia:Christian Research Association, July 2001).
46. Elinor Ostrom, *Governing the Commons,* pp. 182–215.
47. Ibid.
48. Russell Hardin, *Collective Action* (Baltimore, MD: The Johns Hopkins University Press, 1982).
49. Ibid., pp. 182–215.
50. Christopher McMahon, *Collective Rationality and Collective Reasoning* (Cambridge, UK: Cambridge, University Press, 2001).
51. Fikret Berkes, " Cross-Scale Institutional Linkages: Perspectives from the Bottom Up," in Elinor Ostom et al., eds., *The Drama of the*

Commons (Washington, D.C.: National Research Council, 2001), pp. 293–321.

52. Oran Young, "Institutional Interplay: The Environmental Consequences of Cross-Scale Interactions," in Ostrom et al., eds., *The Drama of the Commons,* pp. 263–291.
53. Bonnie J. McCay, "Emergence of Institutions for the Commons: Context, Situations, and Events," in Ostrom et al., eds., *The Drama of the Commons,* pp. 369–401.
54. Julian Wolpert, "Decentralization and Equity in the Public and Nonprofit Sectors," *Nonprofit Research Fund, Working Paper,* 1994.
55. Astrid E. Merget, "Equity in the Distribution of Municipal Services," in Herrington J. Bryce, ed., *Revitalizing Cities* (Lexington, MA: Lexington Books, 1979), pp. 161–191.
56. John D. Donahue, *The Privatization Decision: Public Ends, Private Means* (New York: Basic Books, 1989).
57. Klaus Schmidt, "The Cost and Benefits of Privatization," *Journal of Law and Economic Organization,* Vol. 12, No.1, 1996, pp. 1–24.
58. Andrew Shlerfer and Robert Vishny, "Perspective of Government, Theory and an Application to Prisons," *Quarterly Journal of Economics,* 1997, pp. 1127–116.
59. Walter E. Oates, *Fiscal Federalism* (New York: Harcourt Brace, 1972).
60. Susan A. Ostrander, "Elite Domination in Private Social Agencies: How It Happens and How It Is Challenged," in G. William Domhoff and Thomas R. Dye, eds., *Power Elites and Organizations* (Newbury Park, CA: Sage Publication, 1987), pp. 85–102, and Susan A. Ostrander, "Voluntary Social Service Agencies in the United States," *Social Service Review,* Vol. 59, No. 3, 1985, pp. 435–445.
61. Luiz R De Mello Jr,, "Can Fiscal Decentralization Strengthen Social Capital," *Public Finance Review,* Vol. 32, No. 1, January 2004, pp. 4–35.
62. Michale Woodcock, "Social Capital and Economic Development: Toward a Theoretical Synthesis and Policy Framework," *Theory and Society,* Vol. 27, 1998, pp. 151–208.

Chapter 4

1. http://www.aaas.org/aboutaaas.
2. David Guston, *Between Politics and Science: Assuring the Integrity and Productivity of Research* (Cambridge: UK: Cambridge University Press, 2000).
3. *Church of the Lukumi Buballu Aye v. City of Hideah, Florida* (508 U.S. 528, 1993).
4. Revenue Ruling 8–62 1981 establishes the role of nonprofit tax-exempt organizations as advancing public welfare and so to do Revenue Ruling 70–186, 1970–1, Revenue Ruling 76–94, 1976–1, and Revenue Ruling 54–296, 1954–2.

5. Dennis R. Young, "Complementary, Supplementary, or Adversarial? A Theoretical and Historical Examination of Nonprofit-Government Relations in the United States," in Elizabeth T. Boris and C. Eugene Steuerle, *Nonprofits & Government* (Washington, D.C.: The Urban Institute, 1998), pp. 31–67.
6. Lester M. Salamon, *Partners in Public Service,: Government-Nonprofit Relations in the Modern Welfare State* (Baltimore, MD: Johns Hopkins University Press, 1995).
7. Terry Moe, "The New Economics of Organization," *American Journal of Political Science,* Vol. 28, No.4, 1984, pp. 739–777.
8. Revenue Ruling 8–62, 1981,and Revenue Ruling 70–186, 1970–1. Revenue Ruling 76–94, 1976–1, and Revenue Ruling 54–296, 1954–2.
9. http://www.anl.gov/about.html.
10. Herrington J Bryce, *Financial and Strategic Management for Nonprofit Organizations,* 3rd ed. (San Diego: Jossey Bass, 2002), pp. 3–22.
11. Sharon M. Oster, *Strategic Management for Nonprofit Organizations* (New York: Oxford University Press, 1995), p. 22.
12. James G. March and Herbert A. Simon, *Organizations* (New York: John Wiley, 1958).
13. Ibid.
14. Michael M. Ting, "A Strategic Theory of Bureaucratic Redundancy," *American Journal of Political Science,* Vol. 47, No 2, April 2003, pp. 274–292.
15. Edward A. Zelinsky, "Are Tax Benefits for Religious Institutions Constitutionally Dependent on Benefits for Secular Entities," *Boston College Law Review,* Vol. 42, 2001, pp. 804–842.
16. Political Action Committees (PACs) are exceptions. Sources on PACs include the Center for Responsive Government and others cited here.
17. James Snyder, "On Buying Legislatures," *Economics and Politics,* Vol. 3, 1991, pp. 93–110A. Avinash K.Dixit and John Londregan, "The Determinants of Success of Special Interests in Redistributive Politics," *Journal of Politics,* Vol. 5, 1996, pp. 1132–1155.
18. Elhanan Helpman and Torsten Persson, "Lobbying and Legislative Bargaining," *Advances in Economic Analysis and Policy,* Vol. 1, No. 1, 2001, Art. 3.
19. Steven Bronars and John Lott, "Do Campaign Donations Alter How Politicians Vote Or Do Voters Support Candidates Who Value the Same Thing That They Do?" *Journal of Law and Economics,* Vol. 40, October, 1997, pp. 317–350.
20. Gordon Tullock, "The Theory of Public Choice," in Gordon Tullock, Arthur Seldon, and Gordon L. Brady, *Government Failure* (Washington, D.C.: Cato Institute, 2002), pp.29–51.
21. Yew-Kwang Ng, *Welfare Economics: Introduction and Development of Basic Concepts* (New York: Wiley, 1980).
22. April Witt, "Afghan Poppies Proliferate; As Drugs Widen, Labs and Computers Flourish," *Washington Post,* July 10, 2003, p. A01.

23. Denise L. Anthony, "Micro-Lending Institutions: Using Social Networks to Create Productive Capability," *International Journal of Sociology and Social Policy,* Vol. 17, 1997, pp. 156–178.
24. Karen S. Cook and Russell Hardin, "Norms of Cooperativeness and Networks of Trust," Michael Hechter and Karl-Dieter Opp, eds., *Social Norms* (New York: Russell Sage Foundation, 2001), p. 332.
25. H. Naci Mocan, "Can Consumers Detect Lemons: Information Asymmetry in the Market for Child Care." *National Bureau of Economic Research,* No. 8291, May 2001.

Chapter 5

1. James M. Ferris and Elizabeth Grady, "Production Costs, Transaction Costs, and Local Government Contractor Choice," *Economic Inquiry,* Vol. 29, July 1991, pp. 541–554.
2. Kim W. Chan and Renee Mauborgne, "FAIR Process: Managing in the Knowledge Economy," *Harvard Business Review,* January 2003, pp. 127–136.
3. James Ferris, "The Decision to Contract Out: An Empirical Analysis," *Urban Affairs,* Vol. 22, No. 2, December 1986, pp. 289–311.
4. Julian Wolpert and Thomas Reiner, "The Nonprofit Sector in the Metropolitan Economy," *Economic Geography,* Vol. 57, 1981, pp. 23–33.
5. Government Accounting Office, *Social Service Privatization: Ethics and Accountability Challenges in State Contracting* (Washington, D.C.: Government Printing Office, April 1999).
6. Richard W. Roper, *A Shifting Landscape: Contracting for Welfare Services in New Jersey* (Albany, NY: Rockefeller Institute of Government, December 1998).
7. Jocelyn Johnson and Barbara Romzek, *Implementing State Contracts for Social Services: An Assessment of the Kansas Experience* (Washington, D.C.: The Pricewaterhouse Endowment for the Business of Government, May 2000).
8. Steven Kelman, *Procurement and Public Management* (Washington, D.C.: The American Enterprise Institute Press, 1990), pp. 95.
9. Frank Sloan, "Not-for-Profit Ownership and Hospital Behavior," in J. P. Cuyler and J. Newhouse, eds., *Handbook of Health Economics,* chapter 12 (New York: Elseiver, 2000).
10. Ibid.
11. Herrington J. Bryce, "Profitability of HMOs: Does Non-Profit Status Make a Difference?" *Health Policy,* Vol. 28, 1994, pp. 197–210.
12. United States General Accounting Office, *Privatization: Lessons Learned by State and Local Governments* (Washington, D.C.: United States General Accounting Office, 1997) and United States General

Accounting Office, *Social Service Privatization: Expansion Poses Problems of Ensuring Program Accountability and Results* (Washington, D.C.: Government Printing Office, October 1997).

13. State of California Department of Health and Human Services Agency, Department of Social Services, *All County Information Notice I-70–03, Implementing Public Authorities and Nonprofit Consortia to Deliver In-Home Supportive Services* (Sacramento, CA: October 2003).
14. John Bartle and Ronnie LaCourse Korosec, "A Review of State Procurement and Contracting," *Journal of Public Procurement,* Vol. 3, No. 2, November 2, 2003, pp. 192–214.
15. Yuhua Qiao and Glenn Cummings, "The Use of Qualifications-Based Selection in Public Procurement: A Survey Research" *Journal of Public Procurement,* Vol. 3, No. 2, 2003, pp. 215.
16. Kenneth Arrow, "Uncertainty and the Welfare Economics of Medical Care," *American Economic Review,* Vol 53, 1963, pp. 941–973.
17. Oliver Williamson, "Prologue," in *The Mechanism of Governance* (New York: Oxford University Press, 1996).
18. Oliver Williamson, "Calculativeness, Trust and Economic Organizations," *Journal of Law and Economics,* Vol. 36, No. 1, April 1993, pp. 453–486. Oliver Williamson, "Calculated Trust: A Reply to Craswell's Comments to Williamson," *Journal of Law and Economics,* Vol. 36, No. 1, April 1993, pp. 501–502.
19. Richard Craswell, "On the Uses of Trust, Comment on Williamson 'Calculativeness, Trust and Economic Organizations,'" *Journal of Law and Economics,* Vol. 36, No. 1, April 1993, pp. 487–500.
20. Michael C. Jensen and William C. Meckling, "The Theory of the Firm: Managerial Behavior, Agency Costs and Ownership Structure," *Journal of Financial Economics,* Vol. 3, 1976, pp. 305–360.
21. Oliver Williamson, "Calculativeness, Trust, and Economic Organization," *Journal of Law, Economics and Organization,* Vol. 36, April 1993, pp. 453–486.
22. Mark Granovetter, "Economic Action and Social Structure: The Problem of Embeddeness," *American Journal of Sociology,* Vol. 91, 1985, pp. 481–510.
23. Sharon Zukin and Paul DiMaggio, *Structure of Capital: The Social Organization of Economy* (New York: Cambridge University Press, 1990).
24. Herrington J. Bryce, *Financial and Strategic Management for Nonprofit Organizations,* 3rd ed. (San Diego: Jossey Bass, 2000), pp. 31–32.
25. Oliver E. Williamson, "Public and Private Bureaucracies: A Transaction Economic Cost Perspective," *Journal of Law, Economics and Organization,* Vol. 15, 1999, pp. 306–341. See also Williamson, Oliver E., "The New Institutional Economics: Taking Stock, Looking Ahead," *Journal of Economic Literature,* Vol. 38, No. 3, 2000, pp. 595–613.

26. Eugene F. Fama and Michael C. Jansen, "Ownership and Control," *Journal of Law and Economics,* Vol. 26, 1983, pp. 301–325.
27. Henry B. Hansmann, "The Role of Nonprofit Enterprise," *The Yale Law Journal,* Vol. 89, April 1980, pp. 835–898.
28. Nancy Wolff, Burton A. Weisbrod and Edward Bird, "The Supply of Volunteer Labor: The Case of Hospitals," *Nonprofit Management Leadership,* Vol. 4, 1983, pp. 23–45.
29. Frank Sloan, "Not-for-Profit Ownership and Hospital Behavior."
30. Karen Eggleston and Richard Zeckhauser, "Government Contracting for Health Care," in John Donahue and Joseph Nye, eds., *Market-Based Governance: Supply Side, Demand Side, Upside and Downside* (Washington, D.C.: Brookings Institution Press, 2002), pp. 29–65.
31. David Aaker, "Leveraging the Corporate Brand," *California Management Review,* Vol. 46, No. 3, spring 2004, pp. 6–18.
32. American Association of Fund-Raising Council, *Giving* (New York: 1986–2004).
33. The Independent Sector, *Giving and Volunteering* (Washington, D.C: 2003).
34. L. H. Choi, "Factors Affecting Volunteerism among Older Adults," *Journal of Applied Gerontology,* Vol. 22, No. 2, June 2003, pp. 179–196.
35. E. Frank, J. Breyan, and L. K. Elon, "Pro Bono Work and Nonmedical Volunteerism among U.S. Women Physicians," *Journal of Women's Health,* Vol. 12, July 2003, pp. 689–598.
36. Kristin Gronbjerg and Brent Never, "The Role of Religious Networks and Other Factors in Different Types of Volunteer Work," *Nonprofit Management and Leadership,* Vol. 14, No. 3, spring 2000, pp. 263–290.
37. David E. Campbell and Steven Yonish, "Religion and Volunteering in America," in Corwin Smidt, ed., *Religion as Social Capital: Producing the Common Good* (Waco, TX: Baylor University Press, 2003), pp. 87–106.
38. Ibid., p. 105.
39. Roger J. Nemeth and Donald A. Luidens, "The Religious Basis of Charitable Giving in America," Corwin Smidt, ed., *Religion as Social Capital: Producing the Common Good* (Waco, TX: Baylor University Press, 2003), pp. 107–120.
40. For examples of religious organizations in this connection, see Herrington J. Bryce, *Financial and Strategic Management for Nonprofit Organizations* (Upper Saddle, NJ: Prentice Hall, 1986).
41. Derek P. Apanovitch, "Religion and Rehabilitation: The Requisition of God by the State," *Duke Journal of Law,* Vol. 47, No. 4, February 1998, pp. 785–851.
42. Independent Sector, *Giving and Volunteering in the United States* (Washington, D.C.: Independent Sector, 2001).

43. Fermida Handy, N. Sirinivasan, "Valuing Volunteers: An Economic Evaluation of the Net Benefits of Hospital Volunteers," *Nonprofit and Voluntary Sector Quarterly,* Vol. 33, March 2004, pp. 28–54.
44. Frank Jones, *The Potential for Increased Volunteering in Religious Organizations* (Ottawa, Canada: Christian Commitment Research Institute, April 2002).
45. Lisa Keister, "Religion and Wealth: The Role of Religious Affiliation and Participation in Early Adult Asset Accumulation," *Social Forces,* Vol. 182, No. 1, September 2003.
46. Michael Lipsky and Steven Smith, "Nonprofit Organizations, Government, and the Welfare State," *Political Science Quarterly,* Vol. 104, No. 4, winter 1989/90, pp. 625–648. Steven Rathgeb Smith and Michael Lipsky, *Nonprofit for Hire: The Welfare State in the Age of Contracting* (Cambridge, MA: Harvard University Press, 1993).
47. Kirstin Gronbjerg, "Purchase of Service Contracting Versus Government Service Delivery: The View of State Human Service Administrators," *Journal of Sociology and Social Welfare,* Vol. 23, No. 2, June 1996, pp. 107–119.
48. Alfred J. Kahn and Sheila B. Kamerman, *Big Cities in the Welfare Transition* (NewYork: Columbia University School of Social Work, 1998).
49. Donald Kettl, *Sharing Power: Public Governance and Private Markets* (Washington, D.C.: Brookings, 1993).
50. Lester Salamon, *Partners in Public Service: Government-Nonprofit Relationships in the Modern Welfare State* (Baltimore, MD: Johns Hopkins Press, 1995).
51. Sheila B. Kamerman and Alfred J. Kahn, eds., *Privatization and the Welfare State* (Princeton, N.J.: Princeton University Press, 1989). Sheila B. Kamerman and Alfred J. Kahn, "Social Services for Troubled Children, Youth, and Families in the United States," *Children and Youth Services Review,* Vol. 12, No. 1/2, 1990, pp. 1–84. Sheila B. Kamerman and Alfred J. Kahn, eds, *Child Welfare in the Context of Welfare Reform* (New York: Columbia University School of Social Work, 1997). Sheila B. Kamerman and Alfred J. Kahn, "Privatization, Contracting, and Reform of Child and Family Social Services," prepared for *The Finance Project,* June 1998. Available at *www.financeproject.org/private.htm.*
52. Peter Frumkin, "Service Contracting with Nonprofit and For-Profit Providers: On Preserving a Mixed Organizational Ecology," in John Donahue and Joseph Nye, Jr., eds., *Market-Based Governance* (Washington, D.C.: Brookings Institution Press, 2001), pp. 66–87.
53. James M. Ferris, "The Double-Edged Sword of Social Service Contracting: Public Accountability Versus Nonprofit Autonomy," *Nonprofit Management and Leadership,* Vol. 3, summer 1993, pp. 363–376.

54. Oliver Williamson, "Opportunism and Its Critics," *Managerial and Decision Economics,* Vol. 14, March–April 1993, pp. 97–107.
55. Jeffrey Pfeffer, and Gerald Salancik, *The External Control of Organizations: A Resource Dependence Perspective.* New York: Harper and Row Publishers, 1978).
56. James M. Ferris, "The Double-Edged Sword of Social Service Contracting."
57. Paul DiMaggio and Walter .W. Powell, "Isomorphism: The Iron Cage Revisited: Institutional Isomorphism and Collective Rationality in Institutional Fields," *American Sociological Review,* Vol. 48, 1983, pp. 147–160.
58. Federal Acquisition Council, *Manager's Guide to Competitive Sourcing,* 2d ed. (Washington, D.C.: Government Printing Office, February 20, 2004), p. 21.
59. Kenneth S. Corts and Jaspit Singh, "The Effect of Repeated Interaction on Contract Choice: Evidence from Offshore Drilling," *The Journal of Law, Economics and Organization,* Vol. 20, No. 1, April 2004, pp. 2–31.
60. Ranjay Gulati, "Does Familiarity Breed Trust? The Implications of Repeated Ties for Contractual Choice in Alliance," *Academy of Management Journal,* Vol. 38, No. 1, 1995, pp. 85–113.
61. Alan Schwartz and Joel Watson, "The Law and Economics of Costly Contracting," *The Journal of Law, Economics and Organization,* Vol. 20, No. 1, April 2004, pp. 2–31.
62. John Seeley and Julian Wolpert "Secular and Faith-Based Human Services: Complimentarities or Competition," Spring Research Forum, The Role of Faith-Based Organizations in the Social Welfare System, Hyatt Regency, Washington, D.C., March 6–7, 2003.

Chapter 6

1. Richard America, ed., *Philanthropy and Economic Development* (Westport, CT: Greenwood Press, 1995).
2. Phillip Clay and Robert M. Holliseter, eds., *Neighborhood Policy and Planning* (Lexington, MA: Lexington Books, 1983).
3. Clarence N. Stone and Heywood Sanders, eds., *The Politics of Urban Development* (Lawrence, KS: University of Kansas Press, 1987).
4. Authors such as Barbara Ferman, Patrick Kaylor, Michael Leo Owens, Julia Koshinsky, and Todd Swanstrom, writing in Richard Hula and Cynthia Jackson Elmoore's edited book on nonprofits in urban America, address institutions, governments, and black churches in community and housing development from a nonprofit perspective See Richard Hula and Cynthia Jackson Elmoore, eds., *Nonprofits in Urban American* (Wesport, CT: Quorum through Greenwood Press, 2000).

5. Bennett L. Hecht, *Developing Affordable Housing: A Practical Guide for Nonprofit Organizations* (New York: John Wiley and Sons, 1999)
6. Rachel Weber, "Do Better Contracts Make Better Economic Development Incentives?" *Journal of the American Planning Association,* Vol. 68, No. 1, 2002, pp. 43–55.
7. Marilyn Taylor, *Public Policy in the Community* (New York: Palgrave Macmillian, 2002)
8. Rachel G. Bratt and William M. Rohe, "Organizational Changes among CDCs: Assessing the Impacts and Navigating the Challenges," *Journal of Urban Affairs,* Vol. 26, No. 2, June 2004, pp. 197–220.
9. Ross Gittell and Margaret Wilder, "Community Development Corporations: Critical Factors That Influence Success," *Journal of Urban Affairs,* Vol. 21, No. 3, September 1999, pp. 325–339.
10. Spencer Cowan, William Rohe, and Esmail Baku, "Factors Influencing the Performance of Community Development Corporations," *Journal of Urban Affairs,* Vol. 21, No. 3, September 1999, pp. 325–339.
11. Pierre Clavel, Jessica Pitt, and Jordan Yin, " Community Option in Urban Policy," *Urban Affairs* , Vol. 32, No. 4, , 1997, p. 435.
12. Michael H. Schill,"The Role of the Non profit Sector in Low-income Housing Production: A Comparative Perspective," *Urban Affairs,* Vol. 30, No. 1.
13. Robert J. Chaskin and Sunil Garg,"The Issue of Governance in Neighborhood-Based Initiatives," *Urban Affairs,* Vol. 32, No. 5, 1997.
14. Richard C. Hula, Cynthia Y. Jackson, and Marion Orr, "Urban Politics, Governing Nonprofits, and Community Revitalization," *Urban Affairs,* Vol. 32, 1997, p. 459.
15. B. C. Smith, "The Impact of Community Development Corporations on Neighborhood Housing Markets: Modeling Appreciation," *Urban Affairs Review,* Vol. 2, No.2, November 2003, pp. 181–204.
16. Norman Glickman and Lisa. N. Servon, "By the Numbers, Measuring Community Development Corporations' Capacity," *Journal of Planning Education and Research,* Vol. 22, No. 3, March 2003, pp. 240–256.
17. Robert Mark Silverman, "CDCs and Charitable Organizations in the Urban South: Mobilizing Social Capital Based on Race and Religion for Neighborhood Revitalization," *Journal of Contemporary Ethnography,* Vol. 30, No. 2, April 2001, pp. 240–250.
18. Patricia Fredericksen and Rosanne London, "Discontent in the Hollow State: The Pivotal Role of Organizational Capacity in Community-Based Development Organizations," *Public Administration Review,* Vol. 6, No. 3, May/June 2000, pp. 203–239.
19. Judith Saidel, " Dimensions of Interdependence: The State and Voluntary Sector Relationships," *Nonprofit and Voluntary Sector Quarterly,* Vol. 8, No. 4, 1989, pp. 335–347.
20. U.S. Government Printing Office, Form 1023, Revised April 1996. See Herrington J. Bryce, *Financial and Strategic Management for Non-*

profit Organizations, 3rd ed. (San Diego, CA: Jossey Bass, 2000), pp. 41–48.

21. Herrington J. Bryce, "Joint Ventures for Affordable Housing," *Virginia Business Report,,* Report No. 326, October 1987, pp. 3–4.
22. Walter W. Powell and Laurel Smith-Doerr, "Networks and Economic Life," in Neil Smelser and Richard Swedberg, eds., *The Handbook of Economic Sociology* (Princeton, NJ: Princeton University Press and Russell Sage Foundation, 1994), pp. 369–402.
23. OECD, *Distributed Public Governance Agencies: Authorities and Other Government Bodies* (Paris, France: OECD, 2002).
24. It is also a memorable day for the Bryce family, since our daughter, Marisa, was one of the few who fled and survived the World Trade Center as it crumbled before the eyes and awareness of her sister Shauna. As fate would have it, Marisa survived as her colleagues on the 106th floor did not. Our condolences.
25. Herrington J. Bryce, "The Authority as a Mechanism for Private Enterprise: The United States Experience," *International Review of Public Administration,* Vol. 6, No. 1, June 2001, pp. 11–20; Harold Seidman, "The Quasi World of the Federal Government," *The Brookings Review,* Vol. l6, No. 3, 1998, pp. 23–27. Donald Axelrod, *Shadow Government: The Hidden World of Public Authorities* (New York: John Wiley, 1992); Jerry Mitchell, ed., "Symposium on Public Authorities and Public Policy," *Policy Studies Journal,* Vol. 18, No.4, 1990; Jerry Mitchell, "Public Enterprise in the United States," in Ali Farazmand, ed., *Public Enterprise Management: International Case Studies* (Westport, CT: Greenwood Press, 1996); and Roger Wettenhall, "Pubic Enterprise Management in Australia: A Pioneer among Developing Countries," in Ali Farazmand, ed., *Public Enterprise Management: International Case Studies* (Westport, CT: Greenwood Press, 1996).
26. I am grateful to my son, Herrington Simon Bryce, an aide to the mayor of Oakland, for making me aware of the Port of Oakland.
27. Vernadette Ramirez Broyles, "The Faith-Based Initiative, Charitable Choice and Protecting the Free Speech Rights of Faith-Based Organizations," *Harvard Journal of Law and Public Policy,* Vol. 26, No.1, winter 2003, pp. 318–353.
28. Philip Hamburger, "Separation and Interpretation," *Journal of Law & Politics,* Vol. 18, No. 1, winter 2002, pp. 7–64.
29. Melissa Rogers, "Traditions of Church-State Separation: Some Ways They Have Protected Religion and Advanced Religious Freedom and How They Are Threatened Today," *Journal of Law & Politics,* Vol. 18, No. 1, winter 2002, pp. 277–322.
30. William P. Marshall, "Remembering the Values of Separatism and State Funding of Religious Organizations (Charitable Choice): To Aid

is Not Necessarily to Protect," *The Journal of Law & Politics,* Vol. 18, No. 2, spring 2002, pp. 479–498.

Chapter 7

1. Gloria J. Bazzoli, Benjamin Chan, Stephen M. Shortell, and Thomas D'Aunno, "The Financial Performance of Hospitals Belonging to Health Networks and Systems," *Inquiry,* Vol. 37, fall 2000, pp. 234–252.
2. Margaret A. Potter and Beaufort B. Longest, "The Divergence of Federal and State Policies on the Charitable Tax Exemption of Nonprofit Hospitals," *Journal of Health Politics, Policy and Law,* Vol. 19, No. 2, 1994, pp. 393–419, and Alice Noble, Andrew Hyams, and Nancy Kane, "Charitable Hospital Accountability: A Review and Analysis of Legal and Policy Initiatives," *The Journal of Law, Medicine and Ethics,* Vol. 26, 1998, pp. 116–137.
3. Commonwealth of Pennsylvania Code, Section 32.21, as amended, December 23, 1994.
4. Office of the Attorney General, *Commonwealth of Massachusetts' Community Benefits Guidelines for Nonprofit Acute Care Hospitals* (Boston, MA: June 1994).
5. Texas Health Safety Code, Chapter 311, 1993.
6. Herrington J. Bryce, "Profitability of HMOs: Does Non-profit Status Make a Difference," *Health Policy,* Vol. 28, 1994, pp. 197–210.
7. Herrington J. Bryce, "Capacity Considerations and Community Benefit Expenditures of Nonprofit Hospitals," *Health Care Management Review,* Vol. 63, No. 3, 2001, pp. 24–39.
8. Regina E. Herzlinger and William S. Krasker, "Who Profits from Nonprofits?" *Harvard Business School,* Vol. 87, 1987, pp. 93–106.
9. D. A. Banks, M. Paterson, and J. Wendell, "Uncompensated Hospital Care: Charitable Mission or Profitable Business Decisions?" *Health Economics,* Vol. 6, 1997, pp. 133–143.
10. James Sutton, Meredith Milet, and Bonnie Blanchfield, *The Role of Private Hospitals in the California Healthcare Safety Net* (Bethesda, MD: Project Hope, June 2002).
11. Lawrence Hattick and Richard Ordos, *Charity Care in Washington Hospital 1999* (Olympia: WA: Center for Health Statistics, Hospital, and Patient Data Systems, July 2001).
12. Christine S. Spencer, "Do Uncompensated Care Pools Change the Distribution of Hospital Care to the Uninsured?" *Journal of Health Politics, Policy and Law,* Vol. 23, No. 1, 1998, pp. 3–73.
13. See Walter Isard, *Location and Space Economy* (Cambridge, MA, The M.I. T. Press, 1956), for a discussion of August Losch and other relevant theories.

14. James A. Brickley and Lawrence Van Horn, "Managerial Incentives in Nonprofit Organization: Evidence from Hospitals," *Journal of Law and Economics,* Vol. 45, No. 1, April 2002, pp. 227–250.
15. Bryce, "Profitability of HMOs."
16. Herrington J. Bryce, "Capacity Considerations and Community Benefit Expenditures of Nonprofit Hospitals" *Health Care Management Review,* Vol. 26, No. 3, 2001, pp. 24–39.
17. Bazzoli, Chan, Shortell, and D'Aunno, "The Financial Performance of Hospitals Belonging to Health Networks and Systems."
18. James Sutton, Meredith Milet, and Bonnie Blanchfield, *The Role of Private Hospitals in the California Healthcare Safety Net* (Bethesda, MD: Project Hope, June 2002).
19. Karen Eggleston and Richard Zeckhauser, " Government Contracting for Health Care," in John D. Donahue and Joseph S. Nye, eds., *Market-Based Governance* (Washington, D.C.: Brookings Institution Press, 2002), p. 16.
20. Ibid., pp. 35–36.
21. Nichelson Sean, Mark Pauly, Lawton Burns, Agrieshka Bauemritter, and David Asch, "Measuring Community Benefits Provided by For-Profit and Nonprofit Hospitals," *Health Affairs,* November/December 2000, pp. 168–177.
22. Uwe Reinhardt, "The Economics of For-Profit and Not-for-Profit Hospitals," *Health Affairs,* Vol. 19, December 2000, pp. 178–185.
23. Kenneth Thorpe, Curtis Florence, and Eric Seiber, "Hospital Conversions, Margins and the Provision of Uncompensated Care," *Health Affairs,* Vol. 19, No. 6, December 2000, pp. 187–194.
24. Jack Needleman, "The Role of Nonprofits in Health Care," *Journal of Health, Politics, Policy and Law,* Vol. 26, No. 5, October 2001, pp. 1112–1130.
25. Lawrence Casalino, "Managers, Uncertainty, Intermediate Organizations as Triple Agents," *Journal of Health, Politics, Policy and Law,* Vol. 26, No. 5, October 2001.
26. A. J. Hartz, H. Krakauer, E. M. Kuhn, M. Young, S. J. Jacobsen, G. Gay, L. Muenz, M. Katzoff, R. C. Bailey, and A. A. Rimm, " Hospital Characteristics and Mortality Rates," *New England Journal of Medicine,* Vol. 321–1720-1725, No.25, December 1989.
27. Philip Devereau, P.T.L. Choi, C. Laccheti, et al., "Review and Meta-Analysis of Studies Comparing Mortality Rates of Private For-Profit and Private Not-for-Profit Hospitals," *Canadian Medical Journal,* Vol. 166, No. 11, July 2002, pp. 1399–1406. See also a rebuttal by the Canadian Statistical Assessment Service and the Fraser Institute, A Special Bulletin, *Media Private Health Scare,* July 2002.
28. Martin Gaynor and William Vogt, "Competition among Hospitals," *National Bureau for Economic Research,* February 2003.

29. Pauline Vaillancourt Rosenau, "Performance Evaluations of For-Profit and Nonprofit Hospitals in the U.S. since 1980," *Nonprofit Management and Leadership,* Vol. 13, No. 4, June 2003, pp. 401–423.

Chapter 8

1. Mark Granovetter, "Business Groups," *The Handbook of Economic Sociology,* Neil J. Smelser and Richard Swedberg, eds., (Princeton, N.J.: Princeton University Press, 1994), pp. 453–475.
2. Brian Uzzi, "The Sources and Consequences of Embeddedness for the Economic Performance of Organizations: The Network Effect," *American Sociological Review,* Vol. 61, 1996, pp. 674–698.
3. James Buchanan, "The Economic Theory of Clubs," *Economica,* Vol. 32, 1965, pp. 1–14.
4. Charles M. Tiebout, "A Pure Theory of Local Expenditures," *Journal of Political Economy,* Vol. 64, 1965, pp. 416–424.
5. Richard Cornes and Todd Sandler, *The Theory of Externalities, Public Goods and Club Goods* (New York: Cambridge University Press, 1996).
6. Ronald Burt, *Structural Holes: The Social Structure of Competition* (Cambridge, MA: Harvard University Press, 1992) and Ronald Burt, "The Network Structure of Social Capital," in Robert I. Sutton and Barry Staw, eds., *Research in Organizational Behavior* (Greenwich, CT: JAI, Press, 2000).
7. Kathleen A. Getz, "Research in Corporate Political Action: Integration and Assessment," *Business and Society,* Vol. 36, No. 1, pp. 32–72.
8. This limit is about 20 percent of expenditures or greater if a specific status is requested. Herrington J. Bryce, *Financial and Strategic Management for Nonprofit Organizations* (San Diego: Jossey Bass, 2000), pp. 372–378 and 682–683.
9. Asghar Zarhoodi, "On the Political Participation of the Firm in the Electoral Process," *Southern Economic Journal,* Vol. 58, 1985, pp. 187–191.
10. Sharon Zukin and Paul DiMaggio, *Structure of Capital: The Social Organization of Economy* (New York: Cambridge University Press, 1990).
11. Judith F. Kendell and John Frances Reilly, "Lobbying Issues" (Washington, D.C.: *IRS Publication No. 444,* 1992); and Judith F. Kendell and John Frances Reilly, "Election Year Issues" (Washington, D.C.: *IRS Publication No. 441,* 1992).
12. *National Muffler Dealers Association v. United States* 440, U.S. 472 (1979) affg 565 F 2d 845 (2d. Cir.1977) and *Pepsi-Cola Bottlers' Association, Inc. v. United States* 369 F 2d 250 (1966).

13. Herrington J. Bryce, *Financial and Strategic Management for Nonprofit Organizations* (San Diego: Jossey Bass, 2000), pp. 31–31 and 107–108.
14. Ibid., pp. 117–119.
15. Ibid., pp, 275–346.
16. Ibid., pp. 682–683.
17. John Frances Reilly, Carter C. Hull, and Barbara A. Allen, "IRC (c) (6) Organizations," *Exempt Organizations Technical Instruction Program for FY 2003* (Washington, D.C.: Internal Revenue Service, 2002).
18. David Epstein and Sharyn O'Halloran, "Asymmetric Information, Delegation, and the Structure of Policy-Making," *Journal of Theoretical Politics,* Vol. 11, No. 1, 1999, pp. 37–62.
19. Zarhoodi, "On the Political Participation of the Firm in the Electoral Process"; Marick Masters and Gerald Keim, "Determinants of PAC Participation among Large Corporations," *Journal of Politics,* Vol. 47, pp. 1158–1173; L. Salamon and J. Seigfired, " Economic Power and Political Influence: The Impact of Industry Structure on Public Policy," *American Political Science Review,* Vol. 71, 1977, pp. 1026–1043.
20. Zarhoodi, "On the Political Participation of the Firm in the Electoral Process."
21. Murray Weidenbaum, "Public Policy: No Longer a Spectator Sport for Business," *Journal of Business Strategy,* Vol. 3, No.4, 1980, pp. 46–53.
22. David Yoffe, "Corporate Strategies for Political Action: A Rational Model," in Alfred Marcus, Allen Kaufman, and David Beam, eds., *Business Strategy and Public Policy: Perspectives from Industry and Academia* (Westport: CT: Quorum Books, 1987), pp. 43–60.
23. Mancur Olson, *The Logic of Collective Action: Public Goods and the Theory of Groups* (Cambridge: Harvard University Press, 1965), p. 35.
24. Michael Lord, "An Agency Theory Assessment of the Influence of Corporate Grassroots Political Activism," *The Academy of Management Journal (Best Papers Proceedings),* 1995, pp. 396–400.
25. John Alpin and H. Harvey Hegarty, "Political Influence: Strategies Employed by Organizations to Impact Legislation in Business and Economic Matters," *Academy of Management Journal,* Vol. 23, No. 3, 1980, pp. 438–450.
26. Kathleen A. Getz, "Selecting Corporate Political Tactics," in Barry M. Mitnick, ed., *Corporate Political Agency* (Newbury Park, CA: Sage, 1993), pp. 242–273. Kathleen.A. Getz, "Research in Corporate Political Action: Integration and Assessment," *Business and Society,* Vol. 36, No. 1, 1999, pp. 32–72.
27. Michael D. Lord, "Corporate Political Strategy and Legislative Decision-Making," *Business and Society,* Vol. 39, No. 1, 2000, pp. 76–93.

28. Steven D. Levitt "Who are PACs trying to Influence with Contributions: Politicians or Voters?" *Economics and Politics,* Vol. 10, No.1, 1998, pp. 19–35.
29. Alpin and Hegarty, "Political Influence," p. 1.
30. Ivo Bischoff, "Determinants of the Increase in the Number of Interests Groups in Western Democracies: Theoretical Considerations and Evidence from 21 OECD Countries," *Public Choice,* Vol. 114, Nos. 1–2, January 2003, p. 197.
31. Larry Diamond, "Rethinking Civil Society," *Journal of Democracy,* Vol. 5, 1994, pp. 5–17.
32. Gary S. Becker, "Public Policies, Pressure Groups, and Dead Weight Costs," in George Stigler, ed., *Chicago Studies in Political Economy* (Chicago, IL: The University of Chicago Press, 1988), pp. 85–105.
33. Amy Whritenour Ando, "Do Interest Groups Compete? An Application to Endangered Species," *Public Choice,* Vol. 114, Nos.1–2, January 2003, page 137.

Chapter 9

1. Herrington J. Bryce, "The Nonprofit as a Public Corporation," *Financial and Strategic Management for Nonprofit Organizations,* 3rd ed. (San Diego: Jossey Bass, 2000), pp. 65–84, for a discussion of the public support test.
2. Ranjani Krishman, Michelle Yetman, and Robert J. Yetman, "Financial Disclosure Management by Nonprofit Organizations," working paper, University of California Davis, 2004).
3. Daniel Tinkelman, "Factors Affecting the Relation between Donations to Not-for-Profit and Efficiency Ratio," in *Research in Government and Nonprofit Accounting,* Vol. 10 (Stamford, Ct., JAI Press, 1999), pp. 135–161.
4. Philip Kotler and Allen Andreasen, *Strategic Marketing for Nonprofit Organizations,*3rd ed. (Upper Saddle, NJ: Prentice Hall, 1995) , p. 347.
5. Bryce, "The Nonprofit as a Public Corporation," p. 364.
6. Kent E. Dove, *Conducting A Successful Fund-raising Campaign Program* (San Diego: Jossey Bass, 2001), p. 334.
7. James M. Greenfield, *Fund Raising,* 2d ed. (New York: NSFRE/John Wiley, 1999), p. 89.
8. Howard P. Tuckman and Cyril F. Chang, "How Pervasive Are Abuses in Fundraising among Nonprofits?" *Nonprofit Management and Leadership,* Vol. 9, No. 2, winter 1998, pp. 211–221.
9. William R. Barber, Andrea A. Roberts, and G. Visvanathan, "Charitable Organization Strategies and Program Spending Ratios," *Accounting Horizon,* Vol. 15, No. 4, 2001, pp. 329–343.
10. Karen A. Forelich, Terry W. Knoeple, and Thomas Pollak, "Financial Measures in Nonprofit Organization Research Comparing IRS 990

Return and Audited Financial Statements Data," *Nonprofit Voluntary Sector Quarterly,* Vol. 20, No. 2, June 2000, pp. 232–254.

11. The Council of Better Business Bureau, *CBB Standards of Charitable Solicitations* (Arlington, VA: Council of Better Business Bureau, 1982 and 1999). The American Institute of Philanthropy, *Charity Rating Guide and Watchdog Report* (Chicago: American Institute of Philanthropy, 2002). The Maryland Association of Nonprofit Organizations, *Maryland Nonprofit Standards of Excellence* (Bethesda, MD: Maryland Association of Nonprofit Organizations, 1998).
12. See Sec 1, 501 (c) (3)-1 (a) (1), Revenue Ruling 70–186, 1970–1 Cumulative Bulletin 128 and Revenue Ruling 54–296, 1954–2, Cumulative Bulletin 59 and Revenue Ruling 76–94, 1976–1 Cumulative Bulletin 171 and Revenue Ruling 8–62, 1981–1 Cumulative Bulletin 355.
13. *United Cancer Council, Inc. v. Commissioner,* 109 TC 326 (1997).
14. The United States Supreme Court, No. 02–403—decided Monday, June 16, 2003.
15. No. 01–1806—decided Monday, May 5, 2003.
16. Richard Steinberg, "Economic Perspectives on the Regulation of Charitable Solicitation," *Case Western Reserve University Law Review,* Vol. 39, No.3, 1988–89, pp. 775–797.
17. Susan Rose-Ackerman, "Charitable Giving and Excessive Fundraising," *Quarterly Journal of Economics,* Vol. 97, 1982, pp. 193–212. See also Susan Rose-Ackerman, "Altruism, Nonprofits, and Economic Theory," *Journal of Economic Literature* Vol. 34, 1996, pp. 701–728.
18. *Village of Schaumburg v. Citizens for a Better Environment* (1980), *Secretary of State of Maryland v. Joseph H. Munson, Co., Inc.* (1984) and *Riley v. National Foundation of the Blind of North Carolina* (1988).
19. Ibid.
20. *United Cancer Council, Inc. v. Commissioner* 165 109 Fed 1173 (CA 7, 1999).
21. Bryce, "The Nonprofit as a Public Corporation."
22. Alnoor Ebrahim, "Making Sense of Accountability: Conceptual Perspectives for Northern and Southern Nonprofits," *Nonprofit Management and Leadership,* Vol. 14, No. 2, winter 2004, pp. 191–212.
23. Laura B. Chisolm, "Accountability of Nonprofit Organizations and Those Who Control Them: The Legal Framework," *Nonprofit Management and Leadership,* Vol 6, No.2, winter 1995, pp. 171–180.
24. Robert P. Lawry "Accountability and Nonprofit Organizations: An Ethical Perspective," *Nonprofit Management and Leadership,* Vol. 6, No. 2, winter 1995, pp. 171–180,
25. William T. Bogart, "Accountability and Nonprofit Organizations: An Economic Perspective," *Nonprofit Management and Leadership,* Vol. 6, No. 2, winter 1995, pp. 157–170.

26. Cagla Okten and Burton A. Weisbrod, "Determinants of Donations in Private Nonprofit Markets," *Journal of Public Economics*, Vol. 75, 2000, pp. 255–277.
27. American Institute of Certified Public Accountants, *Audit Risk and Materiality in Conducting an Audit SAS 47* (Wesport, CT: AICPA, 1994).
28. Cagla Okten and Burton A. Weisbrod, "Determinants of Donations in Private Nonprofit Markets," Vol. 75, *Journal of Public Economics*, 2000, pp. 255–277.
29. Holly Hall, "Many Boards Are Said to Be Unhappy over Fundraising Costs," *Chronicle of Philanthropy*, Vol. 5, March 9, 1993, pp. 24–25.
30. Holly Hall, "Many Charities Called Reluctant to Spend Money to Improve Fund-Raising," *Chronicle of Philanthropy*, Vol. 4, April 21, 1992, p. 20.
31. James M. Greenfield, "How Fundraising Costs Measurements Assist in Hiring Fundraising Professional," *Network*, Vol. 7, March-April 1990, pp 4–5.
32. Wilson C. Levi, "Increased Giving by Investing More Money in Fund-Raising Wisely," *Philanthropy Monthly*, Vol. 23, April-May 1990, p. 51–60.
33. Burton Weisbord and Nestor Dominguez, "Demand for Collective Goods in Private Nonprofit Markets: Can Fundraising Expenditures Help Overcome Free-Rider Behavior," *Journal of Public Economics*, Vol. 30, 1986, pp. 83–95.
34. Okten and Weisbrod, "Determinants of Donations in Private Nonprofit Markets."
35. Herrington J. Bryce, " The Fund Raising Ratio: Its Utility in Public Policy, Efficiency and Ethics" (unpublished paper, September 2002). Available from the author.
36. At this equilibrium point returns to investment in fundraising are maximized.
37. Regina Herzlinger, "Effective Oversight," *Harvard Business Review*, July/August 1994, pp. 93–106.
38. Herrington J. Bryce, *Financial and Strategic Management*.
39. Elizabeth K. Keating and Peter Frumkin, "Reengineering Nonprofit Financial Accountability; Toward a More Reliable Foundaton for Regulation," *Public Administration Review*, Jan/Feb 2003.
40. See for example, Jack Quarter, Laurie Mook, Betty Jane Richmond, *What Counts: Social Accounting for Nonprofits* (Upper Saddle, N.J: Prentice Hall, 2003).
41. Statements of Financial Accounting Standards, N 116 and 117 (FASB, 1993).
42. Joel L. Fleishman,"To Merit and Preserve the Public's Trust in Not-for-Profit Organizations: The Urgent Need for New Strategies for Regulatory Reform," in Charles Clotfelter and Thomas Erlich, eds.,

Trust, Service and the Common Purpose: Philanthropy and the Nonprofit Sector in a Changing America (New York: American Assembly, 1998).

Chapter 10

1. Andreas Diekmann and Siegwart Lindenberg, "Cooperation: Sociological Aspects," *International Encyclopedia of the Social Behavioral Sciences,* Vol. 4, 2001, pp. 2751–2756.
2. Elinor Ostrom, "How Types of Goods and Property Rights Jointly Affect Collective Action," *Journal of Theoretical Politics,* Vol. 15, No. 3, July 2003, pp. 239–270.
3. Ibid.
4. Ibid.
5. Securities and Exchange Act of 1934, Section 15A.
6. Report of the SRO Consultative Committee of the International Organization of Securities Commissions, *Model of Effective Regulation* (Madrid, Spain: The International Organization of Securities Commissions, May 2000), pp. 2–5.
7. Curtis Milhaupt, "Nonprofit Organizations as Investor Protection: Economic Theory and Evidence of East Asia" in Curtis Milhaupt, ed., *Global Markets, Domestic Institution: Corporate Law and Governance in a New Era of Cross-Border Deals* (New York: Columbia University Press, 2003).
8. Kon Sik Kim and Joongi Kim, "Revamping Fiduciary Duties in Korea: Does Law Matter in Corporate Governance," in Curtis Milhaupt, ed., *Global Markets, Domestic Institution: Corporate Law and Governance in a New Era of Cross-Border Deals* (New York: Columbia University Press, 2003).
9. Report of the SRO Consultative Committee of the International Organization of Securities Commission, *Model of Effective Regulation.*
10. Anjali Kuma, *Self-Regulatory Organizations: Principles and Issues* (Washington, D.C.: The World Bank, 2003).
11. Peter M. De Marzo, Michael J. Fishman, and Kathleen Hagerty, "The Enforcement Policy of a Self-Regulatory Organization," contributed paper, Econometric Society World Congress, Seattle, WA, 2000.
12. National Association of Securities Dealers, *NASD MANUAL* (Washington, D.C.: National Association of Securities Dealers, April 2004) or www.nasd.com.
13. HR 123, 94th Congress, 1st Session, 48–49 (1975), and Bill Singer, "Are Judicial Findings of Quasi-Governmental Status of SROs Inconsistent or Unfair?" September 2001, *RRBDLAW.Com Securities Industries Commentator,* 2004.

14. Herrington J. Bryce, *Financial and Strategic Management of Nonprofit Organizations,* 3rd ed. (San Diego: Jossey-Bass, 2000), especially chapter 5, "Associations and Other Forms of Organizations."
15. Mancur Olson, *The Logic of Collective Action* (Cambridge: Harvard University Press, 1965).
16. Toshio Yamagishi, "The Provision of a Sanctioning System as a Public Good," *Journal of Personality and Social Psychology,* Vol. 51, No.1, 1986, pp. 110–116.
17. Olson, "How Types of Goods and Property Rights Jointly Affect Collective Action."
18. James Dearden, "Efficiency and Exclusion in Collective Action Allocations," *Mathematical Social Sciences,* , Vol. 34, No. 2, October 1997, pp. 153–174.
19. Paul Pecorino, "Can by-product lobbying firms compete?" *Journal of Public Economics,* Vol. 82, No. 3, December 2001, pp. 377–397.
20. Arun Agrawal and Sanjeev Goyal, "Group Size and Collective Action: Third-Party Monitoring in Common-Pool Resources," *Comparative Political Studies,* Vol. 34, No. 1, February 2001, pp. 63–93.
21. Jeroen Weesie, Vincent Buskens, and Werner Raub, "The Management of Trust Relations via Institutional and Structural Embeddness," in Patrick Doreian and Thomas Fararo, eds., *The Problem of Solidarity: Theories and Models* (Amsterdam: Gordon and Breach, 1988), pp. 113–118.
22. Paul Willman, David Coen, David Currie, and Martin Siner, "The Evolution of Regulatory Relationships, and Firm Behavior in Privatized Industries," *Industrial and Corporate Change,* Vol. 12, No. 1, 2003, pp. 69–89.
23. Paul DiMaggio and Walter W. Powell, "Isomorphism: The Iron Cage Revisited: Institutional Isomorphism and Collective Rationality in Institutional Fields," *American Sociological Review,* Vol. 48, 1983, pp. 147–160.
24. James Coleman, "Prologomena to a Theory of Social Institution: Commentary on Social Institutions and Social Theory," *American Sociological Review,* Vol. 55, No. 3, June 1990, pp. 333–339.
25. Douglas Heckathorn, "Collective Sanctions and Compliance Norms: A Formal Theory of Group-Mediated Controls," *American Sociological Review,* Vol. 55, 1990, pp. 366–384.
26. Pamela Oliver, Gerald Maxwell, and Ruy Teixeira, "Interdependence, A Theory of Critical Mass: Interdependence, Group Heterogenity, and the Production of Collective Action," *American Journal of Sociology,* Vol. 91, 1985, pp. 522–536.
27. Colin Scott, "Private Regulation of the Public Sector: A Neglected Facet of Contemporary Governance," *Journal of Law and Society,* Vol. 29, No. 1, March 2002, pp. 56–76.

28. Hayagreeva Rao, "Caveat Emptor: The Construction of Non-Profit Consumer Watchdog Organizations," *American Journal of Sociology*, Vol. 103, 1998, pp. 912–916.

Chapter 11

1. See *The Journal of Contemporary Issues in Fund Raising*, summer 1990, p. 58.
2. See Herrington J. Bryce, *Financial and Strategic Management for Nonprofit Organizations*, 3rd ed. (San Diego: Jossey Bass, 2000), pp. 733–737 for an itemization and description of costs not allowed under federal government contracts.
3. Patrick D. Kennedy and Maeve Cannon, "Government Procurement Basics," *The CPA Journal*, Vol. 74, No. 5, May 2004, pp. 60–64.

Author Index

Subject Index